DEVELOPMENT STRATEGY AND MANAGEMENT OF THE MARKET ECONOMY

VOLUME II

D0075419

Development Strategy and Management of the Market Economy

VOLUME II

Edited by
István P. Székely and Richard Sabot

CLARENDON PRESS · OXFORD

Published for and on behalf of the United Nations

1997

Oxford University Press, Great Clarendon Street, Oxford OX2 6DP

Oxford New York
Athens Auckland Bangkok Bogota Bombay
Buenos Aires Calcutta Cape Town Dar es Salaam
Delhi Florence Hong Kong Istanbul Karachi
Kuala Lumpur Madras Madrid Melbourne
Mexico City Nairobi Paris Singapore
Taipei Tokyo Toronto Warsaw
and associated companies in
Berlin Ibadan

Oxford is a trade mark of Oxford University Press

Published in the United States
by Oxford University Press Inc., New York

© United Nations 1997

British Library Cataloguing in Publication Data
Data available

Library of Congress Cataloging in Publication Data
Data available
ISBN 0–19–829250–3

1 3 5 7 9 10 8 6 4 2

Printed in Great Britain by
Bookcraft (Bath) Ltd, Midsomer Norton, Somerset.

PREFACE

These two volumes are the result of the work of a High-level Group of Experts established by the Secretary-General of the United Nations at the end of 1993 to analyse key aspects of development policy in the light of the new thinking on economic and social issues that has evolved over recent years.

The Members of the Group were Professor Edmond Malinvaud (Collège de France, Paris), Jean-Claude Milleron (Under-Secretary-General for Economic and Social Information and Policy Analysis in the United Nations, New York), Professor Mustapha K. Nabli (University of Tunis, Tunisia), Professor Amartya K. Sen (Harvard University, Cambridge, Massachusetts), Arjun Sengupta (Member of the Planning Commission of India), Nicholas Stern (Chief Economist, European Bank for Reconstruction and Development, London), Joseph E. Stiglitz (Chairman, Council of Economic Advisers to the President of the United States) and Professor Kotaro Suzumura (Hitotsubashi University, Tokyo). Yves Berthelot (Executive Secretary of the United Nations Economic Commission for Europe) and Gert Rosenthal (Executive Secretary of the United Nations Economic Commission for Latin America and the Caribbean) also participated actively in most of the meetings of the Group. In addition, Peter E. de Jánosi (Director, International Institute for Applied Systems Analysis, Laxenburg, Austria) and Mihály Simai (Director, World Institute for Development Economics Research, Helsinki, Finland) participated as *ex-officio* Members of the Group. All Members served in their personal capacity.

The Group elected Professors Malinvaud and Sen as Co-chairpersons, while Jean-Claude Milleron and Arjun Sengupta jointly headed the secretariat of the Group.

The Group held five meetings between 1994 and 1996. In addition to the contributions of the Members of the Group, background papers for these meetings were prepared by John Bonin, Willem Buiter, Thomas Hellmann, Ricardo Lago, Bozena Leven, Kevin Murdock, Andrés Rodríguez-Clare, Richard Sabot, István P.

Székely, Vito Tanzi, Geedreck Uswatte-Aratchi and John Williamson.

Financial support for the Group was provided by a grant from the Government of France. The International Institute for Applied Systems Analysis (IIASA), the World Institute for Development Economics Research (WIDER), and the European Bank for Reconstruction and Development (EBRD) acted as hosts for the Group's meetings, with Shari Jandl, Lorraine Telfer-Tainvainen and Kerrie Quirk respectively playing key roles in taking care of the logistics for these meetings.

Both volumes were copy-edited by Ilyse Zable. Support for the Group, including in the preparation of these two volumes, was mainly provided by members of the United Nations Department for Economic and Social Information and Policy Analysis (DESIPA): Florence-Marie Anyansi, Joyce Ashie, Binta Dieye, Judith Goss, Marcela Guimaraes, Samuel Jan, Leah McDavid, István P. Székely, Marie-Esther Van Note, Alicia Villarama, Li Wang and Nikolai Zaitsev. Valerian Monteiro prepared the camera-ready copy. Ian Kinniburgh, with the assistance of Béatrice Frankard-Little, played an essential role in supervising the finalization of the two volumes. This group benefitted from the extensive cooperation received from those working directly with the Members of the Group and other contributors.

It is apparent from the foregoing that these two volumes resulted from a cooperative international effort. It is hoped that they will enjoy an equally international response.

CONTRIBUTORS

Yves Berthelot, Executive Secretary
   Economic Commission for Europe, Geneva

Willem Buiter, Adviser to the Office of the Chief Economist
   European Bank for Reconstruction and Development, London
   and Professor, University of Cambridge

Thomas Hellmann, Assistant Professor of Strategic Management
   Graduate School of Business, Stanford University
   Stanford, California

Ricardo Lago, Deputy Chief Economist
   European Bank for Reconstruction and Development, London

Kevin Murdock, Assistant Professor, Graduate School of Business
   Stanford University, Stanford, California

Mustapha K. Nabli, Professor
   University of Tunis, Tunis

Andrés Rodríguez-Clare, Professor, Graduate School of Business
   University of Chicago, Chicago, Illinois

Gert Rosenthal, Executive Secretary, Economic Commission for
   Latin America and the Caribbean, Santiago

Richard Sabot, Chair and John J. Gibson Professor of Economics
   Department of Economics, Williams College
   Williamstown, Massachusetts

Nicholas Stern, Chief Economist, European Bank for
   Reconstruction and Development, London

István Székely, General Manager, Economics and Research
   Department, National Bank of Hungary, Budapest

Vito Tanzi, Director, Fiscal Affairs Department
   International Monetary Fund, Washington, D.C.

John Williamson, Senior Fellow
   Institute for International Economics, Washington, D.C.

CONTENTS

Contents

1

Introduction

RICHARD SABOT AND ISTVÁN P. SZÉKELY

This is the second of two volumes, commissioned by the United Nations, to emerge from the deliberations of the High Level Working Group on Development Strategy. Both volumes focus on the role of development strategy in the transformation of poor countries—in which opportunities are severely limited, and people are unable to realize their productive potential and hence are economically deprived—into countries with abundant opportunities and high levels of productivity and economic welfare.

In the 1950s economists and policy-makers were optimistic that they knew how to bring about such a transformation. And for a time their optimism appeared to be justified. But only a few developing countries sustained the initial spurt of economic growth that many more had experienced. Those few have narrowed the gaps in productivity and economic well-being between themselves and high-income countries. The large majority of developing countries have fallen further behind.

The widening gap has generated a greater sense of urgency among leaders in both low- and high-income countries: the world in which our children and grandchildren live in the new millennium will be profoundly influenced by how well poor nations do. Developing countries have the potential to emulate the successes of the few countries that have closed the gap. But that optimism is tempered by caution—warranted because of the magnitude of the stakes, past failures and the realization that it is extremely difficult to move from either economic theory or the study of economic history to sound, specific policy recommendations. Economic models are based on assumptions that take into account only certain aspects of the reality they intend to describe, while generalizations derived from history are frequently based on an extremely limited number of well-documented cases.

The essays in Volume I lay out the argument for development strategy and construct a theoretical framework for assessing the appropriate allocation of responsibilities for finance, production and decision-making in a partnership between government and markets. The essays in this volume, which were prepared as background papers for Volume I, are more empirical and narrower in scope. They attempt to tease out from the economic success stories and failures of the last several decades lessons in particular spheres of economic policy.

The authors of this volume agree on three key components of a successful development strategy. First, competition provides powerful incentives for increasing productivity by using available resources more efficiently and by investing in physical and human capital. Central planning proved effective at mobilizing savings but ineffective at ensuring that investments yield high returns. A successful development strategy will be market-based.

But this conclusion does not imply a minimalist view of the role of government. For example, unless government ensures macroeconomic stability and an appropriate institutional infrastructure, markets, operating on their own, will likely yield socially undesirable outcomes. Government has a disproportionate responsibility for creating a political and economic environment conducive to growth, while the private sector has a disproportionate responsibility for making the high-return investments and improvements in efficiency that generate growth. The impact of government on growth is asymmetrical: while good government may not generate growth, bad government is likely to preclude sustained growth.

It is important to find the optimal mix of markets and government—not a simple matter. The policies that are optimal will vary across countries and over time. The greater are the extent and cost of market failures, the greater is the potential scope for government intervention. But, ironically, where market failures are most costly, the capacity for government to intervene effectively is often most limited. In their summary of Volume I, Stern and Stiglitz emphasize the importance of government credibility, competence and probity. In deciding on the optimal mix of markets and government, they emphasize the quality of private institutions, most notably in the financial sector.

The elimination of biases against, and the stimulation of, exports is a second component of a successful development strategy. A strong test of the competitiveness of enterprises is how well they perform against foreign competition. Efficiently harnessing labour, which, because of its great relative abundance, is low-cost, offers low-income countries a competitive advantage in international markets.

The high-performing economies of east Asia exploited that advantage and demonstrated that export pessimism, which in other regions led to strategies favouring import substitutes, was not justified. Rapid export growth was consistent with a labour-demanding and, ultimately, skill-demanding growth path: it contributed to rapid growth of workers' wages and living standards, it stimulated investment in human capital and the acquisition of technological capability and it minimized rent-seeking behaviour, typical of firms protected from international competition, by both private and public enterprises.

These newly industrialized economies, responding to the change in comparative advantage associated with higher wages, have moved towards producing more skill- and capital-intensive exports. This move will then generate opportunities for more labour-abundant countries to follow in their footsteps—thus export pessimism is no more justified today than it was 20 years ago.

In an open economy a policy mistake tends to be punished more swiftly and severely than in a less liberalized economy, even if other fundamentals are sound. This burden makes it imperative that policy-makers have the capacity to quickly recognize their mistakes and take corrective actions.

The third component about a successful development strategy is that growth is sustainable only if it is inclusive. Low inequality in the distribution of income may stimulate growth; high inequality may constrain growth. Government-mandated income transfers may simply subsidize consumption—and therefore inhibit growth. But market forces can yield low inequality and inclusive growth by steering the economy onto a labour-demanding growth path: one that is consistent with relative factor endowments and prices, and with comparative advantage. The poor may respond to the new economic opportunities by raising their rates of saving and investment—in human capital, for example—thereby further promoting growth.

Moreover, low inequality may contribute to macroeconomic stability by reducing the tendency (in a democratic system) for those who have not benefitted from growth to press for populist redistributional policies that sacrifice fiscal prudence for political expediency. By reducing some of democracy's disadvantages for growth, low inequality may enhance the attractiveness of democratic institutions for developing countries. And, as Stern and Stiglitz note, democratic institutions can improve how a market economy functions by limiting the power of the executive, hence potential abuses of that power, and by focusing attention on serious economic and political problems that might otherwise be neglected.

In chapter 2 Willem Buiter, Ricardo Lago and Nicholas Stern focus on macroeconomic stability and describe economic institutions and policies needed to achieve macroeconomic stability. Without macroeconomic stability, the ability of individuals, enterprises and government to make optimal decisions regarding inter-temporal substitution is severely compromised. And without stability reforms aimed at the microstructure of the economy may yield perverse results. Generating a vicious circle, macroeconomic instability can induce capital outflows and still greater instability. Typically, macroeconomic instability originates from policy inconsistency, which in turn originates from unresolved conflicts of political interests.

The authors discuss four key aspects of the economic environment policy-makers will have to consider when formulating policies in the coming decades: increasing internationalization, market orientation, diminished role of government and high real interest rates. They conclude their chapter by claiming that the quality of government institutions and policies is most likely the most important factor accounting for differential economic performance in the medium and long term. They suggest that a limited but strong state is likely to be a defining characteristic of future economic success. The authors of later chapters in the volume investigate several aspects of this issue.

In Chapter 3 Andrés Rodríguez-Clare looks at the role of positive feedback mechanisms and externalities in economic development. He presents a review of the literature on models that exhibit multiple Pareto-rankable equilibria and path dependence. These models explain the lack of economic growth as a result of a vicious circle of poverty. The main ingredient of this new literature is externalities. When economies are very inter-dependent—as Buiter, Lago and Stern suggest is characteristic of the international economic environment—these externalities, if they are strong and geographically limited, may lead to geographic concentration of economic activities and thus to underdevelopment traps.

As a consequence, one group of countries may persistently grow faster and pay higher wages for similar types of labour than another group of countries, even if capital can flow between countries. Externalities may lead to such an outcome if they generate positive feedback mechanisms. These models can help policy-makers to understand the conditions under which government intervention may be warranted and the kind of information that would be necessary to carry out such interventions successfully.

Richard Sabot focuses on the importance of human capital accumulation to a development strategy in chapter 4. Rapid accumulation can both stimulate growth and reduce inequality. But increasing the supply of human capital is not enough—growth of demand for human capital must also be sustained. The growth payoff to investment in human capital is likely to be much greater when the economy is on an export-oriented labour-demanding growth path than when economic activity is inward-looking, techniques are capital-intensive, enterprises are inefficient and growth does not generate much demand for labour or skills.

With regard to public financing of education, Sabot makes a case for allocating funds to counter capital market imperfections, which preclude the poor from making high-return investments, rather than to exploit positive externalities. This recommendation implies that in allocating public funds, higher priority should be given to primary and secondary than to tertiary education. Sabot holds that a development strategy should increase the productivity of the poor by ensuring that they have access to high-quality educational opportunities and, later, to a labour market in which demand for their skills is strong. The result will be that the poor make a substantial contribution to economic growth and improve their own position in both absolute and relative terms.

In chapter 5 Gert Rosenthal provides an overview of the theoretical and empirical literature on the relationship between growth and equity. As we pointed out earlier, the authors of this volume hold that growth is sustainable only if it is inclusive. This chapter identifies how government can enhance growth while—or rather, through—reducing inequality.

Yves Berthelot discusses the vital role of institutions in chapter 6. Institutions will contribute to growth if they are high-quality and have credibility, competence and probity. Berthelot points out that the concept of good governance—identified in chapter 2 as the most important factor for economic success—highlights the need to establish an organic relationship between the market economy, the state and civil society in order to generate a sustainable process of growth with equity. The essence of this approach is found in the combination of a competitive market economy, a well-managed state and a democratic society. The chapter concludes by examining the obstacles encountered in implementing institutional reforms and undertaking necessary adjustment in the transition economies of central and eastern Europe.

In chapter 7 Mustapha Nabli, taking the same institutional perspective (and in the same vein as the chapter by Malinvaud and Nabli in Volume I), develops the idea that planning can be seen as a valuable institutional arrangement for managing market economies. He views public planning as an institutional framework of mechanisms for enhancing the efficiency of decentralized economic processes, mitigating market failures and, even more significantly, government failures. The chapter shows that planning models—and planning more generally—have had little success in helping developing countries deal with market failures. Nabli explains this failure by the inadequacies of the specification of the economy-wide planning models used, the issues emphasized and their relevance, as well as the mechanisms and policies for the implementation of plans.

In practice, the concerns of planning have concentrated on mitigating government failures, which are found at different levels. First, Nabli shows that a planning organization can be a useful vehicle within the bureaucracy to promote and support efficient outcomes, decisions and policies. Within government analysis and decision-making activities there is wide scope for assuring the coordination and consistency of public investment programmes. Planning processes are also part of national mechanisms for revealing collective choices, such as the provision of public goods, and their rationalization. Planning institutions also help to insulate public policies from excessive special interest influence.

Second, planning is concerned with the feasibility of outcomes and the sustainability of policies and programmes in the long run. Finally, planning may help to enhance the credibility of public policies.

In chapter 8 Vito Tanzi is concerned with situations in which the capacity of government to implement policy is very low to begin with. Sadly, such cases are not that rare. Tanzi emphasizes the important principle of keeping interventions within the capacity of government. It is crucial that government not squander at the outset what little credibility it has.

Tanzi points out that building basic institutions is government's most urgent and essential task in the post-chaos period. Once these institutions are in place, government can begin to establish credibility. Clearly stated policies on the role of the public sector in the medium and long run is an important building block in this regard. He also emphasizes the importance of introducing laws that are relatively simple and enforceable, and building institutions that can operate with limited means.

Thomas Hellmann and Kevin Murdock focus on financial sector development in chapter 9. Because of the central role of the financial system in the allocation of resources, good corporate governance in this sector is particularly important. Hellmann and Murdock believe that government policy must emphasize the development of appropriate governance structures. They point out that when an enterprise has significant reputational capital, its incentives shift from a focus on rent extraction to a focus on rent creation. They identify a set of government policies, which they call financial restraint, by which government can create reputational capital in the financial sector. An outcome of this policy: the banking sector can become an important locus for the development of governance mechanisms for the rest of the economy.

Much work, however, remains to be done on determining how good governance systems can be developed in financial markets. We can add to this line of argument that not only can good government play an important role in creating well-functioning private (financial) institutions, but well-functioning private (financial) institutions can reinforce good government and reduce the risk of bad policies. By imposing financial discipline, sound financial institutions can promote better government policies, too.

In chapter 10 John Williamson focuses on public policy towards international capital flows. Allowing capital mobility across borders can be regarded as the final step of economic liberalization. The potential welfare benefits of international capital flows are faster growth (by investing more than is saved locally), inter-temporal consumption smoothing, diversification of risks, competition in the financial sector and exploitation of foreign-owned intellectual property (through foreign direct investment). Nonetheless, large capital flows can destabilize macroeconomic management or cause financial fragility.

Such inefficient outcomes are the result of misguided government policies, including fixed-but-adjustable exchange rates, large budget deficits or deposit insurance, or of herd instincts in financial markets. Governments can hope to correct for the latter if they focus on long-run fundamentals rather than short-run prospects. Although the Tobin tax does not appear likely to be helpful, there are policies that can minimize the problems of excessive capital flows, including an appropriate choice of exchange rate regime, an international procedure for more systematic workouts by sovereign debtors and the use of a wide range of national mechanisms to deter excessive inflows, including market-oriented controls on capital inflows (such as reserve requirements on foreign-owned bank deposits).

PART ONE

FOUNDATION OF ECONOMIC POLICY

2

Promoting an Effective Market Economy in a Changing World

WILLEM BUITER, RICARDO LAGO
AND NICHOLAS STERN

In this chapter we examine the main challenges in promoting an effective market economy. While the chapter covers the spectrum of economic institutions and policies, the central theme is the importance of macroeconomic stability for economic growth in the medium and long run. Macroeconomic stability may be seen as a public good.[1] Its provision is one of the essential responsibilities of the state in modern market economies and in economies transforming themselves into modern market economies. While our discussion ranges broadly, both theoretically and empirically, we emphasize lessons for and experience from countries attempting to create a market economy.

POLICY-MAKING IN A "NEW" WORLD

The economic environment within which countries, governments, firms and households—as workers, investors and consumers—will operate in the years to come has four fundamental features that are strikingly different from those of the decades following World War II. First, economic activity is increasingly internationalized. Second, economic activity is increasingly market-oriented and market- mediated. Third, the role of government in economic affairs is more limited, reflecting a more pragmatic and modest view of what can be achieved through government action. And fourth, saving and investment take place in a context of high real interest rates.

Internationalization

Internationalization has several dimensions. In the past two decades international trade has grown at an average annual rate twice that of the growth of world GDP (6 per cent compared with 3 per cent). Nations and regions are therefore increasingly open to trade in goods and services, meaning that foreign markets account for an increasing share of domestic production and imports account for an increasing share of domestic expenditure. The international mobility of financial capital has increased continuously since the 1960s. While the tight correlation between national savings and domestic capital formation remains intact (and, on average, current account surpluses or deficits are small relative to the flows of domestic savings and capital formation), this link is weakening with each passing decade.[2] In addition, small *net* international flows of funds do not rule out very large *gross* flows of funds—and for international portfolio diversification and insurance against national shocks, gross rather than net flows matter.[3] While a strong home bias remains in financial portfolio composition, international diversification and risk sharing are increasingly important for portfolio holders everywhere. Today, the average daily turnover in foreign exchange markets worldwide is in excess of $1 trillion.[4]

Enterprise is becoming increasingly "footloose". Even if corporate headquarters do not yet skip easily across national boundaries, individual production plants, research and development (R&D) establishments and other production or support activities relocate more and more freely in search of new markets and lowest cost production and distribution. Foreign direct investment (FDI) enables the international reallocation of bundled finance, managerial capacity and technical know-how.

Increasing financial openness has given rise to sudden surges of capital inflows or outflows that have complicated macroeconomic management in countries as diverse as Italy and the United Kingdom on the one hand, and the Czech Republic, Malaysia, Mexico and Thailand on the other.[5] Several sets of issues arise. The first relates to the causes of these capital surges. In addition to capital account liberalization measures, these include domestic and external causes. The second concerns the consequences of surges of capital inflows or outflows. After determining the causes and consequences, we can consider possible remedies or policy interventions. At the level of an individual country these range from the (re-)imposition of administrative or tax barriers to capital inflows or outflows and other kinds of foreign exchange controls, to changes in domestic financial regulation and supervision, and changes in the conduct of fiscal, monetary and exchange rate policy. At the systemic level they include international cooperation and surveillance to achieve a more coordinated set of national economic policies and to improve the quality of national economic management.

A third aspect of growing international openness has been increasing international labour mobility.[6] Despite restrictive immigration policies imposed by industrial countries, increasing levels of education and training in much of the developing world and steadily falling transportation and information costs have resulted in an increasing supply of young immigrants to industrial countries (SOPEMI, 1995). The "youth deficit" in industrial countries makes it likely that immigration will be a prominent economic, social and political issue in the decades to come. Finally, the international mobility of ideas, knowledge, know-how and culture is a potent force for change in economic, social and political affairs. No government striving for national technological development will be able to stop its citizens from "surfing the Web".

Moving in the direction of increased openness will benefit the "representative citizen" of a nation if two conditions are satisfied. The first is that there be no unfavourable terms-of-trade effects. If expanding trade generates a lower relative price of exports for a large country, then that country will share in the potential global gains from the removal of obstacles to trade only if it imposes a(n optimal) tariff or receives international compensatory transfers. Lump-sum international compensation would constitute the global first-best solution. The second condition that must be satisfied is that a sufficiently rich set of tax and subsidy instruments is available domestically to cope with scale economies and/or domestic distortions (labour market monopoly, product market distortions, externalities) that could interact unfavourably with increased trade or factor flows.

Even if increased openness benefits the representative consumer, it may harm particular individuals or groups. This possibility holds even when markets function efficiently. In general, policies that promote increasing international openness generate only *potential* Pareto improvements. Unless losers are compensated—and the compensation mechanisms themselves do not create large distortions or inefficiencies—owners of adversely affected factors of production can lose out. For instance, the Stolper-Samuelson theorem reminds us that the factor of production used intensively in the import-competing sector will be hurt when trade liberalization results in an expansion of the exporting sector and a contraction of the import-competing sector. Owners of sector-specific factors of production (or, more generally, of productive inputs whose mobility between sectors is restricted) are likely to suffer capital losses if increased openness shifts demand away from the sectors in which these inputs have been "sunk". Only if the government has a sufficiently rich arsenal of internal redistribution instruments and compensation is actually paid, will increased openness improve the welfare of all.

The ability to impose tariffs is increasingly being restricted by international agreements and treaties. National governments may also not possess, or be able to administer effectively, the corrective tax and regulatory instruments or the domestic redistribution instruments to turn a potential welfare gain into an actual Pareto improvement. A further problem associated with increasing internationalization is that winners and losers will often belong to different national jurisdictions. The new trade theories, emphasizing imperfectly competitive behaviour, product differentiation, static and dynamic scale economies and cumulative conglomeration or agglomeration processes, suggest that without effective international compensation and assistance, enhanced economic integration may make an entire nation worse off, even if it potentially improves welfare for the world as a whole. Compensation mechanisms and assistance are, however, generally defined and financed nationally. There may be a future role for the World Trade Organization (WTO) or other international arrangements to address the international distributional consequences of increasing economic interdependence.

One key impact of increasing internationalization is that change will come with greater frequency and enhanced severity. There will be fewer and fewer "non-traded" or sheltered sectors. And thus the ability to react flexibly and constructively to external change will become increasingly important. Another important effect of increased internationalization is that it creates pressure for increased investment. Chasing an ever-changing dynamic comparative advantage is a resource-intensive business. Both defensive restructuring and strategic investment in newly emerging technologies and industries require enhanced accumulation of physical and human capital. It is also essential, of course, that there be no artificial obstacles to the flexible operation of factor and product markets or to the reallocation of human and other productive resources from declining to expanding sectors. The quality or productivity of any investment will depend on the efficiency of the key input and product markets and on the quality of enterprises' internal resource allocation mechanisms—the "micro-command economies" that are crucial to overall economic performance, even though the macro-command economy has been relegated to the scrap heap of history.

Markets and mixed economies

There is now virtually universal agreement that economic relations among enterprises; between enterprises and consumers, workers and owners of other productive inputs; and between savers and investors are best mediated through markets.[7] This consensus is not a result of the fact that the world has, at last, understood the first and second fundamental welfare theorems[8] or has concluded that, in the debate between Lange-Dobb-Lerner and von Mises-von Hayek, the latter has, belatedly, won the logical argument.[9] Rather, it is the result of the accumulation of experience with the failings of overambitious governments. This experience came from different places, at different times and in different ways, but the disillusion with government performance rose particularly rapidly in the 1970s. In the 1980s this was manifested politically in the United Kingdom and United States with the Thatcher and Reagan administrations. And the most powerful evidence came from the brutal experiment performed by history on the centrally planned economies of eastern and central Europe and of the Soviet Union (now the former Soviet Union) that made it clear by the 1980s that central planning was incapable of producing sustained increases in standards of living beyond relatively modest levels. Milder experiments had been performed at various times from the 1950s until the late 1980s in many Latin American countries pursuing inward-looking, populist policies, in much of Africa, in the Middle East, in India, in Indonesia and in the Philippines.[10] The experience of Chinese agriculture in 1979–83 provides an excellent example of the dramatic increase in productivity resulting from some basic (and no doubt imperfect) reforms that tied private effort to private reward (Lin, 1992).

This consensus in favour of markets coexists with a much greater degree of understanding of the prevalence and significance of market failures (and of their causes, consequences and cures). The reconciliation of these two prima-facie contradictory insights comes from recognizing that not every market failure has a non-market cure and that the same conditions that generate market failure often generate government failure also.

Agreeing on the superiority of markets over central planning does not, however, end the debate over the role of government. First, "markets" can be defined many different ways—with variants ranging from Hong Kong neo-liberalism through United States corporate capitalism and the west-European social market economy to the large oligopolies of Japan and the Republic of Korea. Second, without effective government there can be no effective market system. The government will always have a substantial role in setting and enforcing the rules of the market and in regulating economic activity in general. It is self-evident that government influences the market system in many ways: from the nature and quality of the legal system and the courts, through competition policy, regulation, and public procurement, to the provision of a stable currency. Even holding constant these institutional and microeconomic functions, the operation of a market economy is influenced powerfully by the government's fiscal, financial and monetary actions and rules. Fiscal policy has long-run real effects on after-tax real interest rates and the real exchange rate. It also has transitional effects on capacity utilization and the rate of unemployment. Monetary policy influences real interest rates in the short run, nominal interest rates in the short and long run, and the rate of inflation in the medium and long run. Government borrowing in domestic financial markets crowds out domestic investment and other interest-sensitive private expenditures, unless domestic financial markets are perfectly integrated with the world market and the country in question is small. Unsustainable fiscal, financial and monetary policies lead to high, volatile inflation and prevent the price mechanism from functioning efficiently. They also tend to be regressive, both while they are allowed to fester and when, ultimately, painful corrective measures are imposed to restore solvency and sustainability.

Governments therefore influence (and often set) the rules according to which markets operate. They also, as major purchasers or sellers in a broad range of markets for goods, factors of production and financial instruments, influence prices and the volume of transactions in these markets. Finally, through tax-transfer and subsidy mechanisms, a government indirectly influences the behaviour of private transactors in those markets in which it does not operate as a buyer or seller itself. Even the most market-oriented economic systems are therefore *mixed* economies. In direct activities (public sector employment, the provision of public goods and services, and redistributive spending) and in the financing of these and other activities, the role of the government will not and should not be negligible.

The size of the government sector

Attempts to influence the size of government, conventionally measured by spending or revenue as a fraction of GDP, often have a negligible effect. This observation is underlined by the fact that, after 16 years of conservative administrations (from 1979) in the United Kingdom, in fiscal year 1994–95 the government still spent the equivalent of 43 per cent of GDP and raised 37 per cent of GDP in revenue (35 per cent of GDP in taxes). The corresponding figures for 1979 were 41 per cent of GDP for general government spending and 38 per cent of GDP for revenue. While these figures do not support the conclusion that the political complexion of the government has no effect on the size of the government sector, they do support the conclusion that it is very difficult to achieve lasting, sustainable reductions in the size of the public sector.

The decline of government revenue in some early
transition economies

The question of the appropriate size of the government in different countries depends on initial conditions, economic structure and a host of internal and external political and economic circumstances. The determination of the level of current revenue needed to finance, without undue recourse to the inflation tax, the minimal level of public expenditure required to discharge the irreducible roles of the state and to sustain political and social cohesion is an imprecise and subjective science. A case can nevertheless be made that, in a number of transition countries that are in the earlier stages of transition which have not yet achieved macroeconomic stabilization, government revenue is falling to dangerously low levels.

The conceptual and measurement problems with characterizing pre-transition revenue are severe, but they were surely of the order of 60 per cent of GDP or higher.[11] While the transition, by nature, should involve a reduction in revenue and spending, the fall in revenue has been far more rapid than that of spending, leading to rampant inflation.[12] In some countries of the former Soviet Union post-transition revenue is falling to levels that threaten the functioning of even the barest "night watchmen" duties of the state (table 2.1).[13] A key priority of the state under such circumstances is to strengthen its revenue base and improve its tax collection effort.

The decline in revenue can be attributed in part to a decline in traditional tax bases and in part to a decline in the government's ability to extract revenue from any given base. The decline in

Table 2.1: General government revenue in some transition economies, 1991–95 (percentage of GDP)

Country	1991	1992	1993	1994	1995 (estimate)
Kazakstan	25.0	24.6	22.3	17.7	16.4
Kyrgyz Republic	35.7	12.7	23.3	21.6	14.5[a]
Lithuania	41.4	32.1	28.5	24.5	22.4
Russian Federation	n.a.	41.7	37.8	33.3	n.a.
Ukraine	36.5	41.5	41.1	44.3	41.3[b]
OECD	37.3	37.3	37.6	37.5	37.8

Note: General government revenue includes central, state and local government revenue, social security funds and some off-budget transactions.

[a] Government expenditure and net lending plus government balance.
[b] State budget revenue.
n.a. = not available
Source: 1991–1994: IMF; 1995: EBRD.

traditional tax bases, mainly taxes on turnover and enterprise profits, mirrors the sharp decline in output that occurred in the early years of the transition. In several eastern European countries, the cumulative (measured) output decline over 1990–92 ranged between 20 and 40 per cent.

Equally important has been the weakening of the government's institutional and administrative capacity for collecting key traditional revenues such as that from the business profits tax. Under central planning the tax on state enterprise profits was effectively a business withholding tax. With government setting input and output prices, the tax authorities had direct knowledge of and access to state enterprise profits. Transferring these profits to the centre was essentially a simple accounting transaction. The unified ("mono-bank") banking system further facilitated tax collection by centralizing relevant information. Privatization of state enterprises, the break-up of the old mono-bank system and private banking sector and price liberalization made for a dramatic reduction in the quantity and quality of information available to the centre concerning the former state enterprises. This reduction worsened the administrative capacity of the state for transferring revenue from the enterprises to the centre.

It remains a serious challenge in virtually all transition economies that much of the new private sector falls outside of the net of the enterprise profit tax. Tax compliance is generally poor. Avoidance and evasion are rife. The difficulties are not confined to profit taxes. The rise of the private sector in retail and administration increases the difficulty of collecting sales and turnover taxes.

The common tolerance for poor tax compliance is boosted by the fact that assessments are frequently arbitrary and by the many distortions in the tax system, which create inefficiencies and inequities. For instance, high inflation in Poland in 1990 (586 per cent per year) combined with historic cost accounting and the taxation of inventory valuation profits meant that accounting profits for tax purposes wildly overstated true profits (measured, say, on a cash-flow basis). This provided the government with a (strictly temporary) revenue boost, and saddled the enterprise sector with a sometimes crippling tax burden. The next year, inflation declined (to 70 per cent at an annual rate) and with it the revenue from the enterprise profit tax disappeared (see Schaffer, 1992).

The collapse of the ability to collect taxes is not confined to the transition economies of eastern Europe and the former Soviet Union. In China (an admittedly rather unique kind of transition economy) local and national government tax revenues were around 9 per cent of GDP, according to an estimate in *The Wall Street Journal*,[14] or 12 per cent of GDP, according to an internal IMF estimate, in 1994—compared with 31 per cent in 1978, when market reforms were first introduced.

The seriousness of the problems that arise when the central government cannot secure adequate revenue to perform its essential functions becomes apparent when we consider the history of the demise of the former Yugoslav Republic. The refusal of some of the key republics to adequately fund the federal government and the inability of the federal government to raise revenue in recalcitrant republics without their cooperation were key contributions to the death of the federal state. While there was undoubtedly two-way causation between the disintegration of the state and the collapse of the government's ability to tax, the conclusion that the ability to raise adequate revenue is a defining characteristic of any viable state is surely robust.

That is the bad news. The good news is that it is not impossible to extract the resources required for the general government to function effectively without excessive distortions, without excessive re-course to the inflation tax, without harming growth and without violating common standards of equity. Both economic theory and practical experience support this assertion. In addition to the reser-voir of theoretical knowledge and practical experience with the design and administration of tax systems in advanced industrial countries, there is now a growing body of knowledge on the special problems and issues associated with designing and administering an effective tax system in developing countries (surveyed, for example, in Newbery and Stern, 1987; Burgess and Stern, 1993; World Bank, 1991a) and in transition economies and countries in post-chaos/post-conflict situations (see, for example, Gil Díaz, 1987; Bagchi, Bird and Dasgupta, 1995; IMF, 1995a; Tanzi, 1992, 1993).

The responsibilities of government in the market economy

That the size of government should not be negligible becomes evident when we think more systematically about the essential tasks of government in a market economy.[15] This process will also highlight the fact that the importance of government is not captured well by its share of employment or GDP, by the magnitude of its total spending or by the revenue it raises. The key issue (and problem) is the integration and harmonization of its functions and those of the market, recognizing their essential complementarity.

The continued presence of a sizeable government sector even in the most market-oriented economic systems should, per se, neither surprise nor worry us. But before any task is assigned to the govern-ment, it first must be established exactly what the government can do that the private sector cannot, or not as well. As a rule it makes sense to be sceptical whenever policies or interventions are advo-cated whose success depends crucially on the government having better information, superior motivation or management capability, or higher moral standards than the private sector. To state this is not to take a cynical view of the motivation of public officials. For instance, it does *not* attribute a greater tendency towards self-serving behaviour to public servants than to the public at large. It only questions the assumption of sustained disinterested behaviour by public servants. There are, of course, many examples of individual public servants and even of groups of civil servants who have been engaged in disinterested sustained efforts in the pursuit of some widely accepted notion of the common good. It is hard to explain the success of the National Health Service in the United Kingdom (at least before Thatcher's reforms) in any other way and, in many ways, the remarkable performance of the United Kingdom's fire services. It is also clear, however, that a public service that relies overwhelmingly and exclusively on its employees' sense of civic duty, or on moral incentives generally, is bound to be fragile. When the opportunities for private gain at public expense—whether through still-legal rent-seeking behaviour or through outright corruption—become too attractive and the pressures for private enrichment mount, the odds lengthen against the public sector serving the public good.

We should never lose sight of the inescapable agency problems that crop up whenever a task is assigned on behalf of a principal (the citizens) to an agent (the government) whose interests and objectives need not be coincident with those of the principal. The individuals, groups and agencies that are charged with performing the functions of the state have their own agendas, possess insider (private) information and cannot be monitored continuously and closely. The omnipotent and benevolent social planner of normative economics has no more grounding in reality than the benevolent unaided invisible hand of libertarian lore. To give one example, it is not advisable to encumber the administration of the state with the task of picking winners among firms or industries. More generally, it is difficult to make a case for the state assuming an entrepreneurial role.

Albert Hirschman (1981), a prominent structuralist thinker, eloquently illustrates government failure in the following way:

In Latin America, new, more difficult tasks were continuously presented to the state and society, *whether or not* the previous tasks had been successfully disposed of. Indeed it almost seemed that the less satisfactorily a previous task had been grappled with, the greater was the jump in difficulty of the new task and the sooner it was introduced. (p. 122)

What makes the public sector unique is that the state alone can legitimately use force, in the sense that it has the power to prescribe or to proscribe physical or legal actions. There is an argument, therefore, that the state should act when the solution to a problem requires the involvement of an agent with the power to compel the behaviour of others, because voluntary exchange or bargaining is not sufficient to generate efficient or equitable outcomes.

In societies governed by the rule of law, the government's monopoly over the legitimate use of force—its power to coerce—is reflected in the following three powers: the power to tax, that is, the power to extract payment without a quid-pro-quo; the power to legislate and to enforce, that is, to prescribe or proscribe behaviour; and the power to declare one or more of its liabilities to be legal tender. Thus a minimalist view of the role of the state could hold that unless the solution to a problem requires at least one of these three powers, there is no prima-facie reason for the state to get involved. From this perspective the burden of proof falls on those advocating a role for the state.

Arguments for a more encompassing role in economic affairs (and in the life of the polity in general) often start from a more organic view of the state and a less dichotomous view of the relationship between the state and the individual than has been maintained in the discussion thus far. The state, the individual (or the family, or the household) and the commercial enterprise are connected through the web of civil society: the nexus of voluntary associations and organizations that influence virtually every aspect of our personal and professional lives. They include religious organizations, political parties, trades unions, professional associations, non-governmental organizations (NGOs), lobbying groups, charitable and other not-for-profit organizations, sports clubs, the temperance movement, neighbourhood watches, consumer associations, citizen's advice bureaus, ombudsmen, the boy scouts, the extended family and many others. Clearly, it is often hard to determine where the state ends and civil society begins. To take the United Kingdom as an example: where do quasi-autonomous non-government organizations (quangos) belong, such as the Arts Council and the various regulatory bodies that have been created as privatization has gathered pace since 1979? Where do we put the National Lottery and its regulatory body? What about the Church of England and other established or state churches? Theocracies throughout the world and history have denied that the distinction between church and state was relevant. When we think of the state and the individual not as a simple dichotomy but rather as two extremes on a continuum of modes of association and social interaction, the model of a minimalist state is less likely to recommend itself.

It is also true that the state can bring together or unify its citizens and focus them on particular issues or activities without any direct or overt use of the three powers mentioned above. Often, the state is identified with a nation and the nation with a culture, making the state a natural guardian or custodian of that culture (and of the nation). This role brings with it a range of obligations. An open question remains, however, as to the extent to which this role as a natural national focal point is, ultimately, derived from its power to coerce.

Whatever one's view on the appropriate tasks to be performed by the government, it is evident that there have been (and continue to be) important differences in the effectiveness with which governments in different countries, with distinct cultures and varied histories, discharge similar tasks. It is important to try to learn from the more successful government bureaucracies and to determine to what extent superior organization and practice are culturally and historically transferable.

It is probably not controversial to assert that there is no prima-facie reason for the government to produce pure private (rival and excludable) goods and services that do not give rise to external effects. Examples include cars, bread, electricity, coal and steel. Even with "impure" private goods or with partial or even pure public goods, the case for public provision (production and distribution) is often weak, although there may be a prima-facie case for some government intervention (such as through direct purchasing subsidization, taxation or regulation). For example, in the case of non-rival but excludable goods (video and audio signals transmitted by satellite but subject to scrambling at little cost), provision by properly regulated private suppliers is likely to be more efficient than public provision. Natural monopolies (for example, rail track, electricity transmission grids, water distribution and sewage collection through pipes) call for state intervention. The optimal form of intervention may be private ownership and operation with subsidization and regulation rather than state ownership and public management. The choice may vary within an industry (an electricity transmission grid may be publicly owned, whereas electricity generation may be private) and across industries—most telecommunications services may be private (but subject to regulation).

Public sector production need not involve subsidization. There are many examples of profitable state enterprises that make net financial contributions to the government, either through the ordinary tax mechanism or through direct transfers of part of their surplus. Two special problems faced by public sector producers are the weakness (sometimes the absence) of incentives for cost minimization and the special problems of political pressures on public sector pricing. When prices are set directly by the government, they are likely to become the subject of popular discontent (as in the case of food prices) or of lobbying by sectoral interests (as in the case of the water and electricity prices paid by agricultural producers). Of course, such pressures do not disappear if production is private and prices are market-determined. Instead, they are transformed into calls for subsidies and other forms of assistance. Nevertheless, calls for subsidies in a reasonably transparent market are likely to be easier to resist than calls for favourable public sector pricing when the government *is* the market.

Pressures for containing costs in public sector production are likely to be more effective when the public producer operates in a competitive market environment for which a regulator or overseer can establish reasonably objective yardsticks for costs and rates of return (see Vickers and Yarrow, 1988, 1991). While this reason is not enough to establish the desirability of public sector production, it does provide a way of improving public sector performance.

In a well-functioning market economy we would expect to see only a small non-financial state enterprise sector and a financial state sector restricted to little more than the central bank. The productive role of the general government sector would include providing intermediate public goods and services, such as public administration, defence and law and order,[16] and investing resources to maintain or expand its future capacity to provide these intermediate public goods and services. For these intermediate public goods and services contracting out is not an attractive option. Law and order and national security are examples. Private justice ("the best judges money can buy") is unlikely to be an idea whose time will come. Defence is an intermediate public good for which private provision is unlikely to dominate public provision. A final example of a public intermediate good—one that will be discussed at greater length in the third and fourth sections—is macroeconomic stability.

This same debate arises over other activities currently performed by the general government sector. There are good efficiency, distributional and merit-good arguments (discussed at greater length below) supporting government funding (partly or wholly) or subsidization of education, health care, child protection, drug rehabilitation, the arts and the collection and treatment of garbage, sewage, and so on. But these arguments do not necessarily imply that these services must be provided (produced and distributed) by the public sector. We may wish to subsidize the arts and education, but the members of the symphony orchestra or of the teaching profession do not necessarily have to be public servants.

The minimum tasks of the government of a modern market economy or of a transition economy are listed below. Note that the arguments for government intervention include but are not restricted to the familiar triad based on standard microeconomic welfare economics: enforcing the rules of the game, intervening in the case of market failures and redistributing income.[17]

- Guarantee the rule of law and the internal (law and order) and external (defence) security of persons and property.
- Correct market failures. This (Pigovian) function of the government consists of attempting to correct, through taxes, subsidies and regulation, those inefficiencies and market failures that cannot, because of transaction costs, such as asymmetric information, be internalized and negotiated away through private (Coase) bargains. These inefficiencies and market failures can result from externalities, missing markets, abuse of market power and other forms of non-competitive behaviour, increasing returns, public goods or imperfect information. It is important not to be overambitious: in many instances of market failure, government failure is also likely to occur, especially when informational problems (par-

ticularly those resulting in moral hazard) are the cause of market failure. Economists from the public choice school go further, asserting that the government itself is an important cause of inefficiency and market failure, because politicians and civil servants have considerable discretion to pursue private sectoral interests that are likely to be at odds with any reasonable notion of the common good. They use their discretion to interfere with the efficient functioning of markets in order to extract private rents.

• Pursue distributional objectives that are not met through voluntary private redistribution, within and across generations, using taxes, transfer payments, spending programs, regulation and other administrative measures. These objectives include the prevention, elimination or reduction of poverty and can also include a more general concern with the distribution of income. Why would individuals be unwilling or unable to voluntarily redistribute income between social groups (or generations—see the fourth point below) and at the same time ask the government to do so? Part of the answer is that the government helps solve the "free rider problem" of redistribution in communities with large numbers of potential contributors and recipients. While I might be willing to pay to prevent poverty elsewhere, I would probably prefer to have someone else pay for it. Purely voluntary contributions could be depressed below the socially optimal level if distributional preferences and willingness to pay can be dissimulated. Notions of fairness, of shared burdens, also are likely to play a role. Once compulsion[18] becomes part of the efficient redistributional mechanism, a role for the state in redistribution cannot be avoided. Once we move beyond the scale of small local communities with direct face-to-face contact, monitoring and enforcement, redistribution is also subject to economies of scope, scale and coordination. While any redistributional monopoly might do in principle, the state seems an obvious choice, although other institutions, such as the church, have in the past assumed many of the distributional functions today exercised by the state.

• Enforce the rights of future generations. These distributional issues are often tied up with efficiency questions, including the inter-generational transmission of environmental externalities.

- Give expression to legitimate paternalism by subsidizing the provision of merit goods, like education, or by enacting policies that affect pensions, health insurance and drugs. Alternatively, such policies can be seen as the government asserting and enforcing the rights of some or all citizens to certain facilities or goods, such as education, health and housing.
- Finance public spending in a non-distortionary and equitable manner.

The relative space given to these items in our discussion should not be seen as an indication of our judgement of their importance. Our concern here is mainly with macroeconomic issues and thus with factors influencing levels of taxation and spending, rather than with the details of its composition.

High real interest rates

Real interest rates in the industrial world have been higher since the early 1980s than in any interval spanning a decade or longer since 1850 (table 2.2). The 5.1 per cent real interest rates achieved on average in Germany, Japan, the United Kingdom and the United States over 1981–93 are unprecedented. Also, the "Keynesian era"—from about 1945 until the end of the 1970s—was one of historically low real interest rates, not only when compared with the 1980s and 1990s, but also when compared with 1850–1929.

The pattern observed for the real interest rate is the same for the excess of the real interest rate over the growth rate of real GDP, which, on average for France, Germany, the United Kingdom and the United States, was negative from 1933 until about 1980, but rose to 3.0 per cent in 1981–83. During the first three years of the Great Depression (1929–32) steep declines in the general price level turned fairly high nominal interest rates into very high ex-post real interest rates. The associated painful process of debt deflation was described accurately by contemporary observers like Irving Fisher (1932). As real GDP collapsed, the excess of the real interest rate over the growth rate was extremely high during the first three years of the Great Depression.

In 1933 the industrial world entered the "Keynesian era", in which real interest rates were low both historically and compared with the growth rate of real GDP. If the interest rate is persistently (if not

Table 2.2: Long-term interest rates in the major OECD countries, 1850–1993

Country	1850s	1860s	1870s	1880s	1890s	1900–13	1924–29	1930–32	1933–39	1956–73	1974–80	1981–93
Nominal interest rate												
United States	5.1	5.1	5.0	3.6	3.5	3.9	3.6	3.4	2.6	4.7	7.9	9.5
Japan										5.6	8.2	6.0
Germany	3.9	4.2	4.3	3.9	3.3	3.7	7.1	9.3	5.2	7.0	7.8	7.7
France	4.5	4.4	4.7	3.7	3.0	3.3	5.1	3.6	4.2	6.6	11.1	11.2
United Kingdom	3.2	3.3	3.2	3.0	2.5	3.1	4.5	4.3	3.2	6.9	13.3	10.5
Italy							5.7	5.0	4.6	5.9	12.6	13.6
Canada						3.8	4.7	4.8	3.5	5.8	9.7	10.9
Four-country average[a]	4.1	4.2	4.3	3.5	3.1	3.5	5.1	5.1	3.8	6.3	10.0	9.7
Real interest rate												
United States	4.3	1.7	7.6	5.2	5.4	2.3	3.6	11.5	1.1	1.1	−0.3	5.6
Japan										0.3	0.5	4.4
Germany	1.8	3.3	3.6	3.8	2.9	3.5	5.3	17.1	4.9	3.0	3.0	4.5
France	2.0	4.7	5.1	3.8	3.8	1.8	0.2	7.1	−1.2	1.0	0.4	5.7
United Kingdom	1.8	2.8	3.2	3.7	1.9	2.7	5.5	6.4	2.1	1.8	−3.3	4.5
Italy							5.7	12.7	0.4	1.1	−5.0	4.2
Canada							4.9	10.0	1.8	2.2	0.3	6.7
Four-country average[a]	2.5	3.1	4.9	4.1	3.5	2.6	3.7	10.5	1.7	1.7	0.0	5.1
GDP growth rate												
United States	3.2	3.1	6.2	3.7	4.5	4.1	3.5	−11.1	4.9	3.5	2.1	2.6
Japan										9.1	3.6	3.6
Germany	2.6	2.1	2.1	3.3	2.7	3.5	2.4	−7.1	10.6	4.7	2.2	1.8
France	1.3	1.8	1.0	1.4	2.1	1.6	3.4	−5.3	2.0	5.2	2.8	1.8
United Kingdom	2.2	3.0	1.8	1.3	2.1	1.7	2.3	−1.7	3.7	2.8	1.0	1.9
Italy								−1.0	3.4	5.2	2.9	1.8

Table 2.2 (cont.)

Country	1850s	1860s	1870s	1880s	1890s	1900–13	1924–29	1930–32	1933–39	1956–73	1974–80	1981–93
Canada						5.1	6.1	–8.9	7.7	5.1	3.8	2.4
Four-country average[a]	2.3	2.5	2.8	2.4	2.8	2.7	2.9	–6.3	5.3	4.1	2.0	2.1
Real interest rate – growth rate												
United States	1.1	–1.4	1.4	1.5	0.9	–1.9	0.2	22.5	–3.8	–2.4	–2.4	3.0
Japan										–8.8	–3.1	0.7
Germany	–0.7	1.3	1.5	0.5	0.1	0.0	2.9	24.2	–5.8	–1.7	0.8	2.7
France	0.7	2.9	4.1	2.4	1.8	0.2	–3.3	12.4	–3.2	–4.3	–2.4	3.9
United Kingdom	–0.4	–0.2	1.3	2.4	–0.2	1.0	3.2	8.1	–1.6	–1.0	–4.3	2.6
Italy							2.7	13.7	–3.0	–4.1	–7.8	2.4
Canada						–3.5	–1.2	18.9	–5.9	–2.8	–3.5	4.3
Four-country average[a]	0.2	0.6	2.1	1.7	0.7	–0.2	0.8	16.8	–3.6	–2.3	–2.1	3.0

[a] Four-country average = United States, Germany, France, United Kingdom.

Source: OECD historical statistics for 1966–90; OECD main economic indicators and OECD National Accounts, supplemented as required by data on interest rates from Homer (1991). Pre-World War II data on interest rates are from Homer (1991); pre-World War II data on GDP and prices are from Mitchell (1992, 1993). Conversion to real terms is based on the GDP deflator.

generally) below the growth rate, the government solvency constraint fails to have any short- or medium-term relevance: it is not necessary to generate future primary surpluses or future seigniorage in order to service the outstanding stock of public debt, no matter how high the debt-GDP ratio is![19]

From the budget constraint of the consolidated general government and central bank (henceforth the government), it follows that the change in the government debt-GDP ratio over some period is the sum of two components. The first, representing the intrinsic debt-GDP dynamics, equals the debt-GDP ratio at the beginning of that period multiplied by the excess of the real interest rate over the growth rate of real GDP during that period. This component shows whether the cost of meeting that period's contractual interest obligations exceeds or falls short of the growth in the government's ability to service the debt. The second represents the discretionary component of the increase in the debt-GDP ratio. It is the government sector's primary (non-interest) deficit as a fraction of GDP, *minus* seigniorage (new issues of government base money) as a fraction of GDP.[20]

For example, ignoring seigniorage, the debt-GDP ratio will fall when real GDP growth exceeds the real rate of interest, as long as the primary deficit is smaller than the outstanding stock of debt multiplied by the excess of the growth rate over the rate of interest.[21] Table 2.2 makes it clear that the days of pain-free deficit financing are gone. With the real interest rate above the real growth rate in all but a handful of rapidly growing economies, the government solvency constraint has become a binding constraint on the ability of governments to spend, whatever their motivation. Likewise, the national solvency constraint also became binding in a very visible and tangible way for a large number of highly indebted developing countries during 1981–82.

In the long run the real rate of interest balances planned saving and planned investment in a financially closed economic system (for example, the world economy as a whole). In the short run monetary policy may have a powerful impact on the real interest rate because of nominal price and wage rigidities. Also in the short run, variations in the level of economic activity may, through the Keynesian multiplier mechanism, balance planned saving and planned investment at rates of unemployment and capacity utilization that can depart significantly from their natural levels. Abstracting from these short-run, cyclical considerations, the real interest rate in a financially closed system is, in the long run, governed by the classical forces of thrift and productivity. A financially open economy can pay for an excess of domestic capital formation over national savings by running an external current account deficit—that is, by borrowing from abroad. It can dispose of excess national savings over domestic capital formation by running an external current account surplus—that is, by investing abroad.

Whether high and/or rising equilibrium real interest rates need cause concern depend on what causes them.[22] There are "good news" increases in the real rate of interest, reflecting buoyant investment demand outstripping even robust and healthy savings performance. There also are "bad news" increases in the real rate of interest, reflecting a disappointing and inadequate savings effort, choking off a not necessarily spectacular investment performance.

The increase in the real rate of interest since 1980 appears to be mainly a "bad news" increase, reflecting a worsening in the savings performance of the industrial countries other than Japan, rather than a booming world demand for capital investment.[23]

We do not anticipate that, in a properly managed world economy, the industrial world's demand for capital will decline in the decades to come. If the benefits from increased global economic integration are to be widely shared by workers, owners of capital and consumers in the industrial world, significant restructuring will have to take place in industrial countries. As noted already, both defensive and strategic restructuring require capital formation, broadly defined. If the new industrial countries of south-east Asia and, more recently, of Latin America are to continue their success, their demands for capital are also bound to remain buoyant. Successful completion of the transition in eastern Europe and the former Soviet Union will require substantial physical capital formation in these countries, given the prevailing imbalance between the high quality of their human capital and the decrepit state of much of their industrial capital stock and physical infrastructure. If the less successful developing countries are to join the community of fast growing nations, they too will have to raise substantially their capital formation rates (both physical and human). And the two largest countries in the world, China and India, are following ambitious programmes involving rapid growth, liberalization and restructuring, which are likely to require high investment.

Realizing the legitimate ambitions of a growing world population for a sustained and high growth rate in standards of living is likely to require a significant increase in the global rate of capital formation. Unless there is a matching increase in the global savings rate, the ex-post reconciliation of ex-ante investment and savings plans that are inconsistent will occur through high real interest rates, crowding out capital formation.

While transition economies and developing countries can contribute some of this required increase in the global savings rate, most of the additional saving will have to come from the industrial world, at least in the next decade or so. Saving behaviour in the transition economies is likely to be subject to a number of influences pulling in different directions. Under the previous (communist) regime risks were socialized, with the government guaranteeing employment (thus eliminating open unemployment risk) and fully funding (and providing) health care and disability compensation. With the collapse of communism, households are faced for the first time with the risk of unemployment, with low and time-limited unemployment compensation and with reduced public provision and financing of health care and disability compensation. The need for private provision of these services to cope with these risks therefore arises, with clear implications for saving behaviour.[24] With incomplete risk markets the accumulation of a stock of liquid financial assets provides a (second-best) way of providing for a rainy day (purchasing rainy-day insurance would be the first-best solution). Such precautionary saving behaviour has been quantitatively significant in industrial countries, and there is no reason to believe that this will not be the case in transition economies.[25]

In transition economies precautionary behaviour would in part be reflected in attempts to build up the ratio of financial wealth to income. Given the highly imperfect financial and capital markets that private savers in transition economies faced, and a wish to provide for retirement, there is likely to be a perceived need to restore the financial wealth—income ratio to more prudent levels than those inherited from the early transition phase. Note that under communism private financial wealth (which consisted mainly of foreign and domestic cash holdings and bank deposits) was already very low relative to income, and that much financial wealth in transition economies was destroyed in the near-hyperinflations of the first phase of the transition. As the market economy grows, we should expect a significant build-up of private financial wealth (including equity in residential housing) towards levels (in relation to income) typical of those in industrial market economies. Such stock-correction effects may be significant.

With a relatively unsophisticated financial sector it is often impossible for households to borrow in order to acquire the funds to make the minimal downpayment for a housing purchase or for the purchase of some other big-ticket consumer durable. Because of the inability to collateralize these consumer assets and the limited domain of secure transactions, households will typically have to save for some time before purchasing a "lumpy" or indivisible durable good in order to build up the liquid balances necessary to make the downpayment. Improvement in the ability to collateralize real estate and moveable property reduces the need to save prior to making durable purchases. Thus the elimination (or mitigation) of a capital market imperfection could lead to a reduction in the savings rate.

Reinforcing this is the negative effect of a successful transition and structural adjustment on the savings rate, which is likely to come through the "permanent versus current income" channel—a higher anticipated growth rate of future real income will raise permanent income above current income. For standard life-cycle/permanent-income reasons this would depress private savings rates. Another way in which successful transition, stabilization or structural adjustment affects private savings rates is by reducing the volatility and uncertainty concerning future income streams. This will tend to lower precautionary savings.

Demographic developments differ greatly between the "youth-deficit" countries of eastern Europe and the European parts of the former Soviet Union and some of the Islamic countries of the former Soviet Union. The saving implications of these demographic differences are likely to be important in the former group, and they are likely to limit possibilities for raising savings.

On balance, it seems likely that socially desirable investment programmes in the new industrial countries, developing countries and transition economies will outstrip domestic saving capacities. Significant and persistent current account deficits in the non-industrial world will therefore have to be financed by an excess of industrial-country saving over industrial-country domestic capital formation. If an appropriate *full-employment* current account surplus fails to materialize in industrial countries, one of two things will happen. Either financial autarky will be imposed on the would-be capital importers through higher real interest rates and international credit rationing, or a recession in industrial countries will weaken their investment demand to such an extent that the *low-employment* current account surpluses of industrial countries can fund the financial deficit of the rest of the world. Both of these scenarios are unattractive. It is up to the industrial countries to switch their monetary-fiscal policy mix towards a more restrictive budgetary stance and a more expansionary monetary stance, which are necessary if the industrial world is to generate larger full-employment current account surpluses.

Given the mixed prospects for saving behaviour in transition economies and developing countries in the absence of policies specifically designed to raise national savings rates, what are the available policy options? Past research has not documented any significant sensitivity of aggregate private saving to its real after-tax rate of return. If this empirical regularity continues to hold, we must look for policy changes or other exogenous events that raise public saving without reducing private saving, or for developments that shift the private saving function outward, that is, raise the amount saved by the private sector at any given rate of return for a given level of public saving. A number of policy options (most of which can be applied throughout the world) are considered in the fifth section.

THE IMPORTANCE OF MACROECONOMIC STABILITY

Macroeconomic stability is an intermediate public good whose provision cannot be contracted out to the private sector. Not only is its financing the natural province of the state, producing or providing it is one of the inescapable responsibilities of national governments and international agencies and institutions.

Macroeconomic instability—causes, consequences and cures

Macroeconomic stability matters because uncertainty impairs economic performance. Macroeconomic instability contributes significantly to uncertainty faced by enterprises and households (as workers, as savers/portfolio holders and as consumers). We have written at length elsewhere about macroeconomic instability (see Buiter, Lago and Stern, 1995), so we will be relatively brief here. In examining the costs of avoidable macroeconomic instability, it is necessary to consider the implications of loss of control, the damage inflicted by corrective stabilization policy measures necessitated by loss of control and the cost of policy actions intended to forestall future loss of control. All international finance institutions have an interest in these issues. Several of them, such as the IMF and the World Bank, play an important role in macroeconomic adjustment programmes for individual countries. Others, such as the WTO and its predecessor, the GATT (and also the IMF), play a key role in designing, monitoring and enforcing international rules of conduct that can reduce the risk that member states will adopt negative-sum national policies.

There are two distinct kinds of macroeconomic instability that can have a major impact on microeconomic performance. The first concerns global systemic failure and the ensuing collapse of effective demand and economic activity. The Great Depression of the 1930s is the prime example of such a catastrophic development. Fortunately, such systemic coordination failure is as rare as it is serious. In our view we have the knowledge and the means, in principle, to cope with this particular contingency globally— through institutions like the IMF, the Bank for International Settlements (BIS), the G-7 or the OECD—and at the regional and national levels—through multilateral agencies, national governments and central banks. Even in the absence of global economic disaster, there is a role for international policy coordination and cooperation to internalize the international spillovers from national macro-economic policies. Exchange rate surveillance, as practiced by the IMF, is one recognition of inter-dependence and co-dependence. The collective monitoring of the performance of European Union (EU) member states with respect to the Maastricht convergence criteria (for inflation rates, interest rates, exchange rates, public debt and public deficits) is another example of a collective institutional response to the perception of spillovers and international externalities.

The debt crisis of the 1980s is also an example of a systemic macroeconomic problem. Its origins can be traced to national macro-economic mismanagement, both in the creditor countries of the industrial world and in the indebted developing countries, following the oil price shocks of 1973 and 1979 and the oil exporting countries' resulting need to "recycle" their current account surpluses. International financial markets, commercial banks, national economic policy-makers and some international finance institutions overestimated the extent to which the low (ex-post) real interest rates of the 1970s would persist into the future and underestimated the likelihood of sovereign default.

The second kind of macroeconomic instability concerns unsustainable fiscal, financial and monetary policy programmes. It often manifests itself through outright inflationary financing or through a significant rise in the public debt-GDP ratio without a commensurate increase in the government's capacity to generate sufficient future primary (non-interest) budget surpluses. The "technocratic" costs of achieving and maintaining macroeconomic stability are probably not very high—simply the salaries of the (non-corrupt) central bank and treasury officials in charge of the design and implementation of macroeconomic policy. The political costs of eliminating the real resource appropriation patterns associated with high inflation and non-transparent budgetary and quasi-budgetary procedures represent the real obstacles to change. High and rising inflation, occasionally even exploding into hyperinflation, results when domestic and international markets are unwilling to absorb monetary or non-monetary debt in quantities sufficient to finance the government's budget deficit in a non-inflationary manner.

Moreover, as the Mexican crisis of 1994–95 shows, high inflation can also be the ultimate outcome of a sequence of events that starts with an unsustainable increase in externally financed private sector spending and culminates in a banking and foreign exchange crisis with large private losses, which eventually lead to government budget deficits or quasi-fiscal deficits if these losses are subsequently underwritten (wholly or in part) by the public sector. Of course, the anticipation of an eventual public sector bail-out makes this chain of events more likely. Improved supervision of domestic financial institutions (especially banks), a credible commitment not to bail out domestic or foreign investors and financial institutions and controls on capital inflows are the only policy options capable of forestalling such crises.

Increased recourse to the inflation tax when faced with an otherwise unfinanceable public sector deficit is unlikely to provide a lasting solution to the problem of an inconsistent fiscal, financial and monetary programmes. The amount of real resources that can be appropriated through the inflation tax is limited and will ultimately fall when the rate of inflation becomes sufficiently high.[26] This "seigniorage Laffer curve" reflects both direct international currency substitution (away from the local currency and towards hard currencies) and a shift into domestic non-monetary assets that are better hedges against inflation. The ability to avoid the inflation tax is unequally distributed: the inflation tax, in addition to being inefficient, strikes most strongly at the poor and the weak, who are less able to avoid the tax by switching their portfolios towards domestic and foreign assets that are better hedges against inflation. Further, very high inflation may increase the primary deficit—the fiscal deficit excluding interest payments—through the so-called Olivera-Tanzi effect, which arises from delays in settling tax obligations when these are not properly indexed to inflation or subject to an appropriate interest penalty.

When the government or the country is (de facto) rationed out of domestic and international financial markets and when the limits of the inflation tax have been reached, a crunch is unavoidable. Public and private spending will have to be slashed and revenues increased—or the government (or country) will have to default on outstanding debt. Such corrections are both unavoidable and painful. The external manifestations of retrenchment are import compression and the shifting of production of tradable goods towards exports rather than towards domestic absorption. The necessary reduction in domestic absorption typically leads, at least in the short run, to a contraction of production and an increase in open or hidden unemployment.

Two points must be made about the costs associated with macroeconomic tightening. First, it makes no sense to criticize governments, or those international finance institutions that may advise them, for taking corrective actions. The need to adjust arises from unsustainable policies. Second, there is always a non-trivial range of choices concerning the composition of the policy correction. There are choices about which spending categories to cut, which taxes to raise and which categories of debt to default on or reschedule. There may also be flexibility on timing, although this will depend on the cooperation of external agents and on their perceptions of markets.

Aggregate evidence on the relationship between macroeconomic instability and economic growth

Over the last three decades low or moderate inflation and reduced macroeconomic distortions (such as overvalued official exchange rates) have been characteristics of fast-growing economies, as can be seen in table 2.3. Conversely, economies with a poorer growth record have experienced higher inflation and stronger distortions.

Nevertheless, the time-series and cross-sectional evidence on the

Table 2.3: Some macroeconomic characteristics of fast and slow growers, 1960–89

	Fast growers (per cent)	Slow growers (per cent)	t-statistic
Inflation rate	12	31	–1.7
Black market exchange rate premium	14	57	–3.8
Investment/GDP	23	17	5.2
Export/GDP	32	23	2.3

Source: Levine and Renelt (1992, table 3). Sample of 109 countries, fast growers are the 56 countries whose growth rate of per capita income exceeds the mean; slow growers are the remaining 53 countries.

relationship between macroeconomic stability, on the one hand, and microeconomic efficiency and growth, on the other, should be interpreted with care. Both macroeconomic and microeconomic performance are endogenous. There may be no straightforward causal interpretation of the correlation between the two or the incremental predictive content of the one with respect to the other. The possibility of two-way causation—and even of common third factors causing both—is especially relevant at low and moderate rates of inflation. When annual inflation begins to run in the hundreds or when monthly inflation rates get into double digits, there can be little doubt, however, that macroeconomic malfeasance depresses growth and lowers allocative efficiency. Referring to the experience of a group of very high-inflation, middle-income countries, Bruno (1993) states:

The fact that growth is systematically higher after a sharp stabilisation is consistent with the finding that very high rates of inflation are definitely harmful to growth. Stabilisation by itself, even before sustainable resumption of investment and long-run growth, improves resource allocation and total factor productivity.

Support for this proposition can be found in a large number of case studies (see, for example, Cooper and others, 1993; Corden, 1990; Bruno and others, 1991).

On the other hand, at lower rates of inflation (say 15 per cent a year or lower) there is less evidence of any clear pattern of covariation between inflation and growth or between inflation and other observable indices of efficiency, such as total factor productivity. Much of the relevant evidence is surveyed, discussed and extended in Fischer (1991, 1993). These conclusions are confirmed in a recent paper by Barro (1995a), in which the empirical evidence from more than 100 countries over a period of 30 years suggests that the adverse effect of inflation on growth is clear only when inflation is high: the estimated coefficient of growth on inflation is statistically significant (albeit small)[27] when inflation averages more than 15 per cent per year. The estimated coefficient of growth on inflation is not statistically significant when inflation averages less than 15 percent per year.[28, 29] Thus, in speaking of the damaging effects of inflation on performance, one must be clear that it is the high rates of inflation that are at issue.

Macroeconomic instability and enterprises

Technology, the quantity and quality of material inputs and outputs, and the skills of labour and management are clearly essential to enterprise performance. But the macroeconomic environment surrounding the enterprise is no less relevant. Comparable projects and enterprises perform very differently in countries with differing macroeconomic and regulatory frameworks (see, for example, Kaufmann, 1991 and World Bank, 1991b). If these frameworks provide stable signals and low transaction costs, the quality of enterprise decisions, and thus the odds of success, improve. Any factors influencing the cost to firms of entering into contracts (be they implicit or explicit, market-mediated or administratively determined, repeated or one-off, with outsiders or with insiders) and of monitoring and enforcing them will affect enterprise performance. The macroeconomic environment is an important determinant of the transaction costs incurred by the parties that are stakeholders in the enterprise and by the enterprise itself in its market-mediated transactions with other enterprises, households and other customers or suppliers.

The mechanisms linking inflation to microeconomic performance can be spelled out more explicitly. At a qualitative level, the connections are reasonably well understood:[30] the costs associated with fully anticipated inflation are "shoe-leather" costs, borne mainly by households, and "menu costs", borne mainly by firms.[31] They are real but unimportant costs. If there were no other costs associated with inflation, no one would lose sleep because of it.

More important is the empirical fact that high inflation tends to be associated with variable and uncertain inflation, and variable and uncertain relative prices. The reasons for this empirical association lie partly in the nature of private and public sector wage and price-setting mechanisms—and more generally in the range of contracting arrangements among economic agents—and partly in the realm of political economy. High inflation is often the ultimate monetary manifestation of unresolved social conflict about public spending and its financing. Resolving this conflict is a highly uncertain process. Since complete contingent markets are a theoretical abstraction, high inflation increases the incidence of false signals and creates confusion about the interpretation of observed price changes. How can one know whether they are permanent or transitory? Are they relative price changes requiring an allocative response or just "local" manifestations of an increase in the general price level, requiring no resource reallocation? By increasing the "noise-to-signal ratio" of observed price changes, inflation impairs the allocative efficiency of the price mechanism.

Inflation (especially high and uncertain inflation) and the anticipation of (eventual) future fiscal and monetary policy actions taken to control inflation increase uncertainty in the economic environment within which private agents make production and investment decisions. Future fiscal correction may directly affect business profitability if it involves changes in taxes or subsidies. Changes in public sector infrastructure investment may directly impinge on future project performance. In addition, fiscal retrenchment will tend to be associated with a cyclical decline in economic activity, a reduction in employment and a depreciation of the real exchange rate (an increase in the relative price ratio of traded to non-traded goods), as well as with changes in other key relative prices (for example, real wages and energy prices).

Investment involves the commitment of resources today in anticipation of future, uncertain returns. To some degree, the investment decision is irreversible, and the resources committed to investment projects are "sunk"—they cannot be easily recovered or reallocated to alternative uses if the expectations of future profits fail to materialize (see Dixit and Pindyck, 1994). In other words, when a firm installs a unit of capital today, it also acquires the put option of reselling that unit of capital at some future date. The value of that put option will be greater the higher the resale price (net of adjustment costs) relative to the current purchase price and the lower the uncertainty surrounding future returns to the investment. From this perspective, increased uncertainty increases investment.

Other arguments, associated with costs of expansion if plant size proves inadequate, point in the direction of contracting investment in response to greater uncertainty. The argument is developed by Abel and others (1995) and is sometimes summarized as the "limited expandability" effect. Whether the response of investment to increased uncertainty is positive or negative on balance is an empirical issue. Regardless of whether investment is expanded or contracted, delayed or brought forward, real economic performance worsens as a result of the increase in uncertainty, because the firm and the economy are more likely to be stuck with excess capacity or deficient capacity. Recent firm-level empirical evidence for the United States suggests that an increase in uncertainty depresses investment (see Leahy and Whited, 1996). The empirical evidence surveyed by Pindyck and Solimano (1993) suggests that investment is more likely to be delayed and depressed in the aftermath of stabilization in high-inflation countries. If the irreversibility effect dominates the limited expandability effect, investors would rationally exercise such a wait-and-see option (see Dornbusch, 1990). Only when sufficient commitment to the reform process is shown and a track record is established does private investment resume strongly.

Greater caution may therefore be the rational private sector response to macroeconomic instability. This is compounded by the financial short-termism effect of high inflation. Private markets, for reasons that are not wholly understood, often do not fully index the capital value of long-term outstanding debt but do fully index short-term interest rates. In this borrowing environment loans inevitably become very short-term. And long-term financing of investment may be impossible—borrowers are faced continuously with the problem of rolling over their debt, and the risk of a credit crunch is everpresent.

Macroeconomic instability and households

Macroeconomic instability affects households through inflation and through the likelihood and duration of unemployment. Even in countries that have public unemployment insurance[32] programmes, the standard of living of workers falls sharply when they are made redundant. Much of an individual's unemployment and labour income risk is idiosyncratic, that is, specific to the individual. Idiosyncratic risk is, in principle, diversifiable. But because of adverse selection and moral hazard problems, most individual labour income and unemployment risk cannot be insured privately.[33] Unemployment risk does have a common component, however, reflecting economy-wide macroeconomic developments, both cyclical and structural. Since these aggregate or common risks cannot be insured (although the income consequences for the unemployed can be), economic performance can be enhanced only by minimizing the shocks that perturb the unemployment rate.

Without subscribing to the "if it moves, stop it" approach to stabilization policy, we accept the view that not all fluctuations in output and employment represent Pareto-efficient fluctuations in the natural rate of unemployment. Both aggregate demand shocks and aggregate supply shocks can produce (possibly persistent) deviations of the actual unemployment rate from the natural rate and of actual output from capacity output. Well-designed stabilization policy does not amplify such fluctuations with inappropriate monetary and fiscal policies, but tries to buffer and offset shocks producing deviations of the actual from the natural rate originating in the domestic private sector and abroad. At the very least this means letting the automatic fiscal stabilizers do their work.[34] Allowing for predictable endogenous fluctuations in velocity when pursuing monetary targets or interpreting monetary indicators is another necessary ingredient of any well-designed macroeconomic stabilization rule.

Inflation affects households through a number of channels. We have already referred to the shoe leather cost of anticipated inflation. While these costs are likely to be negligible for low or moderate rates of inflation, very high rates of inflation can divert significant resources from socially productive activities to privately rational but socially unproductive activities, such as management of hyperactive financial portfolios and rent seeking. Typically, the financial and public relations managers of enterprises become more senior and better paid than the production manager.

Imperfect indexation in the public and private sectors means that high (and uncertain) inflation is associated with major redistributions of resources from domestic currency creditors to domestic currency debtors and, more generally, from the economically weak and unsophisticated to the economically agile and well-connected. Since workers' financial portfolios in developing countries are largely restricted to transaction cash balances, the inflation tax has been viewed as an outright tax on wages. The regressive nature of the inflation tax and the negative effects of rising inflation on real wages in general have been extensively documented in countries with chronic high inflation, such as Argentina and Brazil (see, for example, Cardoso, 1992 and Cardoso, Paes de Barros and Urani, 1995). In a recent study of Brazil, Kane and Morisett (1993) show, using data disaggregated by income strata, that high inflation hurts the lower and middle classes far more than the upper quintile of the population, who manage to insulate themselves from its effects by taking advantage of high real interest rates and better (less imperfect) indexation devices to shelter their incomes.

Open inflation is not the only manifestation of macroeconomic instability and not the only macroeconomic evil distorting enterprise decision-making and performance. The underlying, fundamental problem is the sustainability of fiscal and financial policies. Frequently, governments are able to "repress" inflation for a while by borrowing heavily, mostly internationally. As Corden (1990) has emphasized, for a given budget deficit governments often confront a short-run trade-off between monetary financing and external borrowing (that is, a trade-off between inflation and the current account deficit). If external finance is available, the inflationary impact of a given budget deficit can be temporarily "repressed" by letting the exchange rate become overvalued. This strategy, however, may eventually lead to a foreign exchange crisis—and to the introduction of foreign exchange controls and/or outright default—and thus to a sharp adjustment of the nominal and real exchange rate and subsequent high inflation. Many of the enterprise decisions—predicated on the relative prices and rules prevailing prior to the crisis—may have translated into investments and production processes that are no longer financially viable after the crunch. The resulting sunk investment costs impose heavy deadweight losses on society.

Countries prone to social conflict and macroeconomic instability often embark on stabilization attempts that they subsequently abandon, following a recurrent pattern. This stop-go policy cycle brings about sharp swings in real GDP, real wages, sales, availability of inputs and so on, introducing volatility and noise in enterprise sales and cash flows, and in household income and employment opportunities.

Macroeconomic stability and economic performance in transition economies

The special experience of central and eastern Europe and of the former Soviet Union have generated important lessons for the whole world. In the 26 countries in which EBRD operates there has been a clear relationship between economic performance at the aggregate level and macroeconomic control. Those countries that have shown the strongest commitment to reform are also the ones that have simultaneously reduced inflation faster, suffered the smallest GDP and fiscal revenue falls, and witnessed an earlier resumption of growth (table 2.4). The medians of all the indicators for each of the three groups of countries show the better performance of the faster reformers. For example, the median contraction of GDP at the trough for the advanced reformers is about one-quarter, whereas that for the early transition countries is about one-half. The same striking result applies to annual inflation, 22 per cent compared with 125 per cent, respectively, in 1995 (the corresponding figures for 1994 were 21 per cent and 100 per cent, respectively).

Support for the view that macroeconomic stability promotes growth by enhancing the quantity and quality of investment can be found in figures 2.1 and 2.2. Figure 2.1 shows a positive relationship between the number of foreign direct investment projects in a country and an index of the degree to which several reforms considered important for a successful transition have been implemented. The relationship is non-linear, suggesting something like a threshold effect. Figure 2.2 shows a negative relationship between a country's rate of inflation and the same measured FDI.

In a recent study De Melo, Denizer and Gelb (1995) (see also World Bank, 1996) calculate the paths followed on average by inflation and real growth in transition economies during the years prior to a reform breakthrough and during the years following that

Table 2.4: Progress in transition and macroeconomic performance (measured by the median of each group)

Group	Private sector share of GDP[a] (%)	Score on enterprise restructuring and privatization[a]	Score on market liberalization[a]	Score on banking reform[a]	Score on investment laws[a]	Government fiscal balance in 1995 (% of GDP)	Cumulative decline (1989–93) in fiscal revenues (% of GDP)	Annual inflation rate (%) 1992	Annual inflation rate (%) 1995	Ratio of lowest registered GDP to 1989 GDP[b]	GDP growth[a] (%) 1995	Increase in infant mortality rate[d] (%)
Advanced transition countries	60	3.7	3.3	3.0	3.0	–1	–5	93	22	76	5	–15.0
Intermediate transition countries	42	2.7	2.8	2.0	2.0	–7	–20	237	28	65	0	7.0
Early transition countries	27	2.0	2.3	1.8	2.0	–4	–18	1,364	125	49	–5	15.6

Note: Advanced transition countries include: Croatia, Czech Republic, Estonia, Hungary, Latvia, Lithuania, Poland, Slovak Republic and Slovenia; Intermediate transition countries include: Albania, Bulgaria, FYR Macedonia, Kyrgyzstan, Romania and Russian Federation; Early transition countries include: Armenia, Azerbaijan, Belarus, Georgia, Kazakstan, Moldova, Tajikistan, Turkmenistan, Ukraine and Uzbekistan.

a. *Source:* EBRD (1995). The qualitative index of reform in columns 2 to 5 ranges from 1 to 4* classed as 5 when medians were calculated. Most advanced industrial economies would qualify for the 4* rating for almost all of these indicators in the qualitative index of reform. A rating of 1 indicates negligible change from the old position.

b. Projection. It excludes the Central Bank quasi-fiscal deficits. Cash balances used when other figures not available. Data not available for Tajikistan, Belarus, Turkmenistan.

c. *Source:* World Bank (1995).

d. *Source:* UNICEF (1994).

Figure 2.1:   Foreign direct investment and transition level for
25 countries in transition

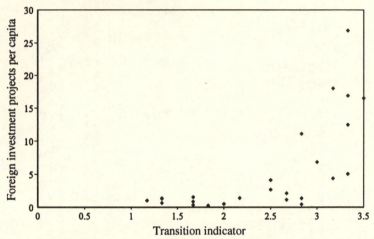

Note: Each point reflects the number of investments in a country that had been undertaken by
the companies in the survey, divided by population size (in millions), and the average of six
scores that a country received in different areas of reform.

Source: Transition indicator from EBRD (1995); foreign investment from EBRD Survey.

Figure 2.2:   Foreign direct investment and inflation
for 25 countries in transition

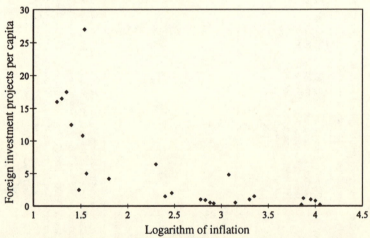

Note: Each point reflects the number of investments in a country that had been undertaken by
the companies in the survey, divided by population size (in millions), and the algorithm of the
rate of inflation.

Source: EBRD (1995).

Figure 2.3: Prototype path of monthly inflation in transition economies before and after reform breakthrough

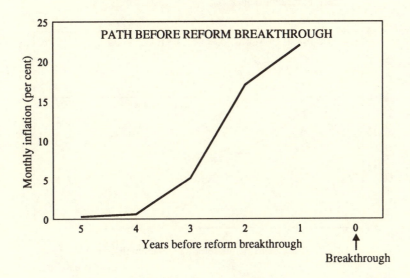

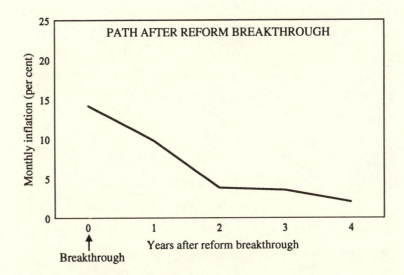

Note: Data for 25 countries in which EBRD operates, plus Mongolia. Results come from statistical method known as "switching regime regression". The breakthrough is defined as the year in which a specific country reached a set of transition indicators comparable to those of Poland as of 1990.

Source: De Melo, Denizer and Gelb (1995).

Figure 2.4: Prototype path of annual real GDP growth
in transition economies before and after
reform breakthrough

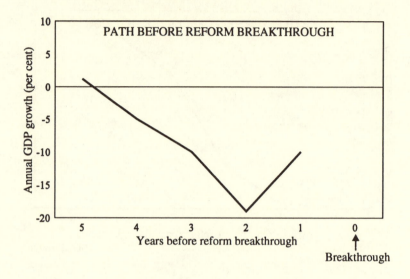

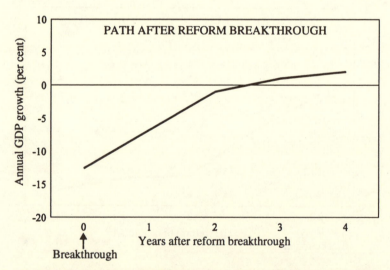

Note: Data for 25 countries in which EBRD operates, plus Mongolia. Results come from statistical method known as "switching regime regression". The breakthrough is defined as the year in which a specific country reached a set of transition indicators comparable to those of Poland as of 1990.

Source: De Melo, Denizer and Gelb (1995).

breakthrough. Their results are summarized in figures 2.3 and 2.4. Radical reformers suffer an initial fall in real income of about 13 per cent and a jump in inflation to 14 per cent per month during the year following the "big bang". Nevertheless, they are able to resume positive growth four years later and control inflation to just below 3 per cent per month during the fifth year. The typical pattern of recovery is one of rapidly expanding private sector activity outweighing the contraction in public enterprise output. A parallel structural change occurs in the sectoral composition of GDP, with the services sector increasing its share of GDP by 10 percentage points and industry—particularly heavy industry—witnessing a similar drop in its GDP share. By contrast, the countries that postpone reform, although they are able in the beginning to limit real income losses and to maintain low "official" inflation (typically with the help of price controls), end up with hyperinflation (average rates of inflation of 23 per cent per month) and deep depression (average yearly income losses of about 10 per cent). The countries, particularly those in the former Soviet Union, that have seen the greatest economic and social traumas, including dramatic increases in age-specific mortality rates, are also the ones that have lost macroeconomic control.[35]

Clearly, in assessing the comparative data, the differences in initial political, social, cultural and economic conditions should not be neglected. The countries of the former Soviet Union embarked on transition two years later than those in central and eastern Europe. Further, the splitting of the former Soviet Republics—the economies of which were tightly integrated and complementary—was a far more traumatic shock than that of the dissolution of the Council for Mutual Economic Assistance (CMEA) for central and eastern European countries. Moreover, the latter had been functioning market economies until the 1940s, some of them even buoyant performers.[36] In contrast, the Russian economy at the time of the Bolshevik revolution of 1917, while growing fast, was a predominately pre-capitalist, agricultural economy. It was also a very statist economy with a high degree of state ownership and control of industry, and a set of repressive institutions. A few of the transition economies (notably Bulgaria, Hungary, Poland, Russia and the Ukraine) started their transitions with a sizeable external debt. Others (notably Romania) had little or no external debt to cope with. Hungary and Poland had considerable prior experience with economic reform. Most of the others had to start from scratch in 1990.

There were also considerable differences in initial economic structure. Belarus, Russia and Ukraine were burdened with a legacy of large homogeneous state farms. Memories of the location and operation of old family farms were more than 70 years old. This gap greatly complicates land reform and the recreation of a private agricultural sector. In contrast, Poland preserved private ownership in agriculture throughout the communist period. Land reform in China and Albania benefited from surviving memories and identification of private farms and farming (collectivization having taken place no more than 40 years earlier)[37] and from the often smaller size and lesser homogeneity of the collective farms. As a result, land reform in Albania was virtually instantaneous. Belarus and Ukraine were also saddled with an industrial structure biased heavily towards industries producing heavy capital goods for which post-reform market demand was extremely limited.

POLICIES AND INSTITUTIONS FOR PROMOTING MACROECONOMIC STABILITY

The uncertainties and deterrents to investment and good decision-making associated with macroeconomic mismanagement—and the ex-post dead-weight losses imposed by decisions based on misguided signals—apply across the economy. These uncertainties are like public bads, and macroeconomic stability, a public good. In order for the government in a market economy to provide this public good, institutions are needed that are conducive to satisfactory macroeconomic performance. The chronicle of macroeconomic developments over the last three or four decades is laced with unsuccessful stabilization attempts, which started off with vigour but failed to take hold because the appropriate institutions that would provide continuity to the process were absent. This concern is particularly relevant to transition economies, which have inherited the "wrong" or "missing" institutions and thus need to develop these tailored to a market economy. Given that a moderate degree of macroeconomic stability is a precondition for efficient enterprise decisions and for the productivity of investments, governments must place building institutions necessary to achieve and preserve macroeconomic stability at the top of the reform agenda. Both domestic and international institutions must be redesigned or created from scratch in order to achieve the best possible global economic performance in the next century.

Building domestic institutions

What can be done at the national or subnational level, through institutional development and the design, implementation and enforcement of proper rules, to avoid unnecessary inflation and unemployment, and create the conditions within which the private sector can flourish and generate sustained growth? This issue is clearly not only technical, but concerns political economy. It may require redesigning major institutions and even changing the political system.

One general lesson of the post-War period is the following: do not impose burdens on a country's public administration that it cannot handle. The experience of the transition economies emphasizes that even if virtually all former state enterprises have been privatized,[38] the enduring weakness of the general government sector (public administration) remains a problem. Lack of skills, lack of transparent legal incentives, inadequate pay and flawed career structures result in rent seeking, dishonesty and corruption. These weaknesses constitute major constraints on the speed of transition and reform.

It follows from this discussion that the transition of the state may be the most important transition of all. Also, outside of the transition economies there are many cases in which reform of general government institutions should have very high priority. The possession (or early creation) of a professional, high-status and well-motivated civil service seems to be a defining characteristic of all the recent economic success stories. We must, of course, avoid confusing necessary with sufficient conditions. It is also important that the highly qualified and competent civil service be content to limit the scope of its actions and interventions to the domains outlined in the second section of this chapter.

A strong but limited state is required. Too many countries still find themselves saddled with a weak but overstretched, quasi-ubiquitous and interfering state. It is vitally important that government regulation and intervention do not create huge incentives for corruption and rent-seeking. Any government regulation and intervention will inevitably create some such incentives. Price controls, rationing and licensing are all subvertible. Transparency and accountability are key to minimizing the incidence and severity of these by-products of regulation and intervention. In order to provide macroeconomic stability, economies in transition must develop the institutions required to perform the following key tasks, among others.

Enforcing hard budget constraints

Enforcing hard budget constraints is the first rule of a market economy. Without it, liberalizing markets, freeing prices and privatizing state enterprises are pointless. A hierarchy of hard budget constraints can be visualized. The government and/or the central bank should impose a hard budget constraint on the banking sector, thereby prompting commercial banks to enforce hard budget constraints on their borrowers, be they enterprises or households. The government should also refrain from extending credit, directly or indirectly, to the non-financial enterprise sector. Any subsidies should be explicit line items in the general government budget. Unless hard budget constraints can be imposed on the enterprise sector, stabilization is virtually guaranteed to go by the board. Explicit or implicit government subsidies will sooner or later show up in either the conventionally measured fiscal deficit, the quasi-fiscal deficit of the central bank or the deferred fiscal deficit (the contingent future claims on public finances currently hidden in the balance sheets of the enterprise sector and/or the banking sector).

It is interesting to note that governments throughout the world are attempting to impose hard budget constraints on themselves by establishing independent central banks and by passing constitutional amendments restricting the government's ability to borrow, spend and tax.[39] While not every one of these attempts to restrict the state's fiscal-financial elbow room makes much sense (some, indeed, make no sense at all), we can appreciate the sense of frustration with the government's inability to stay with long-term fiscal-financial commitments, which prompted this Ulyssian attempt to tie oneself to the mast in order to resist the siren song of "fiscal restraint tomorrow, but a little more jam today".

Choosing a nominal anchor and establishing price stability

In a closed economic system the nominal anchor must be an internal one, such as a domestic monetary aggregate, the general price level or nominal income. In an open economic system the nominal anchor can either be internal or external (the nominal exchange rate). Unless full monetary union is opted for, the pursuit of an exchange rate target will, however, imply constraints on the behaviour of domestic nominal variables and instruments. Domestic credit expansion (monetary base growth net of the increase in external assets of the central bank) cannot systematically exceed the growth of money demand at the target exchange rate. If it did, the country would eventually run out of reserves, and the external peg would have to be abandoned. Likewise, domestic unit cost inflation cannot systematically exceed the foreign rate of unit cost inflation plus the target depreciation rate of the nominal exchange rate. If it did, the country would become increasingly uncompetitive, and the credibility of the government's commitment to the exchange rate peg would be undermined. In a fundamental sense, therefore, even an external nominal anchor ultimately relies on the pursuit of prudent domestic monetary and budgetary policies for its credibility. Anti-inflationary credibility cannot be imported—it can at most be borrowed from abroad. Ultimately, anti-inflationary credibility is home-made (see IMF, 1995b).

Granted that the ultimate source of anti-inflationary credibility is domestic fiscal and monetary restraint, an open economy still has the option of pursuing an exchange rate peg (or some other rule for managing or targeting the exchange rate). This can be done through a conventional central bank or through a currency board. A currency board issues domestic currency only in exchange for convertible currencies at a fixed exchange rate. The whole monetary base is fully backed by international reserves and is demand-driven. Small, very open economies may be advised to opt for a currency board. Hong

Kong in Asia, Argentina in Latin America and, more recently, Estonia and Lithuania in eastern Europe have successfully stabilized inflation with the help of currency boards. One downside of currency boards is that the arrangement prevents the central bank from acting as lender of last resort in the event of a systemic banking crisis. Latvia was recently faced with this dilemma, when its main commercial bank collapsed. Argentina, too, found itself with its public sector hands tied in the face of a major banking crisis. The difference between a country managing a unilateral currency board and belonging to a common currency area became painfully obvious: with a common currency the common central bank has the option and the capacity to act as lender of last resort to banks in all member countries.

Faced with banking crises or major capital inflows or outflows, any fixed exchange rate regime other than a common currency is either unsustainable or (as with a currency board) extremely costly. A floating exchange rate (in which the float can be managed or controlled when circumstances permit) is likely to be the only realistic medium-term choice of exchange rate regime for any country that is unable to control international capital flows and unwilling to forsake the lender of last resort function of the central bank. Whatever the regime, credibility is key: unless a particular institutional arrangement is adopted lastingly and in substance, it is unlikely to survive. Formal independence of the central bank is not strictly necessary, but there is evidence that independence helps ensure macroeconomic stability and signals to domestic and international financial markets that opportunistic devaluations or depreciations of the currency are less likely.[40]

Supervising the banking system

The supervision and regulation of the financial sector should be a top priority. High real interest rates and changing profitability across enterprises and sectors—both inherent to transition—can, in the absence of strong banking supervision, easily lead to non-performing portfolios. A large portion of the "bad loans" will eventually be absorbed by the state.

Administering taxes

The ability to levy taxes on a broad base, with acceptable marginal rates and revenue levels, is key to the state discharging its obligations effectively and without recourse to the inflation tax. As noted above, this challenge is formidable in economies in transition.

Supplying the social safety net

Providing the safety net traditionally supplied by state enterprises constitutes another major fiscal challenge in transition economies. Even in advanced industrial countries the tension between declining active-inactive population ratios and lower trend growth of productivity on the one hand and the demands made on the budget by social expenditures (especially health and pension benefits) on the other is never far below the surface in political and economic debates. There is increasing recognition that the government need not directly supply the services that it finances—a part can be contracted out to the private sector or the "civil society"/not-for-profit sector. But note that, except insofar as private provision is more efficient in administering social benefits and providing social services, privatization merely changes the label on the sacrifices made by the currently active population, without reducing their nature and magnitude.

Transition economies confront in extreme form the issue of inter-generational equity, also faced throughout the world. Older generations have shorter time horizons, and opportunities to accumulate wealth bypass them in favour of skilled, dynamic younger workers and entrepreneurs able to earn high incomes in the private sector. Transition thus focuses attention on the role of the state in effecting inter-generational income transfers in a cost-effective way.

Coping with international capital flows

In principle, the ability to run current account deficits and surpluses is welfare-improving. A country that can lend abroad or borrow abroad can decouple domestic absorption and domestic income. International inter-temporal trade permits improved consumption smoothing. Even pure consumption loans—loans that do not result in increased domestic capital formation—can be welfare-enhancing as long as the constraints implied by the need to maintain inter-temporal solvency are recognized and respected. In short, the existing stock of net foreign liabilities must be matched, in present discounted value terms, by a stream of future primary external surpluses.[41] In addition, foreign borrowing that finances productive domestic capital formation (domestic investment whose rate of return is at least equal to the cost of foreign borrowing) further enhances the borrowing nation's current and future private and public consumption programme. Finally, in addition to permitting international inter-temporal trade, the ability to engage in international financial transactions allows for international risk-sharing. Such international insurance can be obtained even without any net international inflows or outflows, with matching gross external assets and liabilities.

Granted that the ability to bring the current account out of balance enhances a country's opportunity set and that, with well-functioning markets and appropriate policies, there will be gains from international inter-temporal trade and from international risk-sharing, it is nevertheless apparent that there have been cases in which poorly functioning markets and/or inappropriate policies have turned this potential blessing into a curse (see, for example, Williamson, 1996).

Many of the new industrial countries, some of the Latin American countries that have successfully initiated macroeconomic stabilization and structural reform, and a growing number of the more advanced and successful transition economies have experienced very significant gross and net capital inflows. Typically, the result has been an appreciation of the real exchange rate (either through an appreciation of the nominal exchange rate and/or through an increase in the domestic rate of price and cost inflation); a rapid increase in the money stock (fueled by increasing international reserves rather than by domestic credit expansion); a financial market boom, characterized by rapidly rising stock market valuations and fast growth of bank lending; and a rapid expansion of domestic economic activity, often driven by domestic capital formation.

Qualitatively, all of these responses are consistent with a proper equilibrium adjustment to a correctly perceived improvement in the rate of return to financial and real investment. The appreciation of the real exchange rate (or increase in the price of non-traded goods relative to traded goods) could be the manifestation of a beneficial version of "Dutch disease" in which a windfall (say a natural resource discovery) raises national permanent income and thus causes an increase in the price of non-traded goods relative to traded goods and a movement of resources into the non-traded goods sector. Quantitatively, however, the responses could be excessive and harmful for a number of reasons.

The perceived improvement in the rate of return to investing in the country experiencing capital inflows could be based on an unrealistic assessment of the country's fundamentals. Domestic and international financial markets are subject to bouts of euphoria and gloom that at times seem completely detached from the fundamentals. Incomplete markets, bandwagon effects, herding behaviour, noise traders and speculative bubbles (rational or irrational) can drown out the fundamentals that efficient financial markets are supposed to reflect and transmit. Capital inflows are therefore potentially ephemeral. They could be reversed suddenly for reasons no better than those that prompted the original inflows. If real resources are invested and reallocated domestically in response to relative price changes whose degree of permanence is overestimated by enterprises and households, unexpected reversals of these relative price movements could inflict significant real resource costs, as capital formation and real resource reallocation are always characterized by sunk, (partly) irreversible costs.

This problem is aggravated by the fact that domestic factor markets and markets for industrial goods and services are typically much less flexible and efficient than international financial markets. The interaction of a floating exchange rate, determined in a reasonably efficient foreign exchange market, and domestic labour and output markets full of nominal and/or real rigidities can generate ugly results. The example of real exchange rate overshooting, caused by the interaction of a flexible nominal exchange rate and sticky money wages in response to restrictive monetary policy under conditions of high international capital mobility, is familiar: anticipating the success of the anti-inflationary monetary policy, operators in the foreign exchange market bid up the value of the domestic currency (see Dornbusch, 1976). Unlike the nominal exchange rate, domestic costs and prices are not continuously renegotiated in fully flexible auction markets. When a sharp nominal appreciation meets a level of domestic costs that responds sluggishly, a sharp real appreciation and loss of competitiveness results.

A further complicating factor is that domestic financial markets in reforming economies are often rudimentary. Evaluating the commercial merits of projects clamouring for loans is always difficult and risky. The capacity to screen projects adequately is often insufficient in countries faced with sudden capital inflows.

Absent unlimited deposit insurance, banking systems are always vulnerable to runs. The reason is that deposits have a fixed price and can be withdrawn on demand, while the majority of bank assets (mainly loans) cannot be securitized and are highly illiquid. The same fundamentals are consistent with a good equilibrium—in which individual depositors do not find it rational to withdraw their deposits, as they do not expect anyone else to do so—and a bad equilibrium—in which it is rational for individual depositors to run, because they expect everyone else to do likewise. Bank runs are socially costly because banks are, especially in developing countries and transition economies, the main intermediary between ultimate savers and investors, and because they play a key role in the country's payment mechanism. The two solutions to the bank run problem—unrestricted deposit insurance and bank holidays (limits on the amount that can be withdrawn by any depositor)—have obvious drawbacks. In the case of deposit insurance the problem is moral hazard. Bank holidays are indiscriminate because they penalize those who need to withdraw funds for good business reasons. The anticipation of possible future restrictions on withdrawals also encourages disintermediation by undermining the attractiveness of depositing money in banks.

Responding nationally to disruptive capital flows

The first-best approach to establishing coexistence between flexible, efficient financial markets and inefficient, rigid factor and product markets would be to "flex" the inflexible, rigid markets. While measures to improve the functioning of domestic factor and product markets are clearly desirable and should be pursued resolutely, even in the absence of a capital inflow or outflow problem, turning all markets into perfectly functioning Arrow-Debreu markets is not a practical option. In addition, the problem of disruptive capital flows that are not a proper response to the underlying fundamentals would not disappear even if domestic factor and product markets functioned efficiently. Recognizing this, Tobin (1982) and others have proposed, as a second-best solution, to throw sand in the wheels of some of the highly flexible financial markets to prevent them from creating havoc when they interact with more sticky factor and product markets. A Tobin tax on foreign exchange transactions (which may be designed so that the tax rate decreases with the length of time between the purchase and sale of the domestic security in order to discourage quick reversals of positions without penalizing long-term portfolio investment and FDI) is one of the more frequently proposed interventions. Others include administrative and fiscal controls on international capital flows, such as punitive reserve requirements on balances used for taking open positions to attack currencies.

When assessing the feasibility and desirability of such capital controls, it is important to differentiate between advanced industrial countries, with their highly sophisticated and developed financial markets, and developing countries and transition economies. Regarding advanced industrial countries, it does not seem possible to put the capital flow genie back in the bottle through fiscal and administrative capital controls. The scope and efficiency with which the global industry can supply the means to avoid and evade controls is awesome. The rewards from taking on the monetary authorities are too high: given the ineffective penalties that are likely to be imposed and the low risk of being caught evading the controls, the odds that capital controls will work effectively are virtually nil. Proposals for imposing non-interest-bearing reserve requirements on balances used for taking open positions to attack currencies appear naive because they ignore key developments of the last two decades in international financial markets. There are now myriad ways of attacking a currency: through spot markets, through futures and swap markets, and through other derivatives markets, including option markets. The authorities now operate in many of these markets, so "net positions" would have to be identified and be subject to reserve requirements in all of them. Tobin taxes on foreign exchange transactions would likewise have to be expanded to cover transactions in option markets and in markets for all other kinds of derivatives. They would also have to be imposed and enforced globally in order to be effective.

For countries that are not yet fully integrated into the global financial system and that have much less developed and sophisticated domestic financial markets, capital controls are a more realistic option. A number of general guidelines should be respected, however.

No restrictions should be made on the purchase and sale of foreign exchange for financing current account transactions. The repatriation of profits and interest on legal investments should likewise be unrestricted. It is well-known that capital account transactions can be disguised as current account transactions: leads and lags in the invoicing of imports and exports, underinvoicing of exports and overinvoicing of imports will cause slippage in the application of any controls that discriminate between current and capital transactions. The question is not whether this kind of evasion exists—but whether it takes place on a scale sufficient to substantially undermine the controls. There are, we would argue, many cases in which controls can be enforced tightly enough to reduce substantially the magnitude of sudden capital flows.

Foreign direct investment should also not be discouraged, as it is often bundled with the international transfer of managerial and technical know-how that would otherwise not enter the capital-importing country on the same scale. We recognize that the distinction between FDI and portfolio investment is not clear-cut, and that it is possible to disguise portfolio investment as FDI. But, again, the question is not whether the controls would work perfectly, but whether they would substantially reduce the volatility of capital flows. Again, the evidence is consistent with the view that they can make a significant difference.[42]

There are some obvious negatives associated with any attempt to impose or reimpose capital controls selectively. First, the authorities would again have to keep records of foreign exchange transactions. In a number of countries liberalization of foreign exchange markets has been accompanied by the complete dismantling of the authorities' information collecting apparatus, as well as of the administrative and legal enforcement capacity. Second, any (re)imposition of capital controls generates new opportunities for administrative discretion and therefore inevitably creates new opportunities for rent seeking and corruption. The new rules must be simple and transparent to minimize such adverse side effects.

There is another important reason for practicing caution in the application of capital controls. It is not difficult to come up with a long list of countries in which the main disruption caused by sudden, sharp capital outflows was the disruption of the government's undesirable and unsustainable policies. If capital flows respond to fundamentals only, they can impose market discipline firmly and swiftly on disruptive governments. Eliminating the scope for funds to enter or leave the country swiftly and with little notice is a positive development only if capital flows are motivated little by fundamentals and/or domestic factor and product markets are inefficient. It is a negative development if capital flows properly respond to the right fundamentals, and if restrictions on these flows encourage delays in policy reform and in the restructuring of domestic factor and product markets.

Consider a small open economy faced with sudden capital inflows. The cause could be internal (such as a combination of international financial liberalization by the country and an improvement in its investment climate attributable, say, to successful macroeconomic stabilization) or external (such as a change in the rules, laws or practices governing investment in emerging markets in one or more of the leading financial centres). If desired net inflows of capital exceed the current account deficit at the prevailing exchange rate, the country has two options. Either it can allow the currency to appreciate or it can continue to peg the exchange rate at the same level, thus allowing an increase in the stock of foreign exchange reserves. If the second alternative is chosen, a further choice has to be made. The country must either permit the increase in foreign exchange reserves to augment the domestic money stock or the increase must be sterilized, that is, domestic credit must be contracted by the same amount as the increase in foreign reserves, leaving the domestic money stock unchanged.

The statement that net capital inflows exceed the current account deficit at the prevailing exchange rate only makes sense as a statement about equilibrium[43] if at the same time the increase in the demand for money at the current exchange rate and the current general price level exceeds domestic credit expansion. The increase in the demand for money (the shift of the conventional money demand function) could, for example, be due to the same improvement in confidence that prompted the capital inflows. Other possible causes of an increase in the demand for money include a reduction in the opportunity cost of holding money (because of lower domestic nominal interest rates, reflecting increased international financial liberalization and/or a lower expected domestic rate of inflation) and an increase in the transactions demand for money, reflecting booming domestic demand and rising real output.

Typically, surging capital inflows are associated with a booming domestic economy. While domestic output may be rising, domestic absorption outstrips domestic production—this is the income-expenditure counterpart to increased net inflows of capital. Even if the proximate cause of the capital inflows is an improvement in domestic supply conditions (an improvement in productivity or a change in the regulatory or tax environment), demand (typically led by investment) is outstripping domestic supply, and an increase in the price of domestic non-traded goods relative to traded goods is required to restore balance. Such an appreciation of the real exchange rate (which may be accompanied by an increase in the price of exportables relative to import-competing goods if the country in question is large in the world markets for its tradable goods and services) is in principle the appropriate equilibrium response to the shocks generating the surge of capital inflows. It is essentially a benign version of Dutch disease. It is possible that the appreciation of the real exchange rate may exceed what is necessary to restore equilibrium, especially if the nominal exchange rate is allowed to float freely. But some real appreciation is both necessary and unavoidable. A key policy issue remaining is whether the required real appreciation is achieved swiftly, through an appreciation of the nominal exchange rate, or more gradually, through an increase in domestic prices and costs at a fixed nominal exchange rate.

Consider the case in which the nominal exchange rate is kept fixed. If financial capital mobility is perfect, sterilization of the reserve inflows is not an option: the increased demand for real money balances (at the prevailing exchange rate and nominal price level) that is the counterpart to the inflows in foreign exchange reserves *must* be accommodated instantaneously. Either domestic credit must be expanded or a stock-shift inflow of foreign exchange reserves will occur to ensure that the endogenous (demand-determined) money supply always equals the demand for domestic money. When capital mobility is imperfect, sterilization can work for a while. Note, however, that sterilization of foreign exchange inflows is likely to increase the quasi-fiscal deficit of the central bank. The reason is that the interest rate earned on the additional foreign reserves acquired by the central bank is likely to be below that paid on the assets (typically treasury debt) given up or the liabilities (such as central bank interest-bearing debt) incurred by the central bank in order to finance the acquisition of the reserves. Even if sterilization is successful in the short run, the increase in domestic interest rates associated with successful sterilization will encourage even larger capital inflows, which will ultimately swamp the ability or the willingness of the authorities to persist in their sterilization efforts. Sooner or later, therefore, the reserve inflows will be monetized (or the exchange rate peg will be abandoned).

If the (nominal) exchange rate is allowed to appreciate, the capital inflows will be associated with an immediate appreciation of the real exchange rate (a loss of international competitiveness, an increase in the relative price of traded and non-traded goods and, if the country has any market power in world markets, an increase in the price of exportables relative to importables). If the nominal exchange rate is kept pegged, the same real appreciation will ultimately occur, but more gradually, with the domestic price level (and especially the price of non-traded goods) rising faster than world prices. The higher domestic price level is supported by the increase in the money stock that is the counterpart of the increased foreign exchange reserves.

Sterilization can further slow down this process. The choice between rapid real appreciation through a nominal appreciation of the currency and slower real appreciation through the gradual inflation of domestic costs and prices is not straightforward. If the capital flows are expected to reverse in the not-too-distant future, and if the authorities believe that the private sector has a tendency to overestimate the degree of permanence of changes in prices and exchange rates, a case can be made for attempting to slow down changes in the real exchange rate by continuing to peg the currency. If the changes are not expected to be reversed (or, if the private sector responds appropriately to correctly perceived temporary changes in the real exchange rate), it may make more sense to float the currency (or to permit a significant nominal appreciation) in the face of a sudden increase in capital inflows.

Responding internationally to disruptive capital flows

Every country's capital inflows are another country's (or countries') capital outflows. Every sudden currency appreciation is matched by a sudden currency depreciation somewhere else in the world. Changes in external economic conditions that are (properly) viewed as exogenous by small or medium-size individual open economies are the endogenous global outcomes of policies and other developments in the world as a whole. A systemic perspective on the problem of disruptive capital flows is therefore essential.

Traditionally, the IMF has assumed the task of dealing with systemic financial issues. Since its inception, the Fund has performed two distinct roles. The first is its systemic role. The second is the provision of short-term financing and technical assistance to individual member countries that are having balance of payments difficulties. The systemic role—managing the adjustable peg system established at Bretton Woods and providing it with sufficient liquidity—effectively ended in 1972 with the collapse of the Bretton Woods exchange rate system. Private capital markets increasingly took over the role of the Fund as provider of global liquidity and source of short-term financing for the more advanced industrial countries. Exchange rate surveillance is the surviving offspring of this systemic role, but it is just a pale reflection of the IMF's earlier systemic function.[44] Regular gatherings such as those of the G-3, the G-7 and the G-10 countries have taken over some of the earlier consultative functions of the IMF. More fundamentally, the IMF has neither the stick nor the carrots to induce the largest industrial countries (or even the medium-size ones) to act on its recommendations. Since Healey went to the IMF in the autumn of 1976, no G-10 country has been in such dire financial trouble that access to the IMF's resources (or obtaining the IMF's stamp of good house-keeping) has been essential for the maintenance of liquidity and solvency.

Still, there are obvious global gains from the collective pursuit of macroeconomic policies that are conducive to low and stable real interest rates and that avoid both short-term excess volatility and medium-term persistent misalignment of the exchange rates of the main industrial countries. Giving teeth to IMF (exchange rate) surveillance would therefore clearly be desirable. If pursued with determination, it would achieve three key objectives. First, it would put greater pressure on the governments of the main industrial nations to recognize the external effects of macroeconomic and other policies pursued for mainly domestic reasons. Benign neglect would no longer be an option. Second, it would improve the quality of macroeconomic management worldwide, especially in developing countries and transition economies. Third, it would ensure that the global sum of policies that are individually rational to member countries is a global monetary-fiscal mix that makes sense from the point of view of the whole international community.

Another desirable global economic policy development that would have a direct impact on capital flows is a move towards greater international cooperation among national tax authorities, so as to minimize capital flows driven purely by tax arbitrage or outright tax evasion. The natural institutional home of such increased cooperation is less apparent than the case for locating the responsibility for enhanced surveillance in the IMF.

Building international economic institutions

There are public goods whose scope extends beyond the boundaries of any nation-state and there are externalities that likewise do not respect national boundaries. Building up institutions or arrangements for supplying supra-national (including global) public goods and for internalizing supra-national externalities is a key task for governments and multilateral institutions (agencies). If, as seems possible, the rest of this decade is a period of relative global stability and reasonable global economic progress, we must strengthen international institutions, agencies and arrangements at this time. Examples include the following:

- Strengthen the WTO and extend its scope to include trade in all goods and services, including agricultural goods. The agency should have the authority to tackle the key (and sensitive) issue of the role of regional preferential trading arrangements in an integrated global economy.

- Create a vehicle through which global environmental issues (greenhouse effects and global warming, the weakening of the ozone layer, pollution of the atmosphere and the oceans, acid rain, reductions in biodiversity, desertification, depletion of oceanic fish-stocks and other renewable resources subject to common property problems and so on) can be monitored and tackled on other than an ad-hoc basis. Perhaps the World Bank could be given this task. Perhaps a new, specially designed institution is required.

- Extend and adapt the Basle agreements for capital adequacy in the global banking sector to other global financial intermediaries.

BEYOND STABILIZATION—THE GENERATION OF RECOVERY AND GROWTH

The one thing we can be certain of is the occurrence of future unanticipated shocks. But on the basis of currently available information, it is not easy to identify major systemic imbalances likely to lead to such shocks. In many parts of the world (Brazil, India and sub-Saharan Africa are obvious exceptions) structural adjustment is largely completed or it is at least well under way. China has proceeded a long way down the road of reform—with striking results. A number of eastern and central European economies have advanced impressively in their transition. How should national and international policy-makers take advantage of this relative absence of foreseeable traumas, that is, of the likelihood of a period of relatively steady growth and systemic stability?

The short answer is that good times should be used to take care of the future. We must pay attention to both the quantity and quality of investment, broadly defined. That means raising savings rates and boosting capital formation, including human capital (through education, training or other learning experiences), environmental capital and knowledge capital, as well as the accumulation of physical capital.

Policies to promote saving in industrial countries

Most industrial countries have a significant unfunded (pay-as-you-go) social security retirement scheme, in which compulsory "contributions" (indistinguishable from regular taxes on labour income) paid by the working population are used to finance the concurrent payment of retirement benefits to the retired population. Such a scheme redistributes lifetime resources from the young to the old.

An unfunded social security retirement scheme

To assess the effect of unfunded social security on private and aggregate saving, consider the introduction of a balanced budget social security retirement scheme in an economy in which previously there was only voluntary private saving for retirement. The scheme consists of a constant per capita contribution by the young (the working generation), shared equally among those currently retired. We assume that households conform to the life-cycle model of saving, without making any inter-generational gifts and bequests. For simplicity, we ignore the possible effects of introducing such a scheme on the age of retirement. Uncertainty and precautionary savings are also not considered at this point, although we will refer to them later. To focus clearly on the direct effect on saving of introducing the scheme, we hold interest rates and wage rates constant, although there will, of course, be general equilibrium repercussions on these variables.

A pure, unfunded social security retirement scheme is a balanced-budget (lump-sum) redistribution from the young to the old. There are thus no direct effects on the government budget and on public saving. When the scheme is introduced, the old generation receives a pure windfall: they receive benefits during their old age without having made any contributions while young. Their consumption will be boosted by the amount of the windfall.[45] For the young, and for all subsequent generations, the effect of introducing the scheme on the present discounted value of their lifetime resources will be positive if the population growth rate (the "biological rate of return" on the scheme) exceeds the real interest rate, and negative if the opposite holds.

The total effect on the saving of the young, and therefore on the total stock of financial wealth in the economy, is unambiguously negative: income is taxed away when people are young, while an unrequited benefit is given during old age. Wishing to smooth consumption over their life-cycle, the young will lower their saving. Since the scheme is balanced-budget by assumption, the capital stock in the next period will be less than it would otherwise have been.[46]

An aggregate funded social security retirement scheme.

Now consider that this unfunded scheme changes to an aggregate-funded scheme, administered again by the government. Contributions remain compulsory and benefits are still paid to individuals in such a way that there is no link (for the individual) between the individual contribution made while young and the individual retirement benefit received while old. The government, however, invests the contributions of each generation (earning the market rate of return). The aggregate retirement benefits of each generation are equal to the aggregate contributions made while young, plus the interest earned from having invested those contributions. As it affects individual saving behaviour, this scheme is not essentially different from an unfunded scheme. The contributions made while young are effectively a lump-sum tax, while the benefits received while old are effectively an unrequited, lump-sum transfer. Again, private saving by the young is discouraged, compared with a situation of only voluntary private saving. The negative effect on private saving is larger with the aggregate funded scheme than with the unfunded scheme if the rate of return on the fund exceeds the population growth rate, and smaller if the opposite condition prevails. Note that such an aggregate funded scheme will not, in general, be a balanced-budget scheme. Assuming that the per capita contributions of the young are constant, the scheme will need money if the interest rate exceeds the population growth rate.

Note that the negative effect of an aggregate-funded social security retirement scheme on private saving behaviour will be the same regardless of whether the scheme is administered by the government or by the private sector. As long as no individual contributor/beneficiary perceives a link between his or her individual lifetime contributions and his or her individual lifetime retirement benefits, that is, as long as the scheme is not an individual-defined contribution scheme, there will be a negative effect on the saving rate.

A social security retirement scheme with individual accounts

Now consider modifying the aggregate-funded scheme to one with individual accounts. The scheme is still compulsory, but each individual's contributions while young are invested (earning the market rate) in a named individual account. When the individual retires he/she receives as a benefit his/her own lifetime contributions plus accumulated returns from that investment.[47] Such a scheme is effectively a compulsory saving scheme. If the rate of return on the individual account is the same as that on discretionary (voluntary) private saving, and if there are no constraints on the ability of the individual to vary discretionary private saving, such a compulsory saving scheme would have no effect on private saving by the young, compared with a situation featuring only voluntary private saving. It would, of course, raise their saving compared with the unfunded scheme or the aggregate-funded scheme.

Compared with a situation of only voluntary private saving, the compulsory private saving scheme we describe would raise aggregate saving by the young, if the young cannot reduce their voluntary, discretionary saving one-for-one in response to the introduction of the compulsory scheme. This effect is likely to be empirically significant if voluntary saving rates are low, private wealth is illiquid and financial markets make it hard to dissave or to borrow. The individually funded, contribution-defined scheme could be administered privately or publicly.

Compulsory saving schemes are attractive if households are myopic or if there are moral hazard problems that affect private provision for one's old age. It could be the case that, without compulsion, the young would not have saved adequately, intending to throw themselves on the mercy of the community when old age arrived. Forced saving (assuming offsetting discretionary dissaving is not possible) helps to solve this problem. The same moral hazard problem would also lead one to favour paying out the retirement benefit not as a lump-sum, but as a stream of annuity payments.

Clearly, the individual-account, contribution-defined scheme could not, without additions or modifications, provide universal old-age security. The low-paid and those without an income could not make the required contributions. One solution would be for the state to contribute to the accounts of poorer citizens, maintaining the individually funded character of the scheme. Another solution would be to preserve a basic unfunded scheme to provide the social retirement minimum.

Unfunded social security retirement schemes not only help smooth income over the life cycle, thus permitting consumption-smoothing over time, they also reduce uncertainty, permitting consumption-smoothing across states of nature. While this feature is clearly desirable in its own right, it may have a further negative effect on private saving if the precautionary saving motive is operative.

Current unfunded social security retirement schemes (and indeed the subsidized public sector health and disability insurance schemes) were designed on the basis of demographic projections that turned out to be wrong. The rapid greying of the populations in industrial countries (and other developments that have lowered the active-inactive ratio for the population as a whole) has created a youth deficit that makes it impossible to finance current and future benefit entitlements (under current laws and regulations) with the contribution rates and obligations embodied in current laws and regulations. Unfavourable demographics (and also to a certain extent disappointing productivity growth) have created conditions under which inter-generational conflict is unavoidable. If younger generations lose, contribution rates will be raised, or the contribution base will be broadened. If older generations give way, benefit rates will be lowered or eligibility restricted.

Beginning reform early will minimize the extent to which governments will have to renege on implicit or explicit clauses of the social contract. It would hardly be a propitious start if among the first acts of the reforming government was the wholesale expropriation of pension rights and entitlements of generations that lived through the Great Depression, World War II and (in the case of the former Soviet Union and eastern and central European nations) the bleak decades of central planning. But the expectations of current and future contributors (based on the pre-reform record of pay-outs) are inconsistent. Either benefits will turn out to be lower than expected or contributions higher than expected, or both. Painless social security reform is not an option.

The way in which this inter-generational conflict is resolved will have important incentive and efficiency effects, as well as distributional consequences. Raising contribution rates, for instance, would adversely affect labour demand and supply. In industrial countries, too, demographic developments and disappointing productivity growth have made the old (implicit) social security contract inconsistent and unsustainable.

Reduction of public debt-GDP ratios

Policies that reduce public debt–GDP ratios by raising current revenues are, similarly, redistributions from current to future generations. In most industrial countries, however, the overall tax burden (and the marginal effective rates of taxation that they imply) is already so high that both on efficiency and political feasibility grounds, it is hard to make a politically convincing case for further increases. Current spending cuts are therefore likely to be the main mechanism through which the burden of the public debt is reduced. In many of the countries of the former Soviet Union and in many developing countries the overall tax burden is much more moderate, and well-designed tax enhancement measures (say through base-broadening, improved enforcement and elimination of exemptions), if well implemented, need not have overwhelming adverse effects on incentives.

An increase in the after-tax real rate of return to saving

Most of the available empirical evidence suggests that aggregate private saving does not respond significantly to moderate changes in the after-tax real rate of return on saving.[48] Policies designed to raise the after-tax rate of return to saving would therefore not have an appreciable effect on aggregate saving rates. Note, however, that the insensitivity of saving to its rate of return reflects the combined impacts of the substitution effect (which would increase saving with its rate of return) and the income effect (which works in the opposite direction for net lenders). Policy reforms that raise the *marginal* rate of return to private saving (say, by reducing the degree of progression in the tax rate on saving and thus lowering the marginal tax rate on saving) without reducing the average return to private saving (by maintaining the same average tax rate on private saving) will therefore affect behaviour only through the substitution effect.

In addition to policies that affect aggregate private saving, considerable efficiency gains can be achieved by reducing or eliminating distortions in the allocation of savings among competing instruments.

Policies to promote investment

The third section dealt at length with the positive effects on private investment of policies that improve macroeconomic stability. Several additional policies that enhance the quantity and quality of investment, broadly defined, should also be pursued. The unique role of the state lies in promoting forms of capital investment that either have a very long gestation and pay-off period or have returns that are non-rival and/or cannot be fully appropriated by private investors.

Promoting education and training

Subsidizing education and training is a natural function of the state. First, as we indicated earlier, there are merit-good and rights arguments for partial or full public funding. Second, not all of the returns to education can be captured privately. More educated citizens make better citizens. Parents who were well-educated, in turn, are more likely to educate their own children. There are significant peer-group effects in education and socialization. There is evidence that a worker's productivity rises with the average productivity of co-workers and associates. Enterprises are likely to underinvest in on-the-job training if such training is costly and if the human capital thus acquired by the worker is portable. Making workers pay for their own training may not be an option, because most workers do not possess the financial resources to finance these training expenses and are not in a position to offer effective collateral for "training loans". Making workers post bond, to be forfeited in case the worker quits soon after being trained at the expense of the firm, has the same problem as that of inadequate financial resources. In addition, this practice would not be legal in many countries.

Education and training facilitate the transmission of knowledge and the creation of new knowledge. Knowledge is the ultimate non-rival good.[49] This characteristic provides an argument both for subsidizing education and training and for subsidizing fundamental R&D.

The arguments are not all one-way, however. Certain kinds of education have certification, or "sheep-skin", value because they are viewed as signals of unobservable desirable characteristics, such as intelligence, knowledge and productivity. Private agents may over-invest in educational qualifications that have these certification properties. The armies of lawyers produced in some developing countries may be the outcome of such a process. These problems are more likely to occur at the university level than at the pre-school, primary and secondary school levels. The merit-good, rights and externality arguments are also likely to apply more strongly at these levels, particularly in developing countries.

Raising the active/inactive population ratio

Another means of raising the effective human capital stock in industrial countries—almost at a stroke—is to change the rules determining the active-inactive population ratio. Policies that reduce dependency ratios may be desirable both from the point of view of economic efficiency and from the point of view of distributional equity among generations. Dependents are the young, the sick and the old. Education, public health, preventive medicine and poverty reduction can have strong effects on morbidity. Education, rising living standards and availability of contraception can influence birth rates. In both cases educating women is especially important. Large-scale immigration by working-age people is likely to be politically controversial in much of the industrial world (which is not to say that it will not happen). From an economic point of view immigration affects different generations in very different ways. The retired population will welcome the contributions that the young immigrant workers make to their unfunded social security retirement schemes. They will also, as owners of much of the domestic capital stock, benefit from any increase in the rate of return to domestic capital brought about by immigration. Younger workers, especially those in the same (lower) skill categories as the immigrants, will view the new arrivals primarily as competitors in labour markets.

That leaves raising the labour force participation rate of the old as the obvious means for boosting the active-inactive ratio in the population as a whole. An increase in the age of retirement by, say, five years would help to resolve many of problems faced by the unfunded social security systems in industrial countries. An increase in the retirement age would mean an increase in the minimum age at which one becomes eligible for a retirement pension, and a matching increase in the number of years one is obliged to make contributions to the social security fund. Such an increase could be combined with the abolition of automatic compulsory retirement at a particular age. The United States recently abolished compulsory retirement for the vast majority of workers. Complementary changes in seniority systems and arrangements will likely be associated with such changes.

The proposed increase in the age of retirement makes sense and is fair, given the increase in life expectancy of both men and women and the improved health and vigour enjoyed by many well into their seventies.[50] Note that raising the number of working years relative to the number of non-working years in an individual's life span, will not necessarily raise the long-run ratio of private wealth to income. But it will, of course, increase the viability, and reduce the disincentive effects associated with any remaining unfunded component, of the social security system.

It may seem strange, with so much of western Europe still plagued by persistent high unemployment and with continued interest in such measures as compulsory work-sharing, reductions in the duration of the working week and encouragement of early retirement, to advocate measures aimed at achieving a sizable increase in the effective supply of labour. Yet, it seems likely that the problem facing industrial nations in the coming decades will be one of insufficient labour (and of insufficiently skilled and educated labour) relative to the real income expectations and aspirations of a greying population. Unemployment in western Europe, except for a cyclical component,[51] is mainly a self-inflicted wound that can be cured by structural measures, including the improvement of the skill level and mix, the reduction of the wedge between take-home pay and gross marginal labour costs, the reduction of the gap between the private and the social cost of hiring and firing workers, the encouragement of mobility of firms and workers, and the facilitation of investment in long-term productive relationships by workers and employers.

Increasing infrastructure and other spending to enhance long-term growth potential

A benevolent, omniscient and omnipotent social planner undertakes public investment projects whenever the social rate of return on the resources that are committed exceeds their opportunity cost— the social discount rate. There is no automatic presumption that the social rate of return on public sector investment is more likely to exceed the social discount rate in good times than in bad times. In the real world, however, political economy considerations produce a robust empirical regularity: whenever the government budget is squeezed (typically when recession, depression or structural decline depress current government receipts), capital budgets are slashed. Public sector investment spending and other productivity-enhancing expenditures (repairs and maintenance, R&D) are the first to be cut. Effective decision horizons shorten dramatically during a fiscal crunch, and any spending category that yields its returns in the future is a likely victim of political expediency. To restore balance in the composition of public spending, public sector infrastructure spending, other public investment, repairs and maintenance, and all other public spending categories that functionally constitute investment (whatever their official designation) should be favoured when the seven lean years are over and the seven fat years arrive. The reason is simple: *if not then, when*?

When it comes to infrastructure spending, it is again important to distinguish between the operation and management of the social overhead capital stock and its financing. Roads and bridges, for instance, have some of the properties of public capital goods: up to the point when congestion sets in, road and bridge use is *non-rival* (marginal cost is below average cost). But, since road and bridge use are, at a cost, *excludable*, controlled-access roads and bridges can, through tolls or other forms of road charges, be privately operated and managed. If the marginal cost is below the average cost, competitive private operation is not feasible. Subsidization and regulation may be required.

The government also need not be the sole financer of infrastructure investment. Many financial constructs for sharing the risks and returns to infrastructure investment between public and private sector partners have been designed and implemented throughout history, and new joint ventures of this kind are being tested in a variety of economic and institutional settings. It is ironic that perhaps the strongest practical argument for involving the private sector in the financing of infrastructure investment is that without access to private funds, made available by private investors with decision horizons longer than those of the government, the public sector alone would be unable or unwilling to undertake a socially worthwhile investment. Political myopia, sometimes institutionalized in myopic public sector budgeting rules (PSBRs) that do not distinguish between current and capital spending (such as PSBR targets or ceilings), prevents the public sector from fulfilling its "Platonic guardian" role of overcoming private sector capital market imperfections (liquidity constraints, and so on) and enabling the economy as a whole to take a long-run view. It would surely be sensible to try to implement political and administrative reforms that encourage the public sector to make use of its unique potential for taking the long-run view, born of its ability to tax current and future generations and to make use of seigniorage revenues.

Reducing the effective marginal tax rate on capital income

Policies to bring the private rate of return to physical capital formation more closely in line with the social rate of return include reductions in the average effective marginal tax rate on capital income and reductions in the dispersion of the effective marginal tax rate around the average. Different forms of private capital formation are subject to wildly different marginal effective tax rates, and most of these differences cannot be rationalized with reference to externalities or other sources of differences between private and social rates of return.

CONCLUSIONS

Macroeconomic policy in the years to come will have to operate in an environment that is more open and international than at any time since the beginning of World War I. It will also have to work through, and will be constrained by, markets (domestic and international) in a way that would be more familiar to the governments of the Gold Standard days than to governments of the post-World War II Keynesian era.

Although our expectations of what governments can do are more modest than those at the founding of the Bretton Woods institutions more than 50 years ago, we still hold that the quality of the institutions of government and of the policies that it pursues may be the single most important factor accounting for differential economic performance in the medium and long term. A limited but strong state is likely to be a defining characteristic of economic success in the decades to come.

Macroeconomic stability is one of the key intermediate public goods that the government alone can provide. Its effect on the quantity and quality of private investment is one important channel through which it, by stimulating capital formation, can take advantage of a relatively favourable global economic environment and lay the groundwork for sustained and shared growth. This should be complemented with policies to boost saving rates (especially in industrial countries), policies to encourage investment in infrastructure and in environmental capital, policies to develop the effective human capital stock through education and training, policies to raise the active-inactive population ratio and policies to add to the stock of human knowledge through research and development.

APPENDIX 1.

The change in the government debt–GDP ratio in period t, $\Delta b(t + 1)$, equals the initial debt-GDP ratio, $b(t)$, times the excess of the real interest rate, $r(t + 1)$, over the growth rate of real GDP, $g(t + 1)$, minus the government sector's primary (non-interest) surplus as a fraction of GDP, $s(t)$, minus seigniorage (new issues of base money) as a fraction of GDP, $\sigma(t)$, that is,

$$\Delta b(t+1) \equiv \left(\frac{r(t+1) - g(t+1)}{1 + g(t+1)} \right) b(t) - s(t) - \sigma(t).$$

Note that the debt-GDP ratio declines ($\Delta b < 0$) when $s + \sigma > b(r - g) / (1 + g)$.

APPENDIX 2.

Seigniorage (as a share of GDP), denoted σ, is the change in the nominal stock of base money (currency plus commercial bank reserves with the central bank), expressed as a fraction of GDP. It represents the real resources appropriated by the state through its ability to issue non-interest-bearing base money. If H denotes the nominal stock of base money and Y denotes nominal GDP then,

$$\sigma \equiv \frac{\Delta H}{Y}.$$

The inflation tax (as a share of GDP), denoted τ^π, is the reduction in the real value of the outstanding stock of base money due to inflation, expressed as a fraction of GDP. If π denotes the rate of inflation, g the growth rate of real GDP, $h \equiv H/Y$ the base money–GDP ratio and a subscript $_{-1}$ denotes a value in the preceding period, we have

$$\tau^\pi \equiv \pi \frac{H_{-1}}{Y}$$

or

$$\tau^\pi \equiv \frac{\pi}{(1+\pi)(1+g)} h_{-1}.$$

The following identity links seigniorage and the inflation tax:

$$\sigma \equiv \tau^\pi + \left(\frac{g}{(1+g)}\right) h_{-1} + \Delta h.$$

Thus, seigniorage exceeds the inflation tax if there is growth in real GDP or if the base money–GDP ratio is increasing (the income velocity of base money is declining).

NOTES

The authors would like to thank Vanessa Glasmacher, Kasper Bartholdy, Anne Sibert and the UN High Level Group on Development Strategy and Management of the Market Economy for guidance and contributions to this chapter. István P. Székely made detailed and wide-ranging constructive comments on an earlier version of the chapter. Rika Ishii provided valuable assistance with the final revisions of the chapter. The opinions and views expressed are those of the authors and do not necessarily reflect those of the European Bank for Reconstruction and Development. Professor R. Rowthorn of Cambridge University provided the database for table 2.2.

1. In the sense that it is non-rival (one person's consumption does not diminish another's) and non-excludable (it is not possible to exclude consumers from using the good).

2. Feldstein and Horioka (1980) and Feldstein (1983), using data for 17 OECD countries over 1960–74, found that the gross national (private plus public) saving–GDP ratio and the gross domestic capital formation–GDP ratio were highly positively correlated. They interpreted this result as indicating a relatively low degree of international capital mobility. If this interpretation is correct, sustained (exogenous) increases in domestic saving rates would induce approximately equal increases in domestic investment rates rather than spilling over into current account surpluses. Both the empirical analysis and the interpretation have been contested.

3. This also holds for trade in real goods and services. Gross inflows and outflows (imports and exports) matter, not just the net trade balance.

4. See Obstfeld and Rogoff (1995). For a detailed discussion of the recent growth of international financial markets see Goldstein and Folkerts-Landau (1994).

5. See, for example, Schadler and others (1993) and Khan and Reinhart (1995).

6. During the days of the gold standard the international movements of both labour and financial capital were subject to few political barriers. While political and administrative obstacles are probably still higher today than they were between 1870 and 1913, the technology of mobility in the 1990s surely dominates that of the earlier "open" era.

7. It must be remembered that markets do not operate in a vacuum—there are many other relationships and institutions that are crucial to effective economic organization and performance. This is a major theme of this paper.

8. The first welfare theorem says that any competitive equilibrium (with complete markets and complete market participation, and without externalities) is a Pareto optimum. The second welfare theorem says that, without externalities and with lump-sum redistribution (and with appropriate convexity assumptions concerning production and consumption), any Pareto optimum can be supported as a competitive equilibrium.

9. This controversy revolved around the possibility of rational and efficient resource allocation under socialism, or, more specifically, in centrally planned economies with publicly owned means of production. See, for example, von Mises (1920), von Hayek (1935a, 1945), Wootton (1935), Lange (1938), Lerner (1944), Bergson (1948) and Eckstein (1971). Von Hayek and von Mises

emphasized the role of private ownership in providing incentives for work, effort, saving and investment, and for revealing economically useful information. In their view private ownership was essential for the price mechanism to aggregate and disseminate information, thus permitting efficient decentralized decision-making. Market prices in an economy with private ownership were therefore fundamentally different from the shadow prices generated by the (mythical) omniscient central planner. Central in von Hayek's theory of informational efficiency and decentralization was his emphasis on the universality and inescapability of bounded rationality, leading him to view the market system not as a static resource allocation mechanism but as a dynamic discovery process.

10. See, for example, Dornbusch and Edwards (1991); Lago (1991); Thomas and others (1991); Bruno and others (1991); Sachs and Larrain (1992) and Easterly, Rodriguez and Schmidt-Hebbel (1994). For the post-Communist experience of some transition economies see Balcerowicz (1993, 1994).
11. See, for example, Burgess and Stern (1993) and IMF (1989).
12. See, for example, EBRD (1996).
13. It would have been more useful to have had comparative figures for developing countries and for some of the newly industrialized countries (NICs), rather than for the OECD. However, figures for *general* government revenue (and spending) are extremely sparse for non-OECD countries. Only *central* government data tend to be available. These are not appropriate for our purposes.
14. See, for example, Hussain and Stern (1991) and *The Wall Street Journal* (1996).
15. This section touches on some of the same issues covered at greater length in the contribution by Stiglitz in Volume I.
16. Note that national accounts classify such activities as public consumption, which makes only limited economic sense in most cases. On the whole, citizens do not consume law and order. Law and order, however essential, are intermediate public inputs to the safe and untroubled consumption of marketed goods and services, and leisure.
17. What follows is based largely on Stern (1991).
18. Note that compulsion is applied with respect to the "isolated" individual only. The reluctant tax payer may rationally vote for higher taxes.
19. Essentially, the rate of growth of the economy is fast enough to absorb service payment on debt. Government solvency means that the initial debt plus the present value of expenditure is no greater than the present value of revenue, including seigniorage. Under reasonable restrictions on the government's ability to tax, this implies an upper bound on the debt-to-GDP ratio in the long term.
20. See Appendix 1 for a more precise statement.
21. See Appendix 1.
22. Like any price change, a change in the interest rate (the reciprocal of the inter-temporal relative price minus one) has distributional consequences. Net lenders (the old, for instance) will benefit from an increase in the real rate of interest; net borrowers will be hurt.
23. On this see Blanchard and Summers (1985), Barro and Sala-i-Martin (1990), Group of Ten (1995), Qureshi (1995) and IMF (1995c).
24. This is not inconsistent with spending on disability compensation (and on pensions) having increased sharply in many transition economies, which have used disability and early retirement as means of reducing recorded open unemployment. The anticipated lifetime degree of protection against ill-health,

disability and unemployment-related income declines can fall for the representative citizen (with the implications for precautionary saving described above) at the same time that total expenditure on these three categories increases on a temporary basis.

25. See, for example, Hubbard, Skinner and Zeldes (1994a,b, 1995) and Caballero (1991).

26. See Appendix 2.

27. An average annual inflation rate ten percentage points higher was associated with a 0.2 to 0.3 percentage point lower average annual growth rate of real GDP between 1960 and 1990.

28. In the popular dissemination of these findings, Barro's argument gets rather muddled (Barro, 1995b). It is, for instance, hard to make sense of the following sentence: "But while the impact is not statistically significant when inflation averages less than 15 percent, this does not mean lower rates of inflation are costless: the adverse effect on growth of inflation below 15 percent is close to the effect when it is in the higher ranges." Even though the point estimates may be similar, the lack of statistical significance of the estimate for the low inflation range surely means that the point estimate should be taken less seriously. Actually, not only is the point estimate of the coefficient of growth on inflation statistically insignificant for low-inflation countries, the magnitude of the estimated coefficient is smaller for low-inflation countries (-0.016 with a standard error of 0.035) than for middle-range-inflation countries (-0.037 with a standard error of 0.017) and high-inflation countries (-0.023 with a standard error of 0.005). Note also that Barro's research, which focuses on the medium- to long-term relation(s) between inflation and output growth, has no bearing on the existence and magnitude of the "sacrifice ratio"—on the (transitional) output or unemployment cost of achieving a sustained reduction in the rate of inflation. That is, it tells us nothing about the existence or absence of a short-term trade-off between inflation and some measure of real economic performance, such as output or unemployment. Here, too, Barro's popularization of his research findings is only loosely connected to the actual research: "There is, in other words, no empirical support for the idea that more inflation must be tolerated to achieve higher output and unemployment" (Barro, 1995b).

29. Sarel (1996) estimates a non-linear relationship between inflation and growth. The author concludes that there is a threshold for the inflation rate below which the effect of inflation on growth is small and insignificant (and may even be slightly positive) but above which the effect is negative, large and significant. The threshold is estimated to be an average annual rate of inflation of 8 per cent. Some scepticism about the reliability of Sarel's numerical estimates is in order, however. He considers only a single structural break, rather than multiple structural breaks (for example, stable price level regimes, moderate inflation regimes, high inflation regimes and hyperinflationary regimes) or a more general non-linear relationship between growth and inflation, without a single key discontinuity. The results are also affected by the surprising choice of the *logarithm* of the rate of inflation as the inflation variable in his regressions. As the inflation rate is negative in a small number of cases, the author is forced to make arbitrary ad-hoc adjustments to his data. Taking the logarithm of (1 + the rate of inflation) as his inflation variable would have avoided this problem (the price *level* did not become negative in any of his observations).

30. See, for example, Fischer and Modigliani (1978).
31. "Shoe leather" costs refers to making frequent trips to the bank so that as little money can be held as possible. "Menu costs" refers to the frequent relabeling of prices in restaurants and other such establishments.
32. The term "insurance" is hardly descriptive. A worker is paid a contingent benefit (contingent on being unemployed). There is no experience rating for individual workers, and only in some countries (like the United States) is there (partial) experience rating for individual firms. Even in the aggregate there is no necessary (actuarial) link between total contributions (by workers and employers) and total unemployment benefits.
33. Compulsory unemployment insurance can mitigate the adverse selection problem; it does nothing to reduce the moral hazard problem.
34. This need not create any tendency towards positive drift in the public debt–GDP ratio.
35. See EBRD (1995), table 2.2, p. 21 and chart 2.2, p. 23 for the behaviour of the social indicators in the transition economies; table 2.1, p. 11 and chart 2.1 for indicators of progress in transition; and Annex 11.1, pp. 185–6 for data on real GDP growth and inflation in the transition economies.
36. The per capita income of Czechoslovakia at that time was only about 30 per cent lower than that of France. In these countries some generational memory of the market persists.
37. In China collectivization was initiated in the 1950s, and the agricultural reforms of the "household-responsibility" system came in 1979–83.
38. Privatization alone does not, of course, solve the problems of enterprise management.
39. A recent extreme example of the sort is New Zealand's Fiscal Responsibility Act, which makes politicians accountable for economic promises.
40. It seems that it is de facto, rather than de jure, independence that matters (see Bruno, 1994 and Cukierman, 1992).
41. The external primary surplus is the current account surplus minus net foreign factor income, roughly the sum of the trade surplus and net transfers from the rest of the world.
42. See, for example, Eichengreen and Wyplosz (1994); Eichengreen, Rose and Wyplosz (1994); Bosworth, Dornbusch and Laban (1994).
43. This is true even if the equilibrium is strictly temporary or momentary.
44. A second surviving feature of its global or systemic role is the Fund's participation, and often leadership role, in putting together financial rescue packages for countries whose financial troubles are of sufficient magnitude to threaten the stability of financial markets generally. The recent Mexican crisis is a frequently cited example of this function.
45. If the introduction of the scheme was anticipated by the older generation during their youth, they would have raised their consumption while they were young by reducing voluntary private saving or, if financial markets are efficient, by dissaving.
46. We are assuming a closed economy for simplicity. In an open economy the stock of net claims on the rest of the world could be reduced.
47. The scheme is technically a defined-contribution scheme.
48. Clearly, moving from a situation in which there is a serious risk of savings being confiscated or wiped out by hyperinflation to one in which positive real rates of return can confidently be expected will boost the savings rate.

49. In the (correct) formal sense that the use of the laws of physics, for example, by one individual does not prevent their use by another. Differential availability of knowledge might, of course, affect the profitability of certain positions, but, while important, it is a different story.
50. Fair, here, is used in the sense that a rising life expectancy implies a higher present value of benefits than was anticipated when the schemes were conceived.
51. The cyclical component of unemployment can also be a self-inflicted wound. An example is the United Kingdom joining the European exchange rate mechanism (ERM) in October 1990 at an overvalued exchange rate and then having to follow German interest rates up in the wake of the German macroeconomic mismanagement of German re-unification after May 1990. The United Kingdom then aggravated its problems by creating doubts about its commitment to ERM, thereby adding a devaluation risk premium to its interest rates.

REFERENCES

Abel, A., A. Dixit, J. Eberly and R. Pindyck. 1995. "Options, the value of Capital, and Investment." NBER Working Paper 5227. Cambridge, Mass.

Bagchi, A., R. Bird and A. Dasgupta. 1995. "Developing a Strategy for Tax Administration Reform."

Balcerowicz, L. 1993. "Common Fallacies in the Debate on the Economic Transition in Central and Eastern Europe." EBRD Working Paper 11. London.

____. 1994. "Understanding Postcommunist Transitions." *Journal for Democracy.* 5:75–89.

Barro, R. 1995a. "Inflation and Economic Growth." *Bank of England Quarterly Bulletin*, May:166–76.

____. 1995b. "Price Stability is the Path to Prosperity." *Financial Times*, May 17, p. 19.

Barro, R. and X. Sala-i-Martin. 1990. "World Real Interest Rates." In Olivier J. Blanchard and Stanley Fischer, eds., *NBER Macroeconomics Annual 1990*. Cambridge, Mass.: MIT Press.

Berg, A. 1993. "Does Macroeconomic Reform Cause Structural Adjustment? Lessons from Poland." IMF, Washington, D.C.

Bergson, A. 1948. "Socialist Economics." In H. Ellis, ed., *A Survey of* Contemporary Economics. Philadelphia: American Economic Association.

Blanchard, O. and L. Summers. 1985. "Perspectives on High World Real Interest Rates." *Brookings Papers on Economic Activity* 2:273–324.

Bosworth, B., R. Dornbusch and R. Laban, eds. 1994. *The Chilean Economy: Policy Lessons and Challenges*. Washington, D. C.: The Brookings Institution.

Bruno, M. 1992. "Stabilisation and Reform in Eastern Europe: A Preliminary Evaluation." *IMF Staff Papers* 39(4):741–77.

____. 1993a. "Inflation and Growth in Recent History and Policy: Applications of an Integrated Approach." Department of Economics, Hebrew University, Jerusalem. Processed.

____. 1993b. "Stabilisation and Reform in Eastern Europe: A Preliminary Evaluation." In M. Blejer et al., eds., "Eastern Europe in Transition: From Recession to Growth." World Bank Discussion Paper 196. Washington, D.C.

____. 1994. "Political Autonomy of Central Banks: Theory and Practice." Keynote Lecture, Conference on the Constitutional Status of Central Banks in Eastern Europe, University of Chicago Law School, April 22.

____. 1995. *The Kuznetz Lectures*. New Haven: Yale University Press.

Bruno, M., S. Fischer, E. Helpman, N. Liviatan, and D. Meridor, eds. 1991. *Lessons of Economic Stabilisation and Its Aftermath*. Cambridge, Mass.: MIT Press.

Buiter, W., R. Lago and N. Stern. 1995. "Enterprise Performance and Macroeconomic Control." EBRD, London. Processed.

Burgess, R. and N. Stern. 1993. "Taxation and Development." *Journal of Economic Literature* 31(2):762–830.

Caballero, R. 1991. "Earnings, Uncertainty and Aggregate Wealth Accumulation." *American Economic Review* 81(September):859–71.

Cardoso, E., R. Paes de Barros and R. Urani. 1995. "Inflation and Unemployment as Determinants of Inequality in Brazil: the 1980s." In R. Dornbusch and S. Edwards, eds., *Reform, Recovery and Growth; Latin America and the Middle East*. Chicago: University of Chicago Press.

Cardoso, E. 1992. "Inflation and Poverty." NBER Working Paper 7006. Cambridge, Mass.

Coase, R. 1937. "The Nature of the Firm." *Economica* 4(November):386–405.

Cooper, R., W. Corden, I. Little and S. Rajapatrana. 1993. *Boom, Crisis and Adjustment: The Macroeconomic Experience of Developing Countries, 1970–1990*. Oxford University Press.

Corden, W. 1990. "Macroeconomic Policy and Growth: Some Lessons of Experience." *Annual Conference on Development Economics*. Washington, D.C.: World Bank.

Cukierman, A. 1992. *Central Bank Strategy, Credibility and Independence: Theory and Evidence*. Cambridge, Mass.: MIT Press.

De Melo, M., C. Denizer and A. Gelb. 1995. "From plan to market: patterns of transition." Paper presented to the First Dubrovnik Conference On Transition Economies, June.

Dixit, A. and R. Pindyck. 1994. *Investment under Uncertainty*. Princeton: Princeton University Press.

Dornbusch, R. 1976. "Expectations and Exchange Rate Dynamics." *Journal of Political Economy* 84(December):1161–76.

____. 1990. "Policies to Move from Stabilisation to Growth." *Annual Conference on Development Economics*. Washington, D.C.: World Bank.

Dornbusch, R. and S. Edwards, eds. 1991. *The Macroeconomic of Populism in Latin America*. Chicago: Chicago University Press.

Easterly, W., C. Rodriguez and K. Schmidt-Hebbel, eds. 1994. *Public Sector Deficits and Macroeconomic Performance*. Oxford: Oxford University Press.

Eckstein, A., ed. 1971. *Comparison of Economic Systems: Theoretical and Methodological Approaches*. Berkeley: University of California Press.

Eichengreen, B. and C. Wyplosz. 1994. "The Unstable EMS." *Brookings Papers on Economic Activity* 1:51–124.

Eichengreen, B., A. Rose and C. Wyplosz. 1994. "Speculative Attacks on Pegged Exchange Rates: An Empirical Exploration with Special Reference to the European Monetary System." NBER Working Paper 4898. Cambridge, Mass.

European Bank for Reconstruction and Development (EBRD). 1995. *Transition Report*. London: EBRD.

———. 1996. *Transition Report Update*. London: EBRD.

Feldstein, M. 1983. "Domestic Saving and International Capital Movements in the Long Run and in the Short Run." *European Economic Review* 21.

Feldstein, M. and C. Horioka. 1980. "Domestic Savings and International Capital Flows." *Economic Journal* 90:314–29.

Fischer, S. 1991. "Growth, Macroeconomics and Development." In *NBER Macroeconomics Annual 1991* Cambridge, Mass.: MIT Press.

———. 1993. "The Role of Macroeconomic Factors in Growth." *Journal of Monetary Economics* 32:485–512.

Fischer, S. and Franco Modigliani. 1978. "Towards Understanding of the Real Effects and Costs of Inflation." *Weltwirtschaftliches Archiv*, 810–32.

Fisher, I. 1932. *Booms and Depressions*. New York.

Gil Díaz, F. 1987. "Some Lessons from Mexico's Tax Reform." In D. Newbery and N. Stern, eds., *The Theory of Taxation for Developing Countries*. Oxford: Oxford University Press.

Goldstein, M. and D. Folkerts-Landau. 1994. *International Capital Markets: Developments, Prospects and Policy Issues*. Washington, D.C.: International Monetary Fund.

Group of Ten. 1995. "Saving, Investment and Real Interest Rates: A Study for the Ministers and Governors by the Group of Deputies." Washington, D.C.

Hirschman, Albert. 1981. "The Turn to Authoritarianism in Latin America and the Search for its Economic Determinants." In Albert Hirschman, *Essays in* Trespassing. Cambridge: Cambridge University Press.

Homer, S. 1991. *A History of Interest Rates*. Third edition. New Brunswick, N.J. and London: Rutgers University Press.

Hubbard, G., J. Skinner and S. Zeldes. 1994a. "The Importance of Precautionary Motives in Explaining Individual and Aggregate Saving." *Carnegie-Rochester Conference Series on Public Policy* 40(June):59–126.

———. 1994b. "Expanding the Life-Cycle Model: Precautionary Saving and Public Policy." *American Economic Review* 84(May):174–9.

———. 1995. "Precautionary Saving and Social Insurance." *Journal of Political Economy* 103(2):360–99.

Hussain, A. and N. Stern. 1991. "Economic Reform in China." *Economic Policy* (April):141–86.

International Monetary Fund (IMF). 1989. *Government Finance Statistics* Yearbook, Vol. 13. Washington, D.C.: IMF.

———. 1995a. *Government Finance Statistics Yearbook*, Vol. 19, Washington, D.C.: IMF.

———. 1995b. "Saving in a Growing World Economy." In IMF, *World Economic Outlook*. Washington, D.C.: IMF.

———. 1995c. "The Design of a Minimal Monetary and Exchange Rate Structure for Countries in Post-chaos/Post-conflict Situations." Background Paper 8, United Nations High Level Group on Development Strategy and Management of the Market Economy, Third Meeting, Helsinki, Finland. July 8–10.

———. 1995d. "Outlines of the 'Architecture' of Minimalist Fiscal Structure for Countries in Post-chaos/Post-conflict Situations." Background Paper 4, United

Nations High Level Group on Development Strategy and Management of the Market Economy, Third Meeting, Helsinki, Finland. July 8–10.

Kane, C. and J. Morisett. 1993. "Who Would Vote for Inflation in Brazil? An Integrated Framework Approach to Inflation and Income Distribution." Policy Research Working Papers, WPS 1183. World Bank, Washington, D.C.

Khan, M. and C. Reinhart. 1995. "Capital Flows in the APEC Region." Occasional Paper 122(March). IMF, Washington, D.C.

Kaufmann, D. 1991. "The Forgotten Rationale for Policy Reform: The Productivity of Investment Projects." Background paper prepared for the *World Development Report 1991*, World Bank, Washington, D.C.

Lago, R. 1991. "The illusion of pursuing redistribution through macropolicy: Peru's heterodox experience, 1985–1990." In R. Dornbusch and S. Edwards, eds., *The Macroeconomic of Populism in Latin America*. Chicago: Chicago University Press.

Lange, O. 1938. "On the economic theory of socialism." In B.E. Lippincott, ed., *On the Economic Theory of Socialism*, Minneapolis.

Leahy, J. and T. Whited. 1996. "The effects of uncertainty on investment: some stylised facts." *Journal of Money, Credit and Banking* 28(1):64–83.

Lerner, A. P. 1944. *Economics of Control*. New York.

Levine, R. and D. Renelt. 1992. "A Sensitivity Analysis of Cross-Country Growth Regressions." *American Economic Review* 82(4):942–63.

Lin, J. 1992. "Rural Reforms and Agricultural Growth in China." *American Economic Review* 82(1):34–37.

Mitchell, B. 1992. *International Historical Statistics: Europe 1750–1988*. Third edition. London: Macmillan.

Mitchell, B. 1993. *International Historical Statistics: the Americas 1750–1988*. Second edition. Basingstoke: Macmillan.

Newbery, D. and N. Stern, eds. 1987. *The Theory of Taxation for Developing Countries*. Oxford: Oxford University Press.

Obstfeld, M. and K. Rogoff. 1995. "The mirage of fixed exchange rates." National Bureau of Economic Research (NBER) Working Paper 5191. Cambridge, Mass.

Pindyck, R.S. and A. Solimano. 1993. "Economic Instability and Aggregate Investment." In *NBER Macroeconomics Annual 1993*. Cambridge, Mass.: MIT Press.

Qureshi, Z. 1995. "Do we face a global 'capital shortage'"? The World Bank, September.

Sachs, J. and F. Larrain. 1992. *Macroeconomics in the Global Economy*. Englewood Cliffs, New Jersey: Prentice Hall.

Sarel, M. 1996. "Nonlinear Effects of Inflation on Economic Growth." *International Monetary Fund Staff Papers* 33(1):199–215.

Schadler, S., M. Carkovic, A. Bennett and R. Kahn. 1993. *Recent Experiences with Surges in Capital Inflows*. Occasional Paper No. 108. IMF, Washington, D.C.

Schaffer, M. 1992. "The enterprise sector and the emergence of the Polish fiscal crisis." London School of Economics. Processed.

SOPEMI. 1995. *Trends in International Migration*. Annual Report. Paris:OECD.

Stern, N. 1991. "Public policy and the economics of development." *European Economic Review* 35:241–71.

Stiglitz, J. 1997. "The Role of Government in the Economy of Developing Countries." In E. Malinvaud et al., eds., *Development Strategy and Management of the Market Economy*. Volume I. Oxford: Clarendon Press.

Tanzi, V., ed. 1992. *Fiscal Policies in Economies in Transition.* Washington, D.C.: International Monetary Fund.

____, ed. 1993. *Transition to Market: Studies in Fiscal Reform.* Washington, D.C.: IMF.

Thomas, V., A. Chhibber, M. Dailami and J. de Melo, eds. 1991. *Restructuring Economies in Distress: Policy Reform and the World Bank.* Oxford: Oxford University Press.

Tobin, J. 1982. "A proposal for international monetary reform." In J. Tobin, *Essays in Economic Theory and Policy.* Cambridge, Mass.: MIT Press.

UNICEF. 1994. *Crisis in Mortality, Health and Nutrition.* Florence, Italy.

Vickers, J. and G. Yarrow. 1988. *Privatisation: An Economic Analysis.* Cambridge, Mass.: The MIT Press.

____. 1991. "Economic Perspectives on Privatisation." *Journal of Economic Perspectives* 5(2):111.32.

von Hayek, F., ed. 1935a. *Collectivist Economic Planning.* London: Routledge & Kegan Paul.

____. 1935b. *Prices and Production.* New York: Augustus M. Kelley.

____. 1945. "The use of knowledge in society." *American Economic Review* 35(4): 519–30.

von Mises, L. 1920. "Economic Calculation in the Socialist Commonwealth." In F. von Hayek, ed. *Collectivist Economic Planning.* London: Routledge & Kegan Paul.

The Wall Street Journal. 1996. 16 July, p. 8A.

Williamson, J. 1997. "Public policy towards international capital flows." In Richard Sabot and István P. Székely, eds., *Development Strategy and Management of the Market Economy.* Volume II. Oxford: Clarendon Press.

World Bank. 1991a. *Lessons of Tax Reform.* Washington, D.C.: World Bank.

____. 1991b. *World Development Report 1991.* Washington, D.C.: World Bank.

____. 1995. *Global Economic Prospects and the Developing Countries 1995.* Washington, D.C.: World Bank.

____. 1996. *World Development Report 1996.* Washington D.C.: World Bank.

Wootton, B. 1935. *Plan or No Plan.* New York: Farrar and Rinehart.

3

Positive Feedback Mechanisms in Economic Development: A Review of Recent Contributions

ANDRÉS RODRÍGUEZ-CLARE

This chapter presents a very selective review of recent attempts to explain the stylized facts of economic development with models that exhibit multiple Pareto-rankable equilibria and path dependence. In essence, this literature explains lack of growth as a result of "vicious circles of poverty": either the economy is at a "bad" equilibrium or its initial conditions are such that there is no equilibrium path along which the economy can move towards an "advanced" steady state. This literature stands in stark contrast to the more standard tradition in economics, which holds that lack of growth is the result of poorly functioning economic institutions and incorrect policies.

The main ingredient of this new literature is externalities. It is well known that when externalities (that are not internalized) arise, the allocation of resources is not optimal. As a result, many people have argued that the government should intervene to alter the allocation of resources, favouring those industries (and more generally those activities, for example, education) that generate positive externalities. Stated this way, however, this argument is equally relevant for industrial and developing countries and thus does not seem particularly important for development policy.

When several economies are inter-dependent through trade or factor flows, these externalities—if they are strong enough and geographically limited—may have more drastic effects: they may lead to geographic concentration of economic activity, multiple Pareto-rankable equilibria (that is, a bad and a good equilibrium) and underdevelopment traps (that is, a situation in which the only equilibrium path involves no long-run growth). In other words, such externalities may lead to a situation in which the countries of the "North" produce "sophisticated" goods that generate important positive externalities, whereas the "South" remains trapped, specializing in "slow", "simple" or "backward" goods that entail no such externalities. As a consequence, the North may exhibit continuous growth and pay higher wages for similar types of labour than the South—and allowing for capital flows will not lead to convergence.

Whether externalities lead to agglomeration economies, multiple equilibria and poverty traps depends on whether they generate positive feedback mechanisms (also called self-reinforcing mechanisms). Recall that the basic neoclassical general-equilibrium model, with its standard convexity assumptions, entails negative feedback mechanisms. For instance, an increase in production leads to a higher marginal cost and a lower price, discouraging further output increases. Externalities are introduced into the neoclassical model usually without changing this basic property: the economy remains convex, only now some markets are missing, preventing Pareto optimality. For instance, an increase in production may lead to lower marginal costs when externalities are sufficiently strong, but it is assumed that the decrease in price is sufficient to offset this decline, so that, again, further output increases are discouraged. In contrast, recent models of economic development assume that such dampening forces are not sufficiently strong. These models thus feature positive feedback mechanisms.

Economists today believe that externalities may be important for at least two reasons. First, most contributions to the new endogenous growth literature attempt to explain the persistence of growth by assuming the existence of aggregate externalities. Second, some recent papers show that increasing returns to scale at the level of the firm may lead to industry-wide (pecuniary) externalities. Hence, the technological or non-pecuniary externalities (such as information spillovers) with which many economists are uncomfortable because of their "invisible" and abstract nature are not necessary to generate the kind of phenomena discussed above (although some sort of non-tradability becomes a necessary assumption). More importantly, assuming increasing returns to scale at the level of the firm has proved very useful in growth theory (to model innovation), in macroeconomic theory (to understand business cycles) and in trade theory (to understand intra-industry trade), leading to the widespread belief that this assumption is warranted.

The ideas that I will review in this chapter have been around at least since the 1950s and 1960s, when they had a strong impact on development policy. But as Krugman (1992) has pointed out, these ideas were not properly formalized and not well understood until recently, when we learned how to work with models that involve increasing returns to scale. Still, the fact that development policies based on those ideas (such as import substitution, investment subsidies, government enterprise) failed dramatically (see Little, 1982) makes one somewhat skeptical about the value of considering these ideas again. I believe there are at least two reasons why we should. First, the ability to capture those old ideas in formal models has led to a better understanding of the conditions under which government intervention may be warranted and the kind of information that would be necessary to carry out such intervention successfully. Second, past policy failures do not constitute proof that these models are empirically irrelevant: those policies could have failed because government institutions were not designed appropriately to carry them out.

The following section of the chapter discusses the stylized facts of economic development to gauge whether we should move beyond the neoclassical growth model, which predicts the existence of "automatic" development mechanisms. The third section discusses some general issues concerning models with externalities and positive feedback mechanisms, and the three sections following discuss particular models in which externalities lead to multiple equilibria or path dependence. The final section concludes with some general lessons for development policy.

I should mention that this chapter will not review the extensive literature on the development experience of particular countries nor the literature on how industrial policy has succeeded or failed in practice (see Little, Scitovsky and Scott 1970; Little 1982; Rodrik 1993; and World Bank 1993 for reviews of these issues). This chapter will also abstract from issues of income distribution and from political economy considerations, such as whether informed politicians are likely to intervene for society's benefit or for their own benefit.

THE NEOCLASSICAL GROWTH MODEL AND ECONOMIC DEVELOPMENT

Should we be interested in models with multiple equilibria or poverty traps? Should we abandon the neoclassical growth model, which predicts that automatic mechanisms will pull an economy out of economic underdevelopment? The neoclassical growth model explains underdevelopment as a consequence of capital scarcity. Accordingly, the rate of return to capital should be high in poor countries, generating strong incentives for foreign investment and domestic capital accumulation. Yet a casual look at the experience of many developing economies since World War II questions whether these automatic development mechanisms exist: in many poor economies per capita income has remained stagnant for decades and both foreign and domestic investment have been relatively low as a percentage of total production.

Moving beyond casual empiricism, Barro (1991) and Barro and Sala-i-Martin (1992) consider whether the neoclassical prediction of convergence of per capita income is consistent with the data. The first finding is that there is no convergence for the whole set of countries, that is, poorer countries are not growing faster than rich countries. In fact, Barro (1991) shows that there is a mild tendency for divergence—there is a mild positive correlation between initial income per capita and subsequent growth.

Barro then introduces the concept of conditional convergence, which modifies the concept of convergence to allow for the possibility that different countries have different steady states. That is, conditional convergence implies that countries that are further away from their own steady states grow at a faster rate than countries that are close to their steady states.[1] Barro confirms the existence of conditional convergence for the whole set of countries. Taking 1960 school enrollment rates as proxies for steady states (that is, countries with high 1960 school enrollment rates have high steady-state incomes per capita), conditional convergence implies that, holding school enrollment rates fixed, countries with a lower initial income per capita should have had higher subsequent growth. Barro verifies this claim by showing a negative partial correlation between the growth of income per capita in 1960–85 and income per capita in 1960. This finding provides one explanation for the absence of convergence: poorer countries need not grow faster than rich countries because their poverty is associated with a lower income per capita steady state, as reflected in lower school enrollment rates. This result of conditional convergence is consistent with the view advanced by Durlauf and Johnson (1992), who argue that different countries are converging to different steady states: there is convergence among subgroups of similar countries, but dissimilar countries may be diverging.

One problem with the conditional convergence approach is that it takes initial school enrollment rates as exogenous. It would seem more natural to regard school enrollment rates as private decisions based on future growth prospects. In this case, as shown in Bils and Klenow (1995), school enrollment rates would be higher in countries with higher growth prospects. Thus we could interpret the previous results as implying that countries that (for some reason) have better future growth prospects have higher initial school enrollment rates. In fact, Bils and Klenow find that this possibility is more plausible than the usual interpretation of the positive correlation between initial school enrollment rates and subsequent growth—that is, they find that the data are more consistent with the view that schooling responds to future growth prospects rather than the view that schooling drives growth.

A second and more important limitation of the conditional convergence approach as a way to think about economic development is that it does not explain why countries have significantly different steady state income per capita levels. Is not this precisely the puzzle that we are trying to solve? In fact, as suggested recently by Islam (1995), such differences in steady state income per capital levels may be almost as large as the differences in the levels observed in the data.

According to the neoclassical model such differences in steady state income per capita levels are a result of differences in taxes on capital. As opposed to rich countries, poor countries have high (implicit and explicit) taxes on returns to capital, decreasing the capital stock per worker in steady state and consequently also decreasing income per capita. The problem with this explanation is that unreasonably high taxes in poor countries would be necessary to generate the large observed disparity in income per capita levels between poor and rich countries. For instance, assuming a Cobb-Douglas production function with physical capital and labour, and a capital share of 0.4 (which implies that capital holders receive 40 per cent of total income), the implied marginal tax on capital returns for a country with an income per capita level of one-tenth the US level would be 98 per cent.[2] The corresponding pre-tax rate of return to capital would be 32 times higher in the poor country than in the United States.

These numbers become more reasonable if it is assumed that the share of capital in total income is higher than 40 per cent. A capital share of two-thirds may be appropriate if we consider human capital as another reproducible factor in addition to physical capital, as is done, for instance, by Mankiw, Romer and Weil (1992) and Chari, Kehoe and McGrattan (1995). In this case the implied marginal tax on capital would be 77 per cent, and the pre-tax rate of return to capital would be three times higher in the poor country than in the United States. These are certainly more reasonable numbers. Of course, we do not observe tax rates of 77 per cent on capital in poor countries, but macroeconomic instability, barriers to trade, weak enforcement of property rights, corruption and even possibly war have a similar effect to taxes in reducing income.

It thus appears that, once modified to take into account human capital, the neoclassical model is consistent with the empirical evidence. The view that emerges from this new version of the neoclassical model is that countries that adopt the right set of economic policies will converge towards the income levels of rich countries.[3] This is consistent with the view advanced by Sachs and Warner (1995), who find an "overwhelming tendency towards convergence" for countries that "have followed standard market-based economic policies, including respect for private property rights and open international trade." This is true "even among countries that start with extremely low levels of human capital endowments and extremely low levels of initial per capita income" (p. 6).[4]

This is not the only possible interpretation of the evidence, however. One could argue instead that the lack of convergence is due to the fact that some countries are caught in a low-level equilibrium or are stuck in a poverty trap. There is virtually no empirical research on the question of whether this "bad luck" story is more or less plausible than the "bad policy" story advocated by economists closer to the neoclassical paradigm. Thus the rest of the chapter simply explores the "bad luck" view and the associated policy implications.

EXTERNALITIES AND POSITIVE FEEDBACK MECHANISMS

I will now review some models that exhibit externalities and positive feedback mechanisms, and consider how they can explain three important stylized facts of economic development: no absolute convergence, the richest and poorest countries are growing at the same rate (Parente and Prescott, 1993) and the existence of "economic miracles", that is, countries that in a few decades have gained membership into the club of rich countries—for example, Hong Kong, the Republic of Korea, Singapore and Taiwan (province of China).

The second fact implies that if we want to consider models with poverty traps as an explanation for the lack of convergence, then we must assume that there are at least two sources of growth: one that is relevant for the long run and applies to all countries (that is, technical change that diffuses to all countries) and one that has to do with catching-up or convergence. In this light a poverty trap is relative—it implies that it may be very difficult for countries with the lowest incomes per capita to catch up to the countries with the highest.

Models with externalities and positive feedback mechanisms explain economic miracles as instances in which an economy jumps from a bad to a good equilibrium. Such a jump would imply a significant increase in the value of production with an unchanged quantity of resources, leading to a high predicted rate of total factor productivity growth over the period in which the miracle occurs. Some economists have agreed that this prediction is inconsistent with Young's (1995) careful estimates of total factor productivity growth for the Asian miracles—Hong Kong, the Republic of Korea, Singapore and Taiwan (province of China). In fact, as argued in detail in Klenow and Rodríguez-Clare (1996), Young's estimates are entirely consistent with the view that the east-Asian miracle was driven primarily by increases in total factor productivity (except in the case of Singapore).

What do we know about the empirical relevance of externalities and the positive feedback mechanisms that they may generate? The existence of cities and regional concentrations of economic activity are an important confirmation of the empirical importance of such positive feedback mechanisms. Furthermore, as Porter (1992) and Krugman (1991) have shown, related economic activity is often geographically concentrated, like high-tech industries in Silicon Valley and along Boston Route 128, fur products in New York and ceramic tiles in Sassuolo, Italy (see also Henderson, 1988).

At a more formal level Ellison and Glaeser (1994) show that the observed geographic concentration of industries is greater than what we would expect to see if location choice was purely random. This occurs even for "footloose" industries, suggesting the existence of significant localized externalities. Furthermore, Ciccone and Hall (1996) show the existence of significant positive density externalities—that is, they find that, other things being equal, firms operating in areas that are economically dense are more productive than firms operating in relative isolation.

AGGREGATE DEMAND SPILLOVERS

Positive externalities may arise from aggregate demand spillovers if production is carried out under decreasing average costs. This basic idea was formulated by Rosenstein-Rodan (1943) with his famous shoe factory example: the wages that factory workers earn making shoes are spent not only on shoes but also on other manufactures and agricultural goods. As a consequence, an entrepreneur will not want to start up shoe production in a poor economy because demand is not sufficient to make such investment profitable. Yet if other entrepreneurs simultaneously invest in other industries, the argument goes, then enough demand may be generated to make all investments profitable. For this story to be relevant it is crucial that industrial production be characterized by decreasing average costs, because it is this feature that makes profitability depend on aggregate demand.

Murphy, Shleifer and Vishny (1989) have recently formalized this argument. Because their paper has been extremely influential in reviving interest in models with externalities and multiple equilibria, it is worth describing it in some detail. In their model the economy is closed to international trade in all goods, and there are two technologies used to produce every good: cottage production and modern technology. Cottage production is characterized by constant average costs, while the modern technology entails a fixed production cost and a marginal cost that is lower than that of cottage production. If an entrepreneur decides to invest in the modern technology to produce a particular good, then he can undercut the competition from cottage production, which produces with higher average costs. He can thus charge a mark-up over costs. But given the fixed start-up cost, the profitability of his investment depends on market size, or aggregate demand. And aggregate demand depends on the purchasing power of workers, which depends in turn on the extent of industrialization (that is, how widespread the use of the modern technology is). This circularity leads to the possibility of multiple equilibria. In the "no-industrialization" equilibrium demand remains small, industrialization does not take place, income per capita is low and hence demand remains small. In contrast, the industrialization equilibrium entails high aggregate demand, which makes industrialization profitable. Industrialization leads to high aggregate income and high aggregate demand for each manufactured good.

Interestingly, Murphy, Shleifer and Vishny find that the conditions necessary for multiple equilibria are more stringent than those loosely expressed in much of the "big-push" literature. In particular, they find that the aggregate demand spillovers that generate multiple equilibria are not the ones that arise as the profits made in one sector are spent on goods made in other sectors. To see this, notice that in order to generate multiple equilibria, industrialization must be individually unprofitable at the bad equilibrium but individually profitable when several other sectors industrialize. If a firm makes negative profits at the no-industrialization equilibrium, however, then it does not contribute to aggregate income. In fact, by decreasing aggregate income, the firm makes it even less profitable to invest in the modern technology. Thus, the existence of a no-industrialization equilibrium precludes the existence of an industrialization equilibrium. See Appendix 1 for a formal derivation of this result.

Murphy, Shleifer and Vishny postulate a mechanism that is close in spirit to Rosenstein-Rodan's (1943) shoe factory parable that leads to multiple equilibria. They assume that firms producing with the modern technology have to pay a wage premium to workers above what they are paid by firms producing with the cottage technology. This obligation could be the result of poorer working conditions at modern factories or the fact that those factories are further away from where workers live. If modern factories have to pay a wage premium, then aggregate demand spillovers arise not only through profits but also through the excess wages that firms operating modern technologies must pay. Thus, starting from a situation with no industrialization, investing in the modern technology may be individually unprofitable because of low demand, yet still generate positive aggregate spillovers when the entrepreneur's losses are lower than the total wage premiums paid to workers. In this case multiple equilibria arise, and the industrialization equilibrium Pareto-dominates the no-industrialization equilibrium: workers are just as well off in the industrialization equilibrium as in the no-industrialization equilibrium, but average income per capita is higher in the first because profits are higher.[5]

Murphy, Shleifer and Vishny mention other mechanisms that also generate multiple equilibria. For instance, if production with the modern technology takes place in the city and cottage production takes place in the rural area, and if city dwellers' demand is more concentrated on manufactures (such as textiles and furniture), then positive spillovers may still arise even with negative profits, because industrialization by some firms leads to an increase in urban population, which increases the share of income that is spent on manufactures.[6] Murphy, Shleifer and Vishny also present a dynamic model in which the start-up investment is made in one period and production in the next period. Then, a firm that makes negative profits still generates positive spillovers as it increases aggregate demand in the second period, leading to higher profits for other firms that invest in the modern technology.

Rosenstein-Rodan's big-push argument and its subsequent formalizations have been repeatedly criticized because their main results depend on the closed economy assumption. Since most modern economies are well integrated with the world market, the argument goes, there is no need to generate domestic demand for industrialization. But it is easy to respond to this criticism by arguing that the existence of transportation costs implies that firms can earn higher per-unit profits on goods sold domestically than on exports. Thus greater domestic demand does confer an advantage to domestic producers.

Krugman shows this in a model of agglomeration economies generated by aggregate demand spillovers. In Krugman's model there are two regions and two sectors: agriculture and manufacturing. Agriculture uses land, which is specific to each location—the location of agriculture is therefore exogenous. In contrast, manufacturing can take place in either location, but transporting manufactured goods involves a cost. Entrepreneurs producing manufactured goods thus have an incentive to locate close to their customers (agricultural and manufacturing workers), but they also have an incentive to service both regions from a single plant to take advantage of economies of scale. Entrepreneurs prefer to produce from a single plant located where demand is higher—and demand is higher where more entrepreneurs locate their manufacturing plants. As in the Murphy-Shleifer-Vishny model, this behaviour leads to a positive feedback mechanism, which, here, generates economies of agglomeration and geographic concentration.

Path dependence

The same forces that lead to multiple Pareto-rankable equilibria in the models mentioned so far may also lead to path dependence. This is shown by Matsuyama (1992), who introduces dynamics in the Murphy-Shleifer-Vishny model by assuming that there is some inertia in resource allocation. In particular, Matsuyama assumes that the choice of technology is partially irreversible: once an entrepreneur chooses to operate with a particular technology (cottage production or the modern technology), then he has to stick with this choice for a certain (random) length of time. Matsuyama shows that this assumption may lead to path dependence. If the economy starts near one of the two steady states (no industrialization or complete industrialization), then the only perfect-foresight path entails convergence to that steady state. This result implies that economies starting with very little industrialization are stuck in a poverty trap: even if everyone expected the economy to converge to the industrialization steady state, no entrepreneur would invest in the modern technology. Poverty in this context is thus more severe than a problem of expectations or coordination failure.

If we explain the lack of convergence with a model that features a poverty trap, we must ask how some countries were able to grow and become richer than the rest in the first place. How were some countries able to industrialize? We can think about this question in the context of Matsuyama's dynamic model, in which the existence of a poverty trap depends on certain parameters—such as country size, the inter-temporal discount rate and entrepreneurship—which Matsuyama identifies as affecting the flexibility with which entrepreneurs can reverse their past decisions. According to this model today's rich countries must have had favourable parameters that allowed them to follow an equilibrium path towards the industrialization steady state.

Evidence

What evidence do we have for the existence of aggregate demand spillovers? Unfortunately, there are not many empirical studies of this phenomenon. Caballero and Lyons (1992) is a notable exception. They show that productivity increases in all industries as overall economic activity rises. This constitutes a case of positive externalities arising from aggregate economic activity. Are these externalities due to a mechanism similar to the one behind the Murphy-Shleifer-Vishny model? Caballero and Lyons claim that the answer is no, since they find no evidence for internal increasing returns—that is, for a single industry production increases one-for-one with increases in total industry inputs. The authors argue that aggregate positive externalities arise through other mechanisms, such as thick markets (as in Diamond, 1982).

We could check the evidence for the main assumptions behind the Murphy-Shleifer-Vishny model: decreasing average costs and significant transportation costs. Because technology is endogenous, however, the existence of decreasing average costs in one economy does not rule out other options for entrepreneurs in other economies. With respect to transportation costs, the export-led development experience of the "economic miracles" of east Asia—Hong Kong, the Republic of Korea, Singapore, Taiwan (province of China)— makes it doubtful that domestic demand can be a significant obstacle to development in practice (Stiglitz, 1991).

BACKWARD AND FORWARD LINKAGES

In addition to aggregate demand spillovers, firms can also generate positive externalities to other firms more directly through their demand for and supply of inputs. This source of externalities has been discussed at least since Hirschman (1958), but not until recently has it been possible to write formal models in which properly defined linkages give rise to pecuniary externalities. The essential feature of these recent models is increasing returns to scale, which implies that not all possible goods will be produced at any point in time. The set of goods actually produced thus becomes another variable, and linkages arise as private decisions change this set.

A simple formalization of this idea is provided in Rodríguez-Clare (1996a) (based in large part on ideas from Dixit and Stiglitz, 1977; Ethier, 1982; Romer, 1990; Fujita, 1990) and presented in Appendix 2. This formalization of linkages is based on three premises: that production efficiency is enhanced by the use of a wider variety of specialized inputs, that for many of these inputs the proximity of the supplier and the user is essential, and that the size of the market limits the equilibrium variety of specialized inputs. These premises can be captured in a simple model by assuming that there is love of variety for inputs in the production of final goods (as in Ethier, 1982b; Romer, 1990), that domestic firms must buy all of their inputs locally and that inputs are produced with increasing returns to scale. Under these circumstances a firm producing final goods generates a positive externality to other final-good producers. By increasing the demand for inputs, the final-good firm helps bring forth more varieties of specialized inputs. This is our concept of backward linkages. In turn, local production of more specialized inputs enables the production of more complex goods (that is, goods that use specialized inputs with high intensity) at competitive costs. This is our concept of forward linkages.[7]

Backward linkages alone give rise to agglomeration economies, as shown by Fujita (1990). As an industry grows in a particular region, so does demand for industry-specific non-tradable inputs, giving rise to a larger variety of such inputs available locally. In other words, a larger industrial scale leads to a deeper division of labour, which in turn increases productivity. The increase in productivity then leads to a larger industry.[8]

As shown in Appendix 2, an economy that features both backward and forward linkages may exhibit multiple Pareto-rankable equilibria. In the good equilibrium the economy specializes in the production of complex goods, demand for specialized inputs is high, a large variety of these inputs is produced and wages are high. In the bad equilibrium the economy specializes in the production of simple goods (labour-intensive goods), demand for specialized inputs is low, a small variety of these inputs is produced and wages are low. In other words, when both forward and backward linkages materialize, the economy develops a deep division of labour and high wages. But such linkages may fail to materialize, in which case the economy would remain underdeveloped.[9]

Counterfactual scale effects

As with most models in which specialization is limited by the scale of the market, this model of backward and forward linkages leads to the prediction that large economies should not have a problem developing, since their large markets should be able to support a high degree of specialization. Most people immediately think of population size as the correct index for the scale of an economy and thus conclude that the low per capita incomes seen in large countries like China and India cast serious doubts on the model. But this conclusion is wrong for two reasons. First, it is not clear that the appropriate economic unit is a whole country. In the context of the model outlined above, not all provinces of a country may have access to the non-tradable inputs available in the country's economic center. It may thus be more appropriate to think about large countries such as China as a collection of differentiated economic units and not as a single integrated economy.

Second, population size may not be the appropriate measure of scale. For instance, in Rodríguez-Clare (1996a) capital is needed to produce intermediate goods, implying that an economy with a large labour force but a low capital stock will not be able to produce a large variety of non-tradable intermediate goods. Such a "large" economy would thus have a low degree of specialization.

Capital mobility

Rodríguez-Clare (1996a) shows that once we allow for international capital mobility, we can generate an equilibrium in which the rich economy (the economy at the good equilibrium) has a deep division of labour (has a large variety of non-tradable intermediate goods), specializes in the complex good and has higher wages and a higher capital-labour ratio than the poor economy (which remains at the bad equilibrium). Yet the rate of return to capital is equalized across the two economies—thus perfect international capital mobility is consistent with such an equilibrium.

Path dependence

Until now we have discussed models that feature multiple equilibria. A natural question that arises is what determines the equilibrium that is chosen. In the context of these models, we cannot say anything about this issue. But some simple alterations of these models allow us to make several interesting points.

When there are multiple equilibria, in principle all firms could coordinate and jump immediately to the good equilibrium. But this statement makes the coordination problem seem simpler than it is. As Matsuyama (1992) has argued, a static model cannot capture the difficulty of the transition to the good equilibrium. Following Matsuyama, Rodríguez-Clare (1993) introduced friction in the allocation of resources across sectors to develop a dynamic version of the model discussed above. With this version of the model we can characterize the conditions necessary for the economy to follow a path from the bad to the good steady state. If these conditions are not satisfied, the poverty trap is more serious than in our static model. When the economy is specialized in the labour-intensive good, that is, trapped in a vicious circle of underdevelopment, there is no equilibrium path that "breaks out of the vicious circle" to reach the good steady state.

We should again ask how today's rich countries were able to reach the good steady state. It can be shown that the existence of an equilibrium path from the bad to the good steady state depends, among other things, on the international relative price of labour-intensive goods. If this relative price is high, then it is less likely that such an equilibrium path exists. When industrialization was confined to a few countries, the relative price of labour-intensive goods must have been low, since only a few countries were able to produce complex goods at a low cost. It is likely that an equilibrium path from the bad to the good steady state existed back then but not today, given that many economies can now produce the complex good relatively cheaply.

Now, if this is the case, how can we explain the remarkable growth of the Republic of Korea, Taiwan (province of China) and the other miracle countries? We could argue that these economies had a lower inter-temporal discount rate or adopted economic policies that made entrepreneurs more flexible in their investment decisions (see Matsuyama, 1992). Alternatively, we could argue that these countries adopted the right policies at the right time; that is, they opened their economies to international trade when world conditions were such that "miracles" were possible—there was an equilibrium path from the bad to the good steady state.

Evidence

One crucial assumption in all the models presented in this section is that significant advantages arise when input suppliers and users locate close to each other. The models above capture this feature by assuming that all inputs are non-tradable, but, of course, this assumption is made only to simplify the analysis. Similar results would arise under the more general assumption that transportation costs (broadly conceived) for certain inputs are significant. But is it reasonable to expect such transportation costs to be high?

The answer is clearly positive for an important group of inputs, namely producer services (such as banking, auditing, consulting, wholesale services, transportation and machine repair). Indeed, producer services are usually regarded as non-tradable goods in empirical research (Kravis, 1985; Kravis and Lipsey, 1988). This classification is consistent with the finding that some non-local firms that sell services to distant regions charge more for their services (see Daniels, 1985). Perhaps the most powerful evidence for the non-tradable character of producer services comes from indirect sources. Firms rely extensively on local sources for their inputs— and more so with service inputs. Marshall (1988) used data from manufacturing establishments in three city regions of the United Kingdom (Birmingham, Leeds and Manchester) to show that almost 80 per cent of the services purchased by manufacturers were obtained from suppliers within the same planning region.

Additional evidence for the non-tradability of services comes from the broad association between employment change in the manufacturing and service sectors in the European Economic Community (EEC), North America and Japan—which can be explained only by significant transportation costs for such services.[10] Appendix 3 contains a more detailed review of the relevant evidence for producer services and shows that the main assumptions made in the previous model are empirically consistent for producer services: manufacturing is more efficient where producer services are available in better quality and higher diversity (love of variety), and producer services are produced with increasing returns technologies, and they are in general non-tradable, so that the location of producer services affects and is affected by the location of manufacturing.

The costs of using physical intermediate goods not produced locally may also be quite high. Many producer services are involved in taking those intermediate goods from the point of production to where they will be used. If these services are lacking or costly, using imported physical inputs may be costly. Moreover, when inputs have to be imported, there is a higher risk that they will not arrive at the right time or with the correct specifications, forcing firms to hold large inventories of such inputs (see Wilson, 1992, pp. 101–4 for some concrete examples). As Porter (1992) argues, the presence of local suppliers is an important determinant of the comparative advantage of nations, because it provides "efficient, early, rapid, and sometimes preferential access to the most cost-effective inputs" (p. 102).[11]

One might think that falling transportation costs would eventually make our multiple equilibria result irrelevant, since all economies would have virtually the same access to inputs produced anywhere in the world. But transportation costs have also fallen for final goods, which could make multiple equilibria more likely. See Krugman (1991) for a more detailed discussion of this point.

Rosenberg (1982) presents several examples in US economic history in which linkages were crucial to the development of particular industries. He shows how the capital-goods industry developed through a process of specialization and division of labour of the kind specified above—with backward and forward linkages playing a crucial part.

Caballero and Lyons (1992) provide direct evidence on the empirical significance of positive externalities through backward linkages. They show that over relatively long horizons intermediate goods are important in accounting for productivity growth—that is, productivity increases in an industry when output increases in industries that supply it with inputs. Additional evidence for positive localized externalities through backward linkages is provided by Holmes (1995), who shows that, as implied by theory, manufacturing establishments located near other establishments within the same industry use purchased inputs more intensively than do relatively isolated establishments. Holmes also finds that industries that are geographically dispersed according to the Glaeser-Ellison criteria do not exhibit this pattern—the importance of input purchases for firms in such industries is not affected by their location. This finding suggests that geographic concentration is connected with the division of labour as it enlarges the local industrial scale and permits the production of more varieties of non-tradable inputs.

Finally, Hummels (1995) notes that most of the richest countries are clustered in relatively small regions of Europe, North America and east Asia, while the poorest are splayed around the rest of the world. More concretely, Hummels shows that income per capita decreases with distance from core countries (United States, Germany and Japan). He argues that transportation costs (broadly conceived) for inputs may partly explain this phenomenon, since it is more expensive to buy specialized inputs in countries that are further away from core countries, where a large variety of such inputs is produced.

DYNAMIC KNOWLEDGE EXTERNALITIES

Perhaps the most well known mechanism through which positive externalities arise is local knowledge spillovers. They are usually cited as an explanation for the concentration of high-tech industries in Silicon Valley and along Boston Route 128. In their static formulation such externalities generate results similar to those derived in the previous section. That is, if we assume that one of the two sectors of the economy enjoys aggregate external increasing returns to scale, then the economy could have a convex production possibilities frontier and multiple equilibria. But the more interesting implications of these types of externalities arise when we realize that they are better seen as dynamic externalities. I will now consider several different types of models that formalize such dynamic knowledge spillovers.

Education and research externalities

Stokey (1991) formulated a model in which positive externalities arise from education. In her model there is a continuum of goods. Workers choose to spend some fraction of their finite lives receiving an education, which is required to produce more advanced, more valuable goods. As a by-product of education, there is an increase in "social knowledge", which in turn makes education less costly. This model leads to a steady state rate of growth in which workers spend a fixed fraction of their lives pursuing an education. But since education becomes less costly with time, the absolute level of education completed by workers continues to increase, which allows for the introduction of more advanced goods.[12]

One of the interesting results of this model concerns the impact of trade on growth. For a poor economy opening up to trade lowers the relative price of advanced goods and the rate of return to education. As a result the time that agents spend in education drops. But this effect is only temporary—eventually, the economy continues to grow at the autarky rate. The classic welfare gains from trade are thus (partially or more-than-completely) compensated by negative dynamic effects.

The recent literature on endogenous growth has focused mostly on the knowledge spillovers that arise from research and development (R&D) as opposed to education or learning by doing. The classic contribution here is Romer (1990). In this model growth is based on the invention of new intermediate goods by firms that recover R&D costs from profits made by selling those inputs. R&D requires skilled labour, which is a fixed factor (or, more generally, a non-reproducible factor), so externalities in R&D are essential to maintain growth in the long run. As in most of the subsequent literature, externalities arise in Romer's model as a by-product of private R&D efforts. In other words, firms devoted to the invention of new inputs produce not only a profitable input design but also public knowledge that benefits other firms in the R&D sector.

Grossman and Helpman (1992) have worked out the implications of this type of model for convergence, trade and development. The results depend critically on whether knowledge spillovers are assumed to be national or international. The interesting results for our purpose are those obtained under the assumption that such spillovers are national in scope (later, I discuss whether this assumption is reasonable). Grossman and Helpman show that when research entails the introduction of new non-tradable intermediate goods that are used in all sectors, the rate of innovation increases in a poor country (that is, a country with a low endowment of skilled labour) as a result of trade, because trade leads to specialization in unskilled-labour-intensive goods, releasing skilled labour from the production of skilled-labour-intensive goods that can be used in the research sector. On the other hand, when research entails the invention of new tradable intermediate goods (or non-tradable intermediate goods that are specific to the production of a tradable final good), hysteresis results: the country that starts with more accumulated knowledge (more experience in research) often ends up conducting all of the research and enjoys a higher income level in steady state. Of course, differences in country size and government policies may offset the role of history.

A more relevant scenario for our present purposes, also considered by Grossman and Helpman (1992) (extending a previous model by Krugman, 1979), arises when the North innovates and the South imitates. Grossman and Helpman assume that knowledge spillovers are stronger within a country than across countries, so the North's superior research experience gives it a comparative advantage in innovation. But the South can imitate the goods and technologies developed in the North, which prevents the South from falling behind. The steady-state income gap between the North and the South is determined such that the North's advantage from its superior experience in research is exactly matched by the South's advantage from its ability to imitate the North's innovations relatively inexpensively.[13]

The types of models we have considered in this subsection can explain both the absence of absolute convergence across countries and the fact that there are no countries falling steadily behind the rest (see Parente and Prescott, 1993). Still, these models do not explain why some poor countries are able to take off in a process of rapid growth and catch-up.

External learning by doing

Perhaps the simplest setting in which to think about the importance of dynamic externalities for economic development is a world in which knowledge is gained accidentally in the production process—and such knowledge spills over to the rest of society. In this case there are no dynamic considerations in the allocation of resources at any point in time. Since learning by doing is completely external to the firm, resources simply flow to those sectors in which the *present* return is higher.

As a start, think about an economy with two goods, y and z, and labour as the only primary factor of production. Suppose there is industry-specific external learning by doing in both industries (knowledge generated in y does not benefit industry z and vice versa), but learning is slower in industry z, say because production of good z is simpler. In this scenario, as shown in Lucas (1988), each country specializes completely according to its present comparative advantage. Whether trading countries converge or diverge depends on the elasticity of substitution in consumption between y and z. The most interesting scenario is the one in which the two goods are substitutes in consumption (that is, they have an elasticity of substitution higher than one). Then, the country that specializes in good y enjoys a faster real rate of growth, since the declining relative price of y does not outweigh its faster rate of learning by doing. The opposite occurs when goods are not substitutes (that is, the elasticity of substitution is lower than one). When the elasticity of substitution is equal to one, the real growth rates are the same (see Appendix 4 for a formal treatment of this issue).

Now suppose that there are inter-industry knowledge spillovers, but knowledge is generated only in sector y. Even with an elasticity of substitution in consumption of one between goods z and y, the countries that initially specialize in good y eventually enjoy a faster real rate of growth. Because they eventually produce both goods, they enjoy faster learning by doing in both the y and z sectors.

This simple model is suggestive of the effects that trade can have on growth when there is external learning by doing. But we must move beyond this model if we want to draw relevant implications for development policy.

Bounded learning by doing and inter-industry spillovers

The simple model we reviewed above assumed unlimited learning by doing for each good. But this assumption is contrary to the available empirical evidence on learning by doing, which suggests that such learning takes place only in the initial stages of production (see references in Young, 1991). After a certain amount of a good has been produced, little can be learned from producing more. In other words, learning by doing is bounded for each good. But bounded learning by doing is important in the long run only if the knowledge generated in the production of a particular good is useful for the production of other goods, that is, only if there are inter-industry spillovers (or spillovers from one generation of goods to the next). Absent such spillovers, the rate of growth is completely determined by other factors, such as the rate of innovation (Young, 1993).

What is the evidence on the existence of inter-industry spillovers? Jaffe (1986) finds that a firm's R&D productivity is higher the higher is the R&D effort of its technical neighbors (see also Bernstein and Nadiri, 1988). Jaffe, Trajtenberg and Henderson (1993) find evidence of localized knowledge spillovers from patent citations. Strictly speaking, this is evidence for R&D spillovers rather than learning by doing spillovers, but it suggests the existence of inter-industry knowledge spillovers in general. Irwin and Klenow (1994) find no evidence of inter-generational spillovers in the semiconductor industry.

Inter-industry spillovers arise not only directly, as ideas flow across sectors, but also indirectly, through input linkages. Rosenberg (1982) provides several examples of how innovations in particular industries extended strong positive pecuniary externalities to other industries. Breshnahan (1986) gives an econometrically well-documented example of this phenomenon. He shows that the banking, finance and insurance industries derived large gains from the use of high-speed computers that were not captured by manufacturers of computers.[14]

Young (1991) considers a model that incorporates both of these realistic features of learning by doing: bounded learning and inter-industry spillovers. His model involves a continuum of goods that differ only in their potential for learning by doing—goods with a higher potential (more advanced goods) have a lower cost after all learning by doing opportunities have been exhausted. At any given time learning by doing will have been exhausted for some goods but will continue in the remainder, and very advanced goods will not be produced because of their high current cost. As learning by doing continues, it generates positive spillovers for more advanced goods, leading to a lower cost of production. As a result such goods are produced eventually, leading to more learning by doing and more spillovers—and ultimately more advanced goods enter the produc-tion stage. The model thus exhibits continuous growth characterized by the production of a changing basket of goods: advanced goods continuously replace relatively simple goods whose learning by doing potential has been exhausted.

The most interesting result of this model is that for a poor country (that is, a country that has had relatively little time to learn and accumulate experience) trading with richer countries always lowers the rate of learning by doing. The intuition is simple: because richer countries have accumulated more experience, they have a compara-tive advantage in more advanced goods. Trade thus has the poor country specializing in backward goods—which have exhausted their learning by doing potential—and the rich country specializing in advanced goods—which still have potential for learning by doing. Of course, trade is not necessarily welfare-reducing because of the classic static welfare gains from trade. But it is a remarkable result that a country's growth rate always decreases as a result of trade with a richer country.

Two effects could change this result.

- *Income effects.* In Young's model preferences are separable, so the rich country consumes more of all goods relative to the poor country. In fact, consumers from the rich country consume goods that are more backward than the most backward goods consumed by consumers from the poor country. A more natural model that allowed for income effects on the composition of the consumption bundle, such that higher incomes lead consumers to purchase more advanced goods, would lead to different results, because trade between a rich and a poor country would involve trade in intermediate goods (backward for the rich country and advanced for the poor country). The poor country has a comparative advantage in the most backward goods, but the rich country does not buy such goods, so trade is less likely to have the negative impact that it has in Young's model.[15]

- *Factor proportions effects.* Young's model features only Ricardian trade, arising from the different levels of experience of each country. But the economic miracles of east Asia started exporting labour-intensive goods. Now, if there are some goods that are both advanced from the poor country's point of view (with high learning by doing potential) and labour-intensive, then the Hecksher-Ohlin comparative advantage may outweigh the Ricardian comparative disadvantage. The poor country would thus specialize in these goods, and the rate of learning by doing need not fall.

Neither of these two effects can by itself lead to higher learning by doing in the poor country as a consequence of trade with a richer country. But together they can: the poor country would export only advanced, labour-intensive goods, thereby accelerating the rate of learning by doing. This may explain how trade positively affected the economic miracles of east Asia. Indeed, the goods that these countries exported during their first stages of industrialization were labour-intensive and relatively advanced. For instance, their typical exports during this period were toys and shoes designed for consumers in the affluent countries of the west that were much more complex than the toys and shoes produced for the local population.

The effect of trade on a small economy

What are the implications of Young's model for a small economy that takes prices as given? Consider a world equilibrium with trade between the South and the North, and assume that the South is composed of a number of identical small economies, all of which take prices as given. Equilibrium considerations do not determine the goods that these small economies will produce, since they determine only resource allocation for the South as a whole. The allocation of resources for any Southern country is a matter of luck: a particular Southern economy is just as likely to be producing goods with high learning by doing potential as goods that do not generate any knowledge (see Lucas, 1993). Since there is no comparative advantage among the Southern countries, a tariff in any one would eliminate all imports from the South. A general import tariff can thus have drastic effects on learning by doing: it would lead to a drastic increase in learning by doing for any country unlucky enough to be producing backward goods with no learning by doing opportunities, while it would have the opposite effect for any country lucky enough to be specialized in advanced goods.

Of course, the result that the allocation of resources for any individual Southern economy is indeterminate is an artifact of our simple framework. For instance, a more realistic framework would have Southern economies with a higher endowment of skilled labour (that is, higher education levels) specializing in more advanced goods and enjoying faster learning by doing. The effects of a general import tariff are thus likely to depend on individual country characteristics, not only on luck.

International knowledge spillovers

The effects of dynamic knowledge spillovers that we have been discussing depend crucially on the assumption that such spillovers are stronger at the national level than at the international level. That is, we have been assuming that knowledge diffuses faster within the country than across borders. What is the available evidence on this issue?

Let us first go back to our discussion of convergence. We focused there on the role of physical and human capital accumulation in the process of growth and convergence. But this is not the whole story. As Solow (1956) showed, a large part of the growth experience must be explained by forces other than factor accumulation. This is the famous Solow residual, which is usually attributed to exogenous technical progress. But as Romer (1986, 1990) has argued, we must be able to explain the process of innovation (that is, we must make technical progress endogenous) if we are to understand the remarkable growth experience of the past centuries. We must also understand the role of ideas in the propagation of growth across countries. How does the diffusion of knowledge explain convergence—or its absence—across countries?

Although, as mentioned above, Barro and Sala-i-Martin (1995) do not find convergence for their whole set of countries, they do find convergence for certain groups: US states and regions (1880–88), Japanese prefectures (1930–90) and the 20 original OECD countries (1960–85). Plausible explanations for convergence within these groups are labour migration and capital mobility. But Barro and Sala-i-Martin show that, at least for US states and regions, migration and capital mobility do not explain a significant part of the convergence process. Is it possible to explain convergence among these economies as a result of the flow of ideas?

Some recent papers suggest that we can. Coe and Helpman (1993) and Coe, Helpman and Hoffmeister (1995) show that both poor and rich countries benefit substantially from R&D performed in other countries and that such spillovers arise at least partially as a result of trade. They show that countries that are more open to international trade benefit more from international R&D spillovers, and that this effect is stronger when trade is biased towards countries that spend more on R&D. The authors argue that trade acts as a conduit for international R&D spillovers by allowing countries to import technologically advanced inputs that make their economies more efficient.

There are two basic ways in which such spillovers materialize from imports of specialized inputs. First, imports of new varieties of inputs generate higher productivity because users of those inputs are able to keep part of the surplus that arises from their use (that is, they keep the area between their demand curve and the price line). Second, as emphasized by Eaton and Kortum (1995), when firms sell higher quality versions of the same input they may extract all the surplus that arises from the use of that input as opposed to the one currently used. But this surplus is only "marginal"—input users capture all of the surplus that arises from using the current version of the input rather than the version with the lowest quality.

Of course, international knowledge spillovers arise not only through trade—ideas may cross borders just as they flow within countries. Irwin and Klenow (1994) show that this is the case for the semiconductor sector. In particular, they show the existence of substantial spillovers from the knowledge accumulated in production (learning by doing) and that such spillovers are just as strong among firms in different countries as they are among firms within a single country.

At a purely theoretical level the geographical scope of knowledge spillovers depends on our definition of knowledge. Knowledge can be of four types: (inarticulate) knowledge embodied in workers, knowledge that is disseminated through human interaction, knowledge that is disseminated through the written word and knowledge incorporated in new varieties of inputs. The first and second types of knowledge are likely to generate spillovers that are geographically limited, maybe even restricted to a smaller geographical unit than a country (such as Silicon Valley). In contrast, the third and fourth types of knowledge are more likely to cross international borders, although the movement of the fourth depends on the tradability of the inputs that incorporate the new knowledge. Even the first two types of knowledge may diffuse to other regions and countries after a lag, possibly when such knowledge develops to the point when it can be disseminated in written form.

This point, together with the recent empirical results of Irwin and Klenow (1994), Coe and Helpman (1993) and Coe, Helpman and Hoffmeister (1995), leads to the presumption that international knowledge spillovers are significant, and thus the results showing divergence in some models with external learning by doing should be interpreted with care. A recent model developed by Klundert and Smulders (1995) highlights the importance of international spillovers for economic development. They show that if international spillovers are strong enough, then there is convergence, whereas intermediate cases (in which international spillovers are present but not strong enough) may entail a steady state in which both the North and the South grow at the same rate, but there is no convergence: the South does not catch up to the North.

POLICY IMPLICATIONS

What are the policy implications that emerge if we accept the view that the observed lack of convergence is due to externalities and the positive feedback mechanisms they generate? What are the correct development policies in a world characterized by multiple Pareto-rankable equilibria and path dependence?

First, it is important that government not make it more difficult for the economy to reach a good outcome. For instance, government should avoid fiscal policies that generate inflation and high interest rates, since those conditions shrink agents' time horizons and make an expansionary equilibrium path less likely to emerge. For the same reason excessive regulation and high investment taxes should be avoided. Moreover, government should not adopt policies that make the effective size of the economy smaller (such as promote large government bureaucracies), because the economy is less likely to be able to sustain the deep division of labour that leads to high wages and high returns to capital. Of course, this policy advice coincides with the well-known policy prescription of the neoclassical model.

There are other policies important in a world characterized by externalities that are also not controversial. Subsidies to education are recommended because of the knowledge spillovers they generate (Stokey, 1991), because they improve the diffusion of knowledge (Shleifer, 1991) and because sectors that generate more linkages and knowledge spillovers are likely to be relatively intensive in skilled labour (Rodríguez-Clare, 1995). Policies to promote competition may be recommended, because the freedoms to enter an industry and invest are important in the diffusion of knowledge (Shleifer, 1991). But we must be careful here, because such policies also decrease the incentives to generate knowledge in the first place. Policies that promote foreign investment also seem beneficial, since foreign firms are likely to be a conduit for technology transfer and knowledge spillovers (Shleifer, 1991). Foreign investment may also generate positive backward linkages if foreign firms produce sufficiently complex goods (Rodríguez-Clare, 1996c).

Are there more radical policy implications arising from the theories of economic development reviewed in this chapter? It would seem that, when there are multiple Pareto-rankable equilibria, government should coordinate entrepreneurs to reach the good equilibrium. Government wants to convince economic agents that there will be a boom in domestic demand (in the Murphy-Shleifer-Vishny model) or in the variety of intermediate goods (in the model with backward and forward linkages), thus inducing entrepreneurs to generate the boom themselves. But we know very little about how expectations are formed and even less about how expectations react to government policies. As Matsuyama (1994) points out, government policies aimed at coordinating expectations may backfire. This could happen if, for instance, economic agents have the general impression that government intervention is bad for the economy. It also seems unreasonable that government could "force" the economy to allocate resources as in the good equilibrium. More generally, as Matsuyama (1994) argues, the problem of coordinating a whole economy is "of such fundamental difficulty that no algorithm can solve it" (p. 2).

Somewhat less radical and more reasonable policy advice could be given if we knew which sectors generate strong positive externalities. What are the implications of the different models in this regard? In the Murphy-Shleifer-Vishny model, because positive externalities arise from aggregate demand spillovers, the appropriate policy would favour industries that pay high wage premiums or industries that direct demand towards industrial goods. In thinking about these policies, we should note that the distribution of income may be important in generating aggregate demand spillovers. For instance, as pointed out by Shleifer (1991), because large public projects are usually capital- rather than labour-intensive, they are unlikely to generate a strong increase in domestic demand for industrial goods.

In the rest of this section I focus on the policy implications that arise in models with linkages and localized knowledge spillovers. In these models the government will want to support industries generating the strongest linkages and localized knowledge spillovers. But is it possible to identify these industries? There are at least two approaches that we can follow. The direct approach involves determining at least an ordinal measure of externalities for each particular industry, so that we can rank industries in terms of the strength of the externalities they generate. The second approach is more indirect. It entails determining the characteristics shown by industries that generate strong externalities.

Measuring externalities

The model of backward and forward linkages presented in the fourth section indicates clearly which measure captures the impact of a firm on the economy through the generation of linkages: the quantity of employment generated in upstream industries per unit of labour employed directly. The higher is this ratio, the more positive is the backward linkage effect of the firm. This measure differs from those commonly used in that, because it is derived in a general equilibrium framework, it considers how the expansion of one activity comes at the expense of other activities that could be generating linkages. This model is thus especially relevant for measuring linkages in economies with no surplus labour.

But this measure relies on several restrictive assumptions made to keep the model tractable. To measure the linkage potential of an industry in a real economy, we must generalize at least the most restrictive of these assumptions.[16]

First, the model assumes that all inputs are non-tradable. But in the real world most inputs are tradable, although subject to transportation costs. All else equal, we would prefer an investment that generates demand for inputs with high transportation costs. Second, the model assumes a simplistic technology for the production of specialized inputs. In reality some inputs may rely intensively on resources that are very scarce locally (that is, skilled labour), in which case the economy cannot take advantage of the linkages that might arise from some new economic activities. In other words, supply constraints may break the chain of reactions that build linkages. Third, different types of inputs may have different degrees of love of variety. Assume there are two inputs, x_1 and x_2, both of which are available in a continuum of varieties. Assume also that production exhibits a stronger love of variety for input x_1 than for input x_2. An investment that generates a strong demand for input x_1 thus benefits the economy more than one that generates a strong demand for x_2.

Fourth, some inputs may be produced with constant returns to scale, in which case an increase in their demand would not generate any positive externalities.[17] Finally, the model assumes that all industries use the same inputs. But in reality some inputs are industry-specific. As a consequence the linkages generated by the expansion of one particular industry may not benefit the rest of the economy.

It should be obvious from this discussion that the measure of linkages obtained after making these generalizations is of little practical use given data constraints. Of course, we could try to determine whether particular industries generate externalities, as has been done in many studies (see Stewart and Ghani, 1991 for a survey of this literature). But it is difficult to use this literature as a basis for policy because most studies do not *quantify* externalities and thus do not determine which sectors generate the strongest externalities. Moreover, most of those studies are not linked tightly to theory, making their findings more difficult to interpret.

The direct measurement of the strength of knowledge externalities for each industry seems even more difficult than that of externalities arising from linkages, since we know very little about the process by which those externalities arise.

Instead of trying to measure externalities directly, we could instead use the degree of geographic concentration of an industry as an indirect measure of the strength of the localized externalities in that industry, since localized externalities lead to geographic concentration. Because there are costs to geographic concentration, we expect to find a higher degree of geographic concentration for industries that exhibit stronger localized externalities. There are two problems with this approach. First, industries may be concentrated geographically for several reasons, such as the natural characteristics of some regions (for example, soil and climatic conditions are important in explaining why 78 per cent of wine industry employment is concentrated in California). Following this approach, it is necessary to know which industries are geographically concentrated because of natural conditions and which are concentrated because of localized externalities. This undertaking seems to be feasible. The second problem arises because the degree of geographic concentration is determined by the balance of the industry-specific benefits and costs of geo-graphic concentration. As long as the costs of geographic concentration vary by industry, we cannot measure the benefits purely from the observed degree of geographic concentration.[18] We need more information about industry-specific costs before we can use geographic concentration as an index of localized externalities.

Characterizing industries that generate strong externalities

Designing a successful industrial policy does not require the know-ledge of which industries generate the strongest externalities—information about the characteristics of those industries may suffice. For instance, if we were to verify that the industries that generate strong backward linkages are intensive in skilled labour or physical capital (as in Rodríguez-Clare, 1996a; Rodrik, 1994a), then it may be beneficial for an intermediate economy (an economy that has an endowment that makes it potentially competitive in industries that are intensive in skilled labour or physical capital) to set high minimum wages as a way to induce the economy to specialize in those industries (see Rodrik, 1994a).

Can we draw some general inferences about the characteristics of the industries that generate strong externalities? For the model with backward and forward linkages we can argue that industries at earlier stages of the industry cycle are more likely to generate strong backward linkages because such industries are more likely to exhibit strong love of variety (since firms at earlier stages of the industry cycle are not sure which inputs they will need) and to use inputs that are less tradable.[19] For the model with bounded learning by doing and inter-industry spillovers, it also seems likely that the industries that generate stronger spillovers are those at the earlier stages of the industry cycle, since these are the industries that still have learning by doing potential.

Insofar as linkages and knowledge spillovers are localized, we would expect to find young industries highly concentrated geo-graphically, since this would allow firms to benefit from knowledge spillovers. To verify this empirically, I regressed total factor produc-tivity growth (a proxy for the age of an industry) on geographic concentration for industries at the four-digit level, as measured by

Ellison and Glaeser (1994), and found no significant correlation.[20] In fact, the 15 industries that exhibit the highest geographic concentration in the United States are not necessarily the glamorous high-tech industries that one might initially think have the strongest externalities (table 3.1). Of course, this could be due to the fact that, as we mentioned above, geographic concentration arises not only from localized externalities but also from natural advantages that pull some industries to particular regions.

In any case, if we verified that young industries generate stronger localized externalities, what are the implied policy recommendations for developing countries? One may think that the obvious answer is protection or support of advanced industries. But this answer is not so clear because, given their resource endowments, it may not be realistic to expect developing countries to "capture" industries at a very early stage of the industry cycle. That is, the industries that are advanced from the point of view of developing countries (those that they could "capture" through special support) may have already passed through the stage of their cycle in which they generate strong localized externalities.[21] We need more research here before we can make a more definitive policy recommendation.

Table 3.1. The fifteen most geographically concentrated industries

Four-digit code	Industry	Ellison-Glaeser index of geographic concentration
2371	Fur goods	0.63
2084	Wines, brandy, brandy spirits	0.48
2252	Hosiery, n.e.c.	0.44
3533	Oil and gas field machinery	0.43
2251	Women's hosiery	0.40
2273	Carpets and rugs	0.38
2429	Special product sawmills, n.e.c.	0.37
3961	Costume jewelry	0.32
2895	Carbon black	0.30
3915	Jewelers' materials, lapidary	0.30
2874	Phosphatic fertilizers	0.29
2061	Raw cane sugar	0.29
2281	Yarn mills, except wool	0.28
2034	Dehydrated fruits, vegetables, soups	0.28
3761	Guided missiles, space vehicles	0.25

Source: Ellison and Glaeser (1994).

Supporting the entire manufacturing sector

As a final point, I should mention that an alternative to a policy of supporting the industries that are believed to generate the strongest externalities is a policy of subsidizing the entire manufacturing sector—a policy that has long been advocated by cautious economists (Balassa, 1981; Little, Scitovsky and Scott, 1970). This policy advice is based on the belief that the manufacturing sector generates strong externalities. Is there any evidence of supporting this belief? Recent papers by Caballero and Lyons (1992), Chan, Chen and Cheung (1995) and Khan and Bilginsoy (1994) point to a positive answer. We must be careful with these results, however. Other sectors (such as agriculture or services) may also display positive externalities, in which case the correct policy prescription would depend on which sector has the strongest externalities.

Still, it is interesting to ask what the correct policy would be if the manufacturing sector has the strongest positive externalities. Recent models of externalities and positive feedback mechanisms may help us in this regard. For instance, in the context of the model of backward and forward linkages presented in the fourth section, if we view the sector producing complex goods as the manufacturing sector, then the appropriate policy may entail subsidizing the production of the complex good or subsidizing entry (as opposed to production) in the intermediate-goods sector. It seems important that future research study the best ways to support the manufacturing sector in terms of information requirements and public costs.

APPENDIX 1. THE MURPHY-SHLEIFER-VISHNY MODEL: A FORMAL TREATMENT

Consider a one-period economy with a continuum of goods indexed by $q \in [0,1]$ and a representative consumer with a utility function:

$$\int_0^1 x(q)dq.$$

Labour, available in quantity L, is supplied inelastically and serves as the numeraire. Cottage production converts one unit of labour into one unit of output. The modern technology involves a fixed requirement of F units of labour and then $1/\alpha$ units of labour for each unit of output, with $\alpha > 1$. If an entrepreneur invests in the modern technology, he becomes a monopolist. Given the unitary price elasticity of demand for each good, it is optimal to charge a price of 1, which is the price charged by the competitive fringe that produces with the cottage technology. Since consumers spend equal shares of their income on each good, when income is y, a monopolist makes profits π given by:

$$\pi = [(\alpha - 1)/\alpha]y - F \equiv ay - F,$$

where a is the markup. When a fraction n of the goods are produced with the modern technology, aggregate profits are $\Pi(n) = n(ay - F)$. And since $y = L + \Pi$, $y(n)$ is given by:

$$y(n) = \frac{L - nF}{1 - na}.$$

Letting $\pi(n) = ay(n) - F$ denote individual profits as a function of n, we can see that $\pi(0) < 0$ implies $ay(0) = aL < F$. But $\pi'(n) = ay'(n)$, which is negative (positive) if $aL - F$ is negative (positive). This implies that if no industrialization is an equilibrium ($aL < F$), then it is the only equilibrium. There will be an industrialization equilibrium only if $\pi(1) > 0$, but this happens only if $aL > F$, which rules out the no-industrialization equilibrium.

Now, let v represent the wage premium and assume that $\alpha - 1 > v$. Firms with the modern technology must pay workers $1 + v$. Then,

$$\pi = [(\alpha - 1 - v)/\alpha]y - (1 + v)F = by - (1 + v)F,$$

where $b \equiv \dfrac{\alpha - 1 - v}{\alpha}$.

Moreover, we have $y(n) = [L + vnF + \prod(n)] / (1 - vn/\alpha)$. $\pi(0) < 0$ implies $bL < (1 + v)F$. But $\pi'(0)$ is equal in sign to $y'(0) = \prod'(0) + vF + L(v/\alpha) = bL - F + vF + (v/\alpha)L$. Therefore, we can have $\pi(0) < 0$ and $\pi'(0) > 0$, which happens when $bL - (1 + v)F < 0$ but $bL - (1-v)F + (v/\alpha)L > 0$.

APPENDIX 2. A SIMPLE MODEL OF MULTIPLE EQUILIBRIA WITH BACKWARD AND FORWARD LINKAGES

Consider an economy in which the only primary factor is labour, available in total quantity L. There are two final goods, z and y, and one intermediate good, x, which comes in a continuum of varieties. Variety is indexed by the real number j. Goods z and y can be traded freely in the world market, and both countries are "small" in the sense that they do not affect the international prices of z and y, denoted respectively by P_z and P_y (in terms of some international numeraire).

The intermediate good x is non-tradable. The measure of varieties of x actually produced will be denoted by the real number $n \geq 0$ (for $j \leq n$, variety j of x is available). $p(j)$ will denote the price of variety j of intermediate good x. Each variety of the intermediate good x is produced with a simple decreasing average cost technology: there is a fixed requirement of one unit of L and each additional unit of $x(j)$ requires one additional unit of L.

Both final goods are produced with a Cobb-Douglas production function using labour and a composite intermediate good, X, which is assembled from a continuum of differentiated intermediate goods:

$$Q_s = \delta(s) L_s^{\beta(s)} X_s^{1-\beta(s)} \tag{1a}$$

$$X_s = (\int_0^n x(j)_s^\alpha \, dj)^{1/\alpha} \tag{1b}$$

for $s = z, y$, where $\delta(z)$, $\delta(y)$, $\beta(z)$, $\beta(y)$ and α are constant parameters, and we assume that $\beta(z)$, $\beta(y)$, $\alpha \in (0,1)$.[22] We also assume that $\beta(z) > \beta(y)$, which implies that the y-industry uses intermediate goods more intensively than the z-industry.

The specification of the production function in equations 1a and 1b implies that there are returns from the division of labour in the production of intermediate goods. To see this, note that because of the symmetric way in which different varieties of x enter in equation 1b and because of concavity ($0 < \alpha < 1$), efficiency requires firms producing final goods to use the same quantity of all available varieties. That is, efficiency requires that $x(j) = x$ for all $j \leq n$. Letting L_x denote the amount of labour devoted to the production of intermediate goods (excluding the labour used to produce the fixed requirement per variety), then:

$$L_x = \int_0^n x(j)dj = nx.$$

The production function for s can then be written as:

$$Q_s = \delta(s)n^{\phi(s)}L_s^{\beta(s)}L_x^{1-\beta(s)},\tag{2}$$

where $\phi(s) \equiv (1 - \beta(s))\,(1 - \alpha)/\alpha$ and $s = z, y$. Equation 2 shows that an increase in the available variety of intermediate goods increases total factor productivity in the production of final goods. This property is commonly referred to as *love of variety* for inputs. Since $\beta(z) > \beta(y)$, then $\phi(y) > \phi(z)$, which implies that producers of y have stronger love of variety than producers of z. This will play an important role in this model.

Each firm producing a variety of x is better off choosing a variety that is not already being produced by another firm. Therefore, variety j of x, if it is produced, is produced by a single firm, which then chooses the price $p(j)$ to maximize profits. In other words, there is monopolistic competition in the intermediate goods sector.

Given n, we have a constant marginal rate of transformation between z and y—the production possibilities frontier is linear. Formally, letting c_s represent the unit cost for good s, then for some constant A, $c_z/c_y = \rho(n) = An^{\phi(y)-\phi(z)}$. Therefore, except for the knife-edge case in which $p \equiv P_z/P_y = \rho(n)$, there will be complete specialization in the production of final goods: there is complete specialization in the production of y if $\rho(n) > p$, there is complete specialization in the production of z if $\rho(n) > p$, and any combination is an n-equilibrium if $\rho(n) = p$.

Since $\phi(y) - \phi(z) = [\beta(z) - \beta(y)]/\theta > 0$, then $\rho(n)$ is increasing (figure A1). Therefore, as n increases, the production possibilities frontier rotates so that the marginal cost of z in terms of y increases. As we can see in figure A1, there is a level of n, n^*, such that if $n > n^*$, there is complete specialization in y and vice versa. The intuition is simple: since y uses intermediate goods more intensively than does z, it benefits comparatively more from an increase in the variety of intermediate goods. Thus as n increases, the unit cost of y falls relative to the unit cost of z.

To characterize the equilibria we now need to consider the zero-profit condition in the intermediate-goods sector. Since the y sector uses intermediate goods more intensively than the z sector, the demand for intermediate goods is higher when there is complete specialization in y than when there is complete specialization in z. Therefore, when the economy specializes completely in y, the equilibrium variety of inputs is higher than when the economy specializes completely in z. Letting $n(s)$ denote the variety of

Figure A1: Input variety and the pattern of production

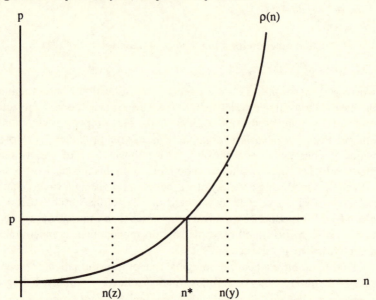

inputs for which the zero-profit condition in the intermediate-goods sector is satisfied when there is complete specialization in s, then $n(y) > n(z)$ (see figure A1).

If n^* lies in the interval $[n(z), n(y)]$, there are multiple equilibria. If $n = n(z)$, then $n < n^*$, so there is complete specialization in final good z, and given the definition of $n(z)$, the zero-profit condition holds. Similarly, if $n = n(y)$, then $n > n^*$. There is complete specialization in final good y and the zero-profit condition holds.

If n^* lies outside the interval $[n(z), n(y)]$, there is a single equilibrium. If $n^* < n(z)$, the unique equilibrium involves $n = n(y)$ and complete specialization in y. There is no equilibrium with $n = n(z)$, because since $n(z) > n^*$, the $n(z)$-equilibrium involves complete specialization in y and hence the zero-profit condition would not be satisfied. Similarly, if $n^* > n(y)$, the unique equilibrium involves $n = n(z)$ and complete specialization in z.

When there are multiple equilibria, the z equilibrium is characterized by a small variety of intermediate goods, low wages and specialization in the simple good z, while the y equilibrium is characterized by a large variety of intermediate goods, high wages and specialization in the complex good y. In the z equilibrium there is a coordination failure: everyone would be better off in the y-equilibrium, but no individual wants to produce y given the small variety of intermediate goods available. But it is not profitable for anyone to produce a new variety of the intermediate good because, since the economy is completely specialized in the production of z, there is a low demand for intermediate goods.

There are two types of distortions that could potentially justify government intervention in this context. First, for each equilibrium, as shown by Dixit and Stiglitz (1977), there is a suboptimal level of entry—that is, n_s is lower than the optimal level of n when the economy is completely specialized in $s = z, y$. Second, there is a coordination problem. The government would like to coordinate economic agents so that the y equilibrium is chosen. One way of doing this is by imposing a tariff on y so that the z equilibrium disappears.

APPENDIX 3. PRODUCER SERVICES, AGGLOMERATION ECONOMIES AND ECONOMIC DEVELOPMENT

Here, I will briefly survey the literature on producer services to explain in more detail what producer services are, their importance in industrial and developing economies, their relation to the manufacturing sector and the locational pattern they follow. The main emphasis is to show that the basic assumptions used in the model with backward and forward linkages have empirical validity for producer services: manufacturing is more efficient if producer services are available in better quality and greater diversity (love of variety), and producer services are produced with increasing returns technologies and they are in general non-tradable, so that the location of producer services affects and is affected by the location of manufacturing.

The idea that non-tradable intermediate goods produced with increasing returns are important for efficiency in the production of final goods has been used often in the urban and regional economics literature to account for the formation of cities and industrial complexes, and to explain differences in economic performance across regions. The main example of non-tradable intermediate goods cited in this literature is producer services, which include services like auditing; administrative and computer consulting; financial, wholesale and transport services; and equipment maintenance.

Producer services began to receive particular attention with the publication of the seminal work by Greenfield (1966), which pointed out the growing importance of producer services as a source of new jobs and as an essential "lubricant" for the manufacturing sector and the economy in general. Since then, the non-tradable character of producer services has been increasingly recognized, and an important literature is now developing on the spatial characteristic of producer services (Stanback 1979; Daniels 1985; Marshall 1988).

Definition of producer services. Marshall (1988) defines producer services as those "services which supply business and government organizations, rather than private individuals, whether in agriculture, mining, manufacturing, or service industries. Based on these criteria, producer services are concerned with financial, legal, and general management, innovation, development, design, administration, personnel, production, technology, maintenance, transport, communication, wholesale distribution, advertising, and selling" (p. 13).[23]

These services can be produced within the organization, or they can be acquired from outside specialized sources. Greenfield (1966) enumerates several reasons why firms may prefer to contract out services rather than produce them "in house". They can be reduced to the following basic argument: the adequate provision of a service necessitates specialized and up-to-date personnel "that many small and medium-size firms cannot afford to employ on a full-time basis" (p. 42). But even larger firms may prefer to contract out the provision of certain services to keep staff at a manageable size, to decrease "influence" and "agency" costs (Milgrom and Roberts 1988; McAfee and McMillan 1990) and to maintain "a small, compact, relatively homogeneous labour force" (Greenfield 1966, p. 43). Demand for outside intermediate services thus arises from a combination of economies of scale due to indivisibilities in the production of such services and "organizational diseconomies of scale" (to paraphrase McAfee and McMillan). In the rest of this section I focus exclusively on the producer services provided to firms by external agents, for these are the producer services that generate the kind of phenomena we are interested in.

The importance of producer services in industrial countries. There is by now wide recognition that the proportion of workers not engaged directly in the production process in firms has been increasing (Gershuny and Miles, 1983). Here, however, we are concerned only with the provision of producer services by specialized external sources, and we will thus concentrate only on the importance of the producer service sector as an independent industry, measured both by its share of the labour force and GNP. This task is difficult because different authors use different classifications of industries. The problem is that some services are sold to firms and some to consumers, so that only part of the industry can be said to be producing producer services. Moreover, problems with data availability compound the problem significantly. Since the purpose here is only to give an approximate idea of the importance of producer services in the economy, we will give the estimates of authors using different classifications without going over the details of the definitions used.

In a study of the industrial structure of employment in EEC countries, Gershuny and Miles (1983) show that producer services account for a proportion of total employment, that ranges from 9.8 per cent in Italy to 14.6 per cent in Belgium. Greenfield (1966) estimates that in 1960 13.2 per cent of the labour force was employed in producer services, and 22.7 per cent of national income originated in that sector. Singlemann (1970) notes that, already in 1970, producer services had surpassed the personal services sector in the United States with respect to the proportion of employment in the service sector. In terms of the importance of producer services as an intermediate-goods industry, Stanback (1979) shows that "more than a fourth of all intermediate outputs are services" (p. 17). We can see from table A1 that rich countries allocate a substantial part of their labour force to this class of producer services.

The importance of producer services for efficiency in manufacturing. The direct evidence of the importance of the availability of a wide range of producer services for the efficiency of manufacturing is still largely anecdotal and relies mostly on qualitative studies. Marshall (1988) cites some studies, which establish that accurate and up-to-date services to management, marketing services, the services of engineering consultants in the organization of goods production, and research, development and technical support services to the innovation process contribute positively to firm performance.

In a study of the service sector in developing countries, McKee (1988) argues that producer services are very important for the efficiency of the leading industrial operations in those countries. Furthermore, he argues that producer services "aid in establishing effective linkages between various stages of the manufacturing process" (p. 20).

Producer services and increasing returns to scale. So far, I have cited studies that support the idea that the availability of a wide variety of locally provided producer services is an important determinant of the efficiency of other industries in the area. This by itself implies only that the location of producer services is influenced by the locational pattern of other industries. However, there is also evidence that many specialized producer services are produced with increasing returns, which implies that producer services play a more active role in the explanation of the uneven development of regions and in the explanation of multiple equilibria.

Table A1. Proportion of employment in selected services for some industrial countries

Canada	10.52	Japan	7.41
Denmark	8.42	Sweden	7.61
France	8.48	Switzerland	9.41
West Germany	6.78	United Kingdom	10.44
Italy	3.78	United States	11.09

Note: The data on employment in selected services are taken from the OECD Summary Statistics, 1990. The services included are financing, insurance, real estate and business services. The year for the data varies with the country, but ranges from 1984 to 1987.

Faini (1984) mentions various studies that support the assumption that increasing returns to scale prevail in the production of producer services (banking, accounting, transportation, electricity, and so on). Moreover, professional services (like consulting, auditing and engineering) are information intensive; and this in itself suggests the presence of decreasing average costs because of the non-rival property of information as an input of production (Romer, 1990). "Overall, available empirical evidence, while not conclusive, provides encouraging support for the assumption that increasing returns to scale prevail in the production of non-traded inputs" (p. 310).

Agglomeration economies and economic development. Together, love of variety, non-tradability and increasing returns lead to the existence of agglomeration economies and the concentration of producer services and manufacturing activities in cities and regions. The possibility of cumulative and uneven regional development arises.

Marshall (1988) surveys some studies that support the argument that remoteness from places in which certain producer services are produced will reduce the efficiency and competitiveness of an industry. He notes that "work examining the relationship between accessibility and economic development in Europe has identified an association between peripherality and relatively low incomes per head" (p. 58).

In her work on the origin, growth and decline of cities and their importance for economic development, Jacobs (1969, 1984) also argues that the abundance of producer services is a consequence and a fundamental cause of the high productivity of economic activity in cities. Stanback (1979) holds similar views: "The modern capitalistic economy has been made possible by the development of a number of strategic business services or service-like activities—transportation, distribution, communication, and financial—many of which individual producing firms could not have performed themselves. The rise of producer service firms has sparked the proliferation and growth of goods-producing firms as well as the other way around" (pp. 21–2).

There is also evidence to support the view that more-developed economies allocate a greater proportion of primary resources to the production of producer services. Singlemann (1970) shows that the higher is the level of per capita income, the larger is the proportion of the labour force in producer and social services.

Moreover, there is evidence indicating that the intensity with which intermediate services are used increases with development and technical change. For instance, Gershuny and Miles (1983) have shown that the intensity with which producer services are used in the primary and manufacturing industries in the United Kingdom increased between 1963 and 1973. Marshall (1988) suggests that a plausible explanation for this trend is that "the pace and complexity of economic and technical change have necessitated greater utilization of more specialized and sophisticated services by the production sector" (p. 42).

APPENDIX 4. A SIMPLE MODEL OF EXTERNAL LEARNING BY DOING WITH TWO GOODS

I now present a simple model that illustrates how trade may have dramatic effects on growth rates when there is external learning by doing. Consider an economy with two goods, y and z, and in which labour is the only primary factor of production. At time t, production of good s ($s = z$ or y) takes place according to:

$$Q_s = A_s(t)\mu_s L,$$

where μ_s denotes the fraction of the total labour force L engaged in production of good s. We assume that $A_z(t)$ and $A_y(t)$ evolve according to:

$$\mathring{A}_s(t) = A_s(t)\delta_s(\beta_{sz}\mu_z + \beta_{sy}\mu_y),$$

where δ_s, β_{sz} and β_{sy} are positive parameters for $s = z, y$, and we assume that $\delta_y > \delta_z$. That is, sector y benefits more from the accumulation of knowledge than does sector z.

Preferences are given by the following CES utility function:

$$U(Q_z, Q_y) = (\alpha_z Q_z^{-\rho} + \alpha_y Q_y^{-\rho})^{-1/\rho},$$

where $\alpha_z, \alpha_z \geq 0$, $\alpha_z + \alpha_y = 1$, $\rho > -1$ and $\sigma \equiv 1/(1+\rho)$ is the elasticity of substitution between z and y.

In autarky a country would simply allocate resources to these two goods depending on the relative cost and preferences at each point in time. The allocation of resources at time t, that is, $\mu_z(t)$ and $\mu_y(t)$, would then determine $\mathring{A}_z(t)$ and $\mathring{A}_y(t)$, the rate of change in prices, and the dynamics of $\mu_z(t)$ and $\mu_y(t)$.

Trade can have dramatic effects on such dynamics. When two countries start trading, specialization is determined according to static comparative advantage. The effect of trade on growth for a particular country then depends both on how trade affects its rate of knowledge accumulation through its impact on the country's allocation of resources and on the rate of change of world relative prices. To see this more clearly, let us consider two simple cases:

(i) $\beta_{zy} = \beta_{yz} = 0$, $\beta_{zz} = \beta_{yy} = 1$ (no inter-industry externalities).

In this case, as Lucas (1988) shows, the initial pattern of specialization is preserved and reinforced through time. The country that has an initial comparative advantage in good y, say country A, specializes in that good, so the relative cost of y in that country falls with time. The opposite happens in the other country, say country B.

Since country A specializes in good y, it enjoys a faster rate of knowledge accumulation. But this is somewhat offset by a decreasing relative price of y. With a unitary elasticity of substitution between z and y ($\sigma = 1$), for example, prices exactly offset the faster rate of knowledge accumulation in country A, so the rate of growth of income in both countries is the same. But if $\sigma > 1$, then the declining price of y only partially offsets the faster rate of knowledge accumulation in country A, so country A has a faster rate of income growth than country B. The opposite occurs when $\sigma < 1$.

Now, if $\sigma > 1$ and $a(t) \equiv A_y(t) / A_z(t)$ is not too low at $t = 0$, then $a(t)$ will be increasing for a country in autarky. Therefore, when countries A and B start trading, the country that "started" earlier (the richer country) will have a comparative advantage in good y, so trade will lead to divergence.

(ii) $\beta_{zz} = \beta_{zy} = 0$, $\beta_{zy} = \beta_{yy} = 1$, $\sigma = 1$.

In this case only production of good y generates new knowledge, but this knowledge also contributes to higher productivity in sector z. When trade is opened up between countries A and B, country A will have a comparative advantage in good y. Hence, trade allows country A to enjoy a faster rate of knowledge accumulation than the poor country (country B), where knowledge accumulation will stop completely (because of complete specialization in good z). But given $\sigma = 1$, the declining price of y completely offsets this advantage, and the real rate of growth of both countries is equalized. However, the world relative price of y is falling faster than country A's relative cost of y, so at some point country A starts to produce both goods. At this point, it is clear that country A's real rate of growth becomes higher than country B's. Concretely, at time t, country A's real rate of growth will be faster than country B's by $\delta_z \mu_y(t)$, where $\mu_y(t)$ is the share of the labour force devoted to the production of good y in country A. It can be shown that $\mu_y(t)$ converges to some $\mu_y^* > 0$, thus countries A and B diverge.

NOTES

I thank Peter Klenow, Randy Krozner, participants in the Second Meeting of the United Nations High-Level Group on Development Strategy and Management of the Market Economy and an anonymous referee for very helpful comments.

1. It is assumed here that steady states entail no growth, as in the pure Solow model with no technical change. With exogenous labour-augmenting technological change the steady state implies a constant income per efficiency unit of labour, not income per capita. The main implications remain the same.

2. This calculation assumes a tax rate on capital of 30 per cent in the United States and also that the after-tax rate of return on capital is equalized across countries. This exercise is very similar to one performed by Lucas (1990), who finds that if the difference in income per capita between India and the United States is to be explained by differences in capital-labour ratios, the marginal product of capital in India would be about 58 times the marginal product of capital in the United States.

3. See Parente and Prescott (1994) for a very interesting paper that argues that the stylized facts of economic development can be explained with a model of technology adoption in which poor countries benefit from their technological backwardness but remain poor because of high barriers to technology adoption.

4. A possible problem with this approach is that it takes economic policy as exogenous, whereas in reality economic policy may be influenced by future growth prospects. If this is the case, it makes the results in Sachs and Warner more difficult to interpret.

5. Wage premia are not crucial; similar results arise when firms operating modern technologies have to pay above-market returns to factors other than labour.

6. Fafchamps and Helms (1996) develop this story formally.

7. Hirschman (1958) made similar assumptions in his analysis of linkages. He argued that domestically produced inputs were more conducive to the development of further economic activity (pp. 99–100), and he believed that there was a "minimum economic size" for the profitable operation of most activities (p. 101). Finally, he implicitly assumed that a set of inputs was indispensable for the production of each good—an extreme form of love of variety.

8. Notice that this argument is based entirely on the scale of the industry. Greif and Rodríguez-Clare (1995) show that there may also be a role for the composition of the industry (the number of firms) in generating agglomeration economies. That is, other things equal, productivity is higher in a region where the industry is composed of many small firms than in a region where the industry has the same scale but is composed of a few large firms. The reason is that when the industry is composed of many small firms, industry-specific intermediate-good suppliers will be less concerned that final-good producers will act opportunistically and pay low prices. More industry-specific inputs will thus be produced, making production more efficient.

9. Closing the economy to international trade is not necessarily optimal when the economy is at the bad equilibrium, however (see Rodríguez-Clare, 1996a).

10. "Those countries such as Portugal, Canada, Japan, and the USA in which manufacturing has grown or remained stable during the last decade have among the strongest service sector growth records, and in all of these apart from Japan, service employment has grown by more than 30 per cent. In contrast in Belgium and the United Kingdom, where manufacturing employment declined by approximately 30 per cent between 1974 and 1984, employment growth of only 15.7 per cent and 12 per cent respectively was recorded in service industries. Employment change in producer services such as transport, storage, communications, and finance and office-based business services are most strongly related to manufacturing performance" (Marshall 1988, p. 40).

11. In regional economics the conventional wisdom seems to be that when the value-weight ratio is low, when the time of need of inputs is uncertain, when low quantities are needed and when quality and time of delivery are essential, then it is very convenient to have the supplier of the input close by (Vernon, 1966; Scott and Storper, 1987).

12. Azariadis and Drazen (1990) also consider a model in which there are externalities in education. They show that in some cases such externalities may lead to path dependence: when the economy starts up with a low level of education, education is costly and no one chooses to become educated. Thus the level of education drops, and the economy eventually reaches a steady state with a low level of education. In contrast, if the economy starts with an education level above a certain threshold, then education is not too costly. People choose to become educated, taking the economy towards a steady state with a high level of education.

13. Rodríguez-Clare (1996b) develops an alternative model to consider what determines the rate of technology adoption in a small open economy. It is shown there that trade barriers have a negative effect on the rate of technology adoption, thereby increasing the income gap between North and South.

14. Glaeser and others (1992) use data on the growth of industries in cities to show the existence of inter-industry externalities. But it is not clear whether such externalities arise through the flow of ideas or as a result of backward and forward linkages.

15. See Lucas (1993) for an interesting argument concerning how this type of income effect may lead poor countries to benefit from trade even when there is bounded external learning by doing.

16. The following discussion is based on Rodríguez-Clare (1996c).

17. Hirshman (1958) was careful on this point. He noticed that certain linkages do not significantly affect the rest of the economy, as in the case of what he called "satellite industries", which require only a small economic size to be profitable (p. 102).

18. To think about industry-specific costs of geographic concentration, suppose that entrepreneurs living all around the country get an idea or an opportunity to enter an industry X. Suppose these entrepreneurs like to locate where they already live because of reallocation costs, because they already know that environment and possibly because of particular advantages of that region. These costs explain why not all entrepreneurs move to the place where the industry is concentrated.

19. The non-tradability of inputs for young industries arises because at earlier stages of the industry cycle firms depend on short delivery times for inputs and

often specify the design of the inputs to their suppliers, making it important to have constant contact with them. The possibilities of doing so are enhanced by proximity between firms and suppliers.

20. The correlation coefficient is 0.027 with a t-statistic of 0.5.

21. There are other well-known problems with protecting infant industries in developing countries, such as the possible decrease in competition and efficiency. Moreover, as shown in Rodríguez-Clare (1995), such a policy may lower the rate of technology adoption.

22. The production function of the composite intermediate good X uses the functional form first proposed by Dixit and Stiglitz (1977) as a specification for a utility function, and later applied to production theory by Ethier (1982).

23. In a classic paper on the service sector Katouzian (1970) provided a different classification of services. The category that comes closest to the group of producer services are what he calls "complementary services". He says that "these services have been complementary to the growth of manufacturing production in two ways: as complementary factors to urbanization, and as necessary links to the process of round-about or capitalistic production" (pp. 366–7).

REFERENCES

Azanadis, C. and A. Drazen. 1990. "Threshold Externalities in Economic Development." *Quarterly Journal and Economics* 105(2):501–26.

Balassa, B. 1981. "The Process of Industrial Development and Alternative Development Strategies." *The Newly Industrializing Countries in the World Economy*. New York: Pergamon Press.

Barro, R. 1991. "Economic Growth in a Cross Section of Countries." *Quarterly Journal of Economics* 106(2):407–44.

Barro, R. and X. Sala-i-Martin. 1992. "Convergence." *Journal of Political Economy* 100(2):223–51.

_____. 1995. *Economic Growth*. New York: McGraw-Hill.

Bernstein, J.I. and M.I. Nadiri. 1988. "Interindustry R&D Spillovers, Rates of Return, and Production in High Tech Industries." *American Economic Review* 78(2):429–34.

Bils, M. and P. Klenow. 1995. "Does Schooling Drive Growth or the Other Way Around?" Graduate School of Business, University of Chicago.

Breshnahan, T. 1986. "Measuring the Spillovers from Technical Advance." *American Economic Review* 76(4):742–55.

Caballero, R. and R. Lyons. 1992. "The Case for External Economies." In A. Cukierman, Z. Hercowitz and L. Leiderman, eds., *Political Economy, Growth and Business Cycles*. Cambridge, Mass.: MIT Press.

Chan, V., B. Chen and K. Cheung. 1995. "External Economies in Taiwan's Manufacturing Industries." *Contemporary Economic Policy* 13(October):118–30.

Chari, V.V., P.J. Kehoe and E.R. McGrattan. 1995. "The Poverty of Nations." Federal Reserve Bank of Minneapolis.

Ciccone, A. and R. Hall. 1996. "Productivity and the Density of Economic Activity." *American Economic Review* 86(1):54–70.

Coe, D. and E. Helpman. 1993. "International R&D Spillovers." NBER Working Paper 4444. Cambridge, Mass.

Coe, D., E. Helpman and A. Hoffmeister. 1995. "North-South R&D Spillovers." NBER Working Paper 5048. Cambridge, Mass.

Daniels, P.W. 1985. *Service Industries: A Geographical Appraisal.* New York: Methuen & Co.

Diamond, P. 1982. "Aggregate Demand Management in Search Equilibrium." *Journal of Political Economy* 90(4):881–94.

Dixit, A. and J. Stiglitz. 1977. "Monopolistic Competition and Optimum Product Diversity." *American Economic Review* 76(1):297–308.

Durlauf, S. and P.A. Johnson. 1992. "Local versus Global Convergence Across National Economies." NBER Working Paper 3996. Cambridge, Mass.

Eaton, J. and S. Kortum. 1995. "International Patenting and Technology Diffusion." NBER Working Paper 4931. Cambridge, Mass.

Ellison, G. and E. Glaeser. 1994. "Geographic Concentration in US Manufacturing Industries: A Dartboard Approach." NBER Working Paper 4840. Cambridge, Mass.

Ethier, W.J. 1982. "National and International Returns to Scale in the Modern Theory of International Trade." *American Economic Review* 72(2): 389–405.

Fafchamps, M. and B. Helms. 1996. "Local Demand, Investment Multipliers and Industrialization." *Journal of Development Economics* 49(1):57–72.

Faini, R. 1984. "Increasing Returns, Non-Traded Inputs and Regional Development." *Economic Journal* 94(2):308–23.

Fujita, M. 1990. *Land Resources and Urban Economics.* Cambridge, U.K.: Cambridge University Press.

Gershuny, J. and I. Miles. 1983. *The New Service Economy.* London: Frances Pinter.

Glaeser, E.L., H.D. Kallal, J.A. Scheihkman and A. Shleifer. 1992. "Growth in Cities." *Journal of Political Economy* 100(6):1126–52.

Greenfield, H. I. 1966. *Manpower and the Growth of Producer Services.* New York: Columbia University Press.

Greif, A. and A. Rodríguez-Clare. 1995. "A Transactions Cost Theory of Agglomeration Economies." Stanford University and University of Chicago.

Grossman, G. and E. Helpman. 1992. *Innovation and Growth in the Global Economy.* Cambridge, Mass.: MIT Press.

Henderson, J. 1988. *Urban Development: Theory, Fact and Illusion.* New York: Oxford University Press.

Hischman, A.O. 1958. *The Strategy of Economic Development.* New Haven: Yale University Press.

Holmes, T. 1995. "Localization of Industry and Vertical Disintegration." Federal Reserve Bank of Minneapolis.

Hummels, D. 1995. "Global Income Clustering and Trade in Intermediate Goods." Graduate School of Business, University of Chicago.

Irwin, D. and P. Klenow. 1994. "Learning-by-Doing Spillovers in the Semiconductor Industry." *Journal of Political Economy* 102(6):1200–27.

Islam, N. 1995. "Growth Empirics: A Panel Data Approach." *Quarterly Journal of Economics* 110(4):1127–70.

Jacobs, J. 1969. *The Economy of Cities.* New York: Random House.

____. 1984. *Cities and the Wealth of Nations*. New York: Random House.

Jaffe, A. 1986. "Technological Opportunity and Spillovers from R&D: Evidence from Firms' Patents, Profits and Market Value." *American Economic Review* 76 (December):984–1001.

Jaffe, A., M. Trajtenberg and R. Henderson. 1993. "Geographic Localization of Knowledge Spillovers as Evidenced by Patent Citations." *Quarterly Journal of Economics* 108 (August):577–98.

Katouzian, M. 1970. "The Development of the Service Sector: A New Approach." *Oxford Economic Papers* 22(3):362-82.

Khan, S. and C. Bilginsoy. 1994. "Industry Externalities Revisited." *Kyklos* 47(1): 67–80.

Klenow, P. And A. Rodríguez-Clare. 1996. "Economic Growth: A Review Essay." Graduate School of Business, University of Chicago.

Klundert, T. and S. Smulders. 1995. "North-South Spillovers and Competition: Convergence versus Divergence." Department of Economics, Tilburg University.

Kravis, I. 1985. "Services in World Transactions." In Robert P. Inman, ed., *Managing the Service Economy*. Cambridge, U.K.: Cambridge University Press.

Kravis, I. and R. Lipsey. 1988. "National Price Levels and the Prices of Tradables and Nontradables." *American Economic Review* 78(May):474–8.

Krugman, P. 1979. "A Model of Innovation, Technology Transfer, and the World Distribution of Income." *Journal of Political Economy* 87(2):253–66.

____. 1991. *Geography and Trade*. Cambridge, Mass.: MIT Press.

____. 1992. "Towards a Counter-Counter Revolution in Development Theory." Department of Economics, Stanford University.

Little, I. 1982. *Economic Development*. New York: Twentieth Century Fund.

Little, I., T. Scitovsky and M. Scott. 1970. *Industry and Trade in Developing Countries*. Oxford: Oxford University Press.

Lucas, R.E. Jr. 1988. "On the Mechanics of Economic Development." *Journal of Monetary Economics* 22(1):3–42.

____. 1990. "Why Doesn't Capital Flow from Rich to Poor Countries?" *American Economic Review* 80 (May):92–6.

____. 1993. "Making a Miracle." *Econometrica* 61(2):251–72.

Mankiw, N.G., D. Romer and D. Weil. 1992. "A Contribution to the Empirics of Economic Growth." *Quarterly Journal of Economics* May 1992:407–37.

Marshall, J.N. 1988. *Services and Uneven Development*. London: Oxford University Press.

Matsuyama, K. 1992. "The Market Size, Entrepreneurship, and the Big-Push." *Journal of the Japanese and International Economies* 6 (December):347–64.

____. 1994. "Economic Development as Coordination Problems." Department of Economics, Northwestern University.

McAfee, R. and J. McMillan. 1990. "Organizational Diseconomies of Scale." Department of Economics, University of Texas, Austin and University of California, San Diego.

McKee, D. L. 1988. *Growth, Development, and the Service Economy in the Third World*. New York: Praeger Publishers.

Milgrom, P. and J. Roberts. 1988. "An Economic Approach to Influence Activities in Organizations." *American Journal of Sociology* 94 (Supplement):154–79.

Murphy, K., A. Shleifer and R. Vishny. 1989. "Industrialization and the Big-Push." *Journal of Political Economy* 97(5):1003–26.

Parente, S. and E. Prescott. 1993. "Changes in the Wealth of Nations." *Federal Reserve Bank of Minneapolis, Quarterly Review* 17(2):3–14.

____. 1994. "Barriers to Technology Adoption and Development." *Journal of Political Economy* 102(2):298–321.

Porter, M. 1992. *The Competitive Advantage of Nations.* New York: The Free Press.

Rodríguez-Clare, A. 1993. *The Division of Labor, Agglomeration Economies and Economic Development.* Unpublished Ph.D. dissertation. Stanford University.

____. 1995. "Technology Adoption and Trade in a Small Economy." Graduate School of Business, University of Chicago.

____. 1996a. "The Division of Labor and Economic Development." *Journal of Development Economics* 49(1):3–32.

____. 1996b. "The Role of Trade in Technology Diffusion." Graduate School of Business, University of Chicago.

____. 1996c. "Multinationals, Linkages and Economic Development." *American Economic Review* 86(4):852–73.

Rodrik, D. 1993. "Trade and Industrial Policy Reform in Developing Countries: A Review of Recent Theory and Evidence." NBER Working Paper 4417. Cambridge, Mass.

____. 1994a. "Coordination Failures and Government Policy: A Model with Applications to East Asia and Eastern Europe." Kennedy School of Government, Harvard University.

____. 1994b. "Getting Interventions Right: How South Korea and Taiwan Grew Rich." Kennedy School of Government, Harvard University.

Romer, P. 1986. "Increasing Returns and Long Run Growth." *Journal of Political Economy* 94(5):1002–37.

____. 1990. "Endogenous Technological Change." *Journal of Political Economy* 98(5):71–102.

Rosenberg, N. 1982. *Inside the Black Box.* Cambridge, U.K.: Cambridge University Press.

Rosenstein-Rodan, P.N. 1943. "Problems of Industrialization of Eastern and South-Eastern Europe." *The Economic Journal* 55(3):210–11.

Sachs, J. and A. Warner. 1995. "Economic Convergence and Economic Policies." NBER Working Paper 5039. Cambridge, Mass.

Scott, A. and M. Storper. 1987. "High Technology Industry and Regional Development: A Theoretical Critique and Reconstruction." *International Social Science Journal* 34(2):215–32.

Shleifer, A. 1991. "Externalities and Economic Growth: Lessons from Recent Work." Department of Economics, Harvard University.

Singelmann, J. 1970. *From Agriculture to Services: The Transformation of Industrial Employment.* Beverly Hills: Sage Publications.

Solow, R. 1956. "A Contribution to the Theory of Economic Growth." *Quarterly Journal of Economics* 70(1):65–94.

Stanback, T.M. 1979. *Understanding the Service Economy: Employment, Productivity and Location.* Baltimore: Johns Hopkins University Press.

Stewart, F. and E. Ghani. 1991. "How Significant are Externalities for Development?" *World Development* 19(6):569–94.

Stiglitz, J. 1991. "Social Absorption Capability and Innovation." Department of Economics, Stanford University.

Stokey, N. 1991. "Human Capital, Product Quality, and Growth." *Quarterly Journal of Economics* 106 (May):587–616.

Vernon, R. 1966. "International Investment and International Trade in the Product Cycle." *Quarterly Journal of Economics* 80(1):190–207.

Wilson, P. 1992. *Exports and Local Development: Mexico's New Maquiladoras.* Austin: University of Texas Press.

World Bank. 1993. *The East Asian Miracle.* New York: Oxford University Press.

Young, A. 1991. "Learning by Doing and the Dynamic Effects of International Trade." *Quarterly Journal of Economics* 106 (May):369–406.

____. 1993. "Invention and Bounded Learning by Doing." *Journal of Political Economy* 101(3):443–72.

____. 1995. "The Tyranny of Numbers." *Quarterly Journal of Economics* 110(3): 641–80.

PART TWO

HUMAN RESOURCES

4

Human Capital Accumulation and Development Strategy

RICHARD SABOT

What role does human capital accumulation play in a market-based development strategy? In this chapter I attempt to answer this question by assessing the contribution that human capital accumulation has made to the marked inter-regional difference in economic performance among developing countries. The difference between east Asia and other developing regions in two key dimensions of economic performance is striking: in recent decades African, Latin American and south Asian countries experienced slow or negative growth and high inequality, while east Asian countries achieved both extremely low inequality and rapid growth. Figure 4.1 relates percentage growth in GDP and income inequality, as measured by the ratio of the income shares of the top and bottom quintiles, during 1965–90 for a number of Latin American countries, which are concentrated in the south-east quadrant,[1] and east Asian countries, which stand alone in the north-west quadrant.[2]

I assess the extent to which differences in the supply of human capital explain east Asia's higher rates of growth and lower levels of inequality. I provide evidence suggesting that the growth payoff to improving the quality of schooling may be at least as great as the payoff to increasing the quantity of schooling, and that among the

Figure 4.1: Income inequality and GDP growth, 1965–90

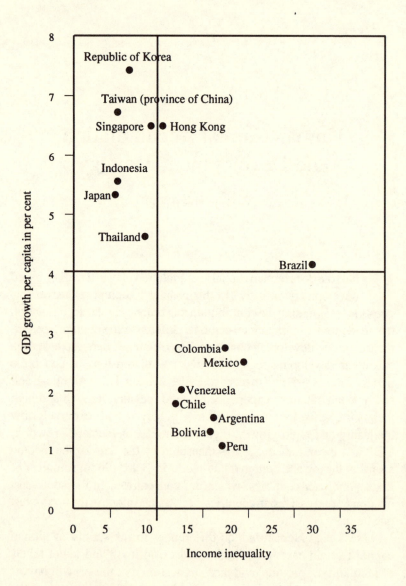

Note: Income inequality is the average ratio of the income shares of the richest 20 per cent and the poorest 20 per cent of the population.

Source: Based on World Bank (1993).

developing regions east Asia alone was able to simultaneously increase quantity and improve quality. I also show that despite lower labour force participation rates of women, the growth payoff to educating girls is as high as the payoff to educating boys, and that some of east Asia's superior performance is due to the changes in household behaviour associated with better educated women.

Countries with large endowments of human capital that nonetheless grow slowly demonstrate that increasing the supply of human capital is not enough. I provide evidence that the growth payoff of human capital accumulation has been greater in east Asia than elsewhere because of its export-oriented labour and skill-demanding development strategy. The inward-oriented policy regimes characteristic of other regions generated slower growth of labour demand and a smaller growth payoff to human capital accumulation.

In addition to its direct effect of increasing labour productivity, educational expansion, by reducing inequality, may also have had an indirect positive effect on growth in east Asia. I provide evidence of negative relationships between educational endowments and income inequality, and between inequality and growth. The first relationship is explained by the erosion of workers' scarcity rents as a result of educational expansion. There are several explanations for the second relationship. In particular, I focus on the possibility that, contrary to conventional wisdom, when income inequality is low and labour demand is strong, the poor's marginal propensity to save may be very high.

Finally, I consider why the east Asian system of basic education performs better than educational systems in other developing regions. Higher levels of expenditure per eligible child are an important part of the story, I assess the contribution to the differential in performance and expenditure per child of such factors as: the strength of governments' financial commitment to education, the allocation of public expenditures among education levels, the degree of administrative inefficiency, the feedback of economic growth on education expenditures, the feedback of reduction in fertility on expenditures per eligible child and the feedback from low inequality to higher rates of investment in human capital among the poor. I conclude with some lessons for policy.

INTER-REGIONAL DIFFERENCES IN EDUCATIONAL PERFORMANCE

Examining regressions of secondary school enrollment rates on per capita national income for more than 90 developing countries in 1965 and 1987, we see that countries in east Asia, with the exception of Thailand, had significantly higher primary and secondary enrollment rates than predicted by cross-country comparisons (figure 4.2).[3] The performance of African, Latin American and south Asian countries is not nearly as strong as that of east Asia and is mixed relative to international norms.[4] In countries where enrollment rates are low, children of poor parents are the least likely to be enrolled. Thus, a corollary of the lower enrollment rates in Latin America is higher inequality of access by socioeconomic background.[5]

Moreover, in contrast to east Asia, where increases in quantity were associated with improvements in the quality of education, the expansion of enrollment in many other regions resulted in the erosion of quality, particularly for the poor. In human capital models inputs matter only to the extent that they affect output: it is the output of schooling—cognitive and other skills—not inputs to educational production, such as years of schooling, that is presumed to affect subsequent productivity. Children with the same number of years of schooling, even if they have similar abilities and similar family backgrounds, do not necessarily have the same level of cognitive skills. It can, therefore, be misleading to look solely at a measure of the quantity of schooling as an indicator of human capital accumulation.

In regions other than east Asia increases in schooling outputs such as cognitive skills have been smaller than increases in inputs such as years of schooling. This pattern suggests that some of the apparent improvement in educational attainment in those regions has been illusory. But there is no cookie-cutter approach to improving school quality. Research on education production functions has not sent clear signals about which inputs will best improve the learning outcomes of students. Not surprisingly, the ingredients needed to improve quality will vary from one school system to the next. And it is not clear that improvements in quality will always require increases in spending. Production function studies in high-income

Figure 4.2: Cross-country regressions for secondary
enrollment rates, 1965 and 1987

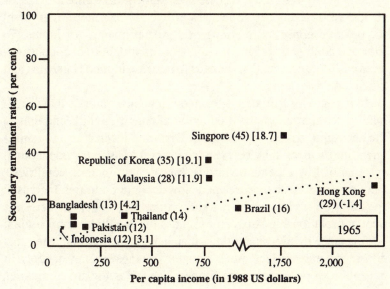

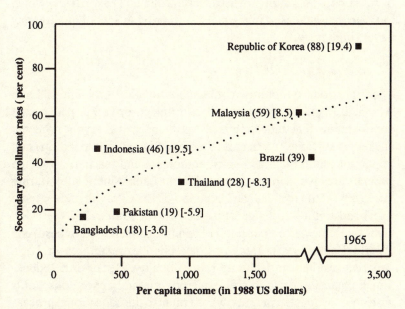

Note: Figures in parentheses are enrollment rates; bracketed numbers show residuals.

Source: Behrman and Schneider (1992).

countries suggest that variations in school expenditures are not systematically related to variations in student performance (Hanushek, 1989). Using resources less efficiently can more than offset the positive impact on learning of a greater quantity of inputs. To improve quality, therefore, it may be as important to change incentives within educational systems as to increase inputs (Hanushek and others, 1994).

There is growing evidence from low-income countries that school quality is important to the production of cognitive skills and thus to the economic payoff to schooling. Distorted incentives and consequent inefficiency may be even bigger problems in the educational systems of low-income countries than in high-income countries.[6] But it is also clear that in many low-income countries increased spending on inputs would markedly improve quality. If there is a stronger relationship between expenditures per student and student performance in low- and middle- than in high-income countries, this difference may reflect much greater variance among schools in expenditures per pupil in the former. The following are summaries of research from Latin America, south Asia and east Africa, which indicate that increased investment in improving school quality may have a high payoff.

Diagnosing poor school quality

There are four symptoms of the school quality problem in Latin America. First, the expansion of enrollment, driven in part by the populist view that education is an entitlement to everyone, was not backed by sufficient resources to maintain per pupil expenditures on important inputs such as books, equipment and teachers. Average expenditures per primary school child in Latin America fell during the 1980s—"the lost decade", a period of slow growth and extreme fiscal constraint—from an estimated $164 in 1980 to $118 in 1989. Over the same period per pupil expenditures increased in east Asia (World Bank, 1993). Declining per pupil expenditures in Latin America resulted in declining school quality. Because the educational expansion drew in children from relatively poor households with poorly educated parents, whose input to the educational process was necessarily limited, cognitive outputs per year of schooling almost certainly declined in many Latin American countries.[7]

Second, repetition rates are high. Twenty-nine per cent of all students in the first six years of primary school fail each year. Forty-two per cent of all first graders repeat. In 1989 less than one-half of all primary school students finished six years of school in six years. The aggregate cost of repetition to Latin American school systems: an estimated $2.5 billion a year (Birdsall, Bruns and Sabot, 1996). Not all of this spending is wasted, however: children do learn more during the year that they repeat.

Third, completion rates are low and may be declining. Trends in dropout rates are an indicator of trends in quality, with quality improvements generally associated with reduced dropouts.[8] As school quality increases, so do the productivity-enhancing cognitive skills acquired in school and, hence, the probability of gaining access to higher-level educational opportunities, rationed by meritocratic criteria, and the expected returns to schooling. Higher probabilities of promotion and higher expected returns are inducements to remain in school.

In Brazil the expansion of primary school coverage was associated with a dramatic decline in completion rates—due to the inability of the system to offer adequate quality schooling to a larger and more diverse pool of students. By contrast, in east Asia, where quantity and quality were improved simultaneously, completion rates remained high. In the 1950s Brazil's primary completion rate was higher than the Republic of Korea's—60 per cent compared with 36 per cent. Over the next three decades Brazil's primary completion rate dropped to 20 per cent, while in the Republic of Korea more than 90 per cent of those enrolled completed their primary education.[9]

A fourth symptom of poor quality is test scores. While studies of cognitive achievement across countries are often as crude as they are scarce, international comparisons of scores on tests that attempt to measure the output of schooling confirm that in Latin America education systems are performing poorly. For example, in one study of reading skills Venezuelan nine-year-olds ranked last among a group of economies that included Hong Kong, Indonesia and Singapore. In a 1992 assessment of math and science skills, 13-year-old students from China, Israel, Jordan, the Republic of Korea and Taiwan (province of China) all out-performed Brazilian 13-year-olds. In another 1992 assessment of math and science skills the performance of 13-year-olds in Argentina, Colombia, the Dominican Republic and Venezuela, with the exception of those attending elite private schools, was significantly weaker than that of students from countries such as Thailand (World Bank, 1993).

The pay-off to raising school quality

Research in Brazil suggests that the returns to improving the quality of schooling could be exceptionally high. As the average quality of basic education declined in Brazil, the variance in school quality increased. Almost all of the decline in average quality over the past two decades is attributable to a worsening at the bottom of the quality distribution. The worst schools in Brazil operate shifts of less than three hours, lack basic facilities, have no books or other learning materials and have teachers who have not completed primary school themselves and are virtually innumerate and illiterate.[10]

Because teachers cannot teach what they do not know, primary schools become day care centers. And this abandonment of the educational mission of schools hinders human capital accumulation. As school quality erodes, children learn less and acquire fewer productive skills, reducing both the likelihood of progressing to the next educational level and the rate of return to schooling when competing in the labour market. Once children in low-quality schools grow old enough to be economically productive, parents no longer face an economic incentive strong enough to keep their children in school through graduation. In Brazil, where school quality is low, repetition rates have risen, and completion rates have declined (Birdsall, Bruns and Sabot, 1996).

The Brazil studies suggest that there are two dimensions to the returns to investment in quality improvement. First, if the quality of schooling is improved, graduates will be more productive and earn more.[11] Second, higher quality schooling leads to lower repetition rates, reducing the costs associated with repetition. It is costly if an educational system takes seven or eight years to put a child through only four or five years of the primary school curriculum. Indeed, the analysis by Hanushek, Batista Gomes-Neto and Harbison (1996) indicates that in Brazil the gains from potential improvements in internal efficiency may be more than enough to pay for the costs of making these improvements. Thus improving school quality need not require a tradeoff with quantity.

Behrman and others (1994) have attempted to measure the relative rates of return to investments in improving the quality of existing schools and in increasing the number of schools in rural Pakistan.[12] The study uses a rich set of micro-data, containing measures of educational inputs and outputs and labour market outcomes, to estimate educational attainment, literacy and numeracy, and cost and earnings functions. The cost and earnings functions are then used to measure rates of return to improvements in quality (holding quantity constant) and to increases in quantity (holding quality constant).[13] The study found that the social rate of return to improving primary school quality exceeds the rate of return to increasing the available quantity of either primary- or middle-school places. With regard to improving school quality, the production function results suggest that larger gains can be made by investments that improve teacher quality (by increasing their cognitive skills) and increase student exposure to teachers (by reducing class size) than by investments that improve physical infrastructure and equipment.

In east Africa rich micro-data were used to decompose the large gap in wages between workers in Kenya and in Tanzania. Estimates of wage functions, which included cognitive skills among the independent variables, demonstrated that literate and numerate workers are more productive and that if the cognitive skills of Tanzanian workers were as high as those of their Kenyan counterparts (29 per cent higher), their mean wages would be roughly 13 per cent higher. Estimates of education production functions indicated that the gap in cognitive skills was due to both more and higher quality schooling in Kenya. Simulations with education production functions and wage functions indicated that increasing the quantity of secondary education in Tanzania to the Kenyan level would increase the cognitive skills of the wage labour force by 4 per cent and mean earnings by 3 per cent. An increase in the quality of schooling in Tanzania to the Kenyan level would increase the cognitive skills of workers by 24 per cent and earnings by 10 per cent. The difference in school quality was not a function of higher expenditures in Kenya—per pupil expenditures in Tanzania were at least as high.[14]

In the sections that follow I focus on two "vicious circles". First, I show how, in a process of cumulative causation, poor educational performance (which limited the supply of human capital) in combination with inward-looking, capital-intensive development strategies (which limited the demand for human capital) contributed to slow economic growth in regions other than east Asia, and how, in turn, slow economic growth contributed to low investment in education. Then, I show how poor educational performance contributed to high income inequality, and how high income inequality constrained growth and investment in education. I also suggest means by which these vicious circles can be converted to virtuous circles.

EDUCATION AND GROWTH

In the past 50 years cross-country comparisons have been a prominent feature of the empirical search for patterns that countries follow as they transform themselves from low-income to high-income nations.[15] The accumulation of human capital has consistently emerged as an essential feature of economic growth and development. But the direction of causality implied by the positive correlation between educational attainment and per capita output in a cross-section of countries is unclear: it could simply indicate that education is a luxury consumer good that is increasingly demanded as incomes rise. This concern has been eased by Barro-style growth regressions, in which the characteristics of economies decades ago are used as predictors of subsequent rates of economic growth.[16] The important contribution of education to growth is one of the most robust findings of the burgeoning literature on the determinants of the variance in growth rates across countries. Its importance is relatively insensitive to changes in the measurement of the education and other independent variables, specification of the regressions or sample composition (Levine and Renelt, 1991).

These results are consistent with human capital theory. The theory of investment in people predicts that education augments cognitive and other skills, which, in turn, augment the productivity of labour (Becker, 1964; Schultz, 1961). Endogenous growth theory predicts the same: a larger stock of human capital facilitates technological progress or, for a country that is not on the technological frontier, relatively rapid acquisition of technological capability (Nelson and Phelps, 1966; Romer, 1990). Moreover, rates of return to human capital may actually be increasing over some range because of spillover benefits—that is, when increasing the education of one worker makes an entire group of workers more productive (Lucas, 1988; Becker, Murphy and Tamura, 1990).

Birdsall, Ross and Sabot (1995) use a modified version of the

Table 4.1: Determinants of GDP growth, (1960–85)

Variable	Basic regression	Excludes education variables	Excludes eight Asian economies
1960 real per capita GDP (in thousands of 1980 US$)	-0.0075 (-3.730)	-0.0020 (-1.801)	-0.0061 (-3.547)
1960 primary enrollment rate	0.243 (3.024)		0.0199 (2.493)
1960 secondary enrollment rate	0.0366 (2.427)		0.0361 (2.189)
Ratio of real government consumption (excluding defence and education) to real GDP, averaged over 1960–85	-0.1229 (-4.380)	-0.1495 (-4.760)	-0.0969 (-3.162)
Number of revolutions and coups (per year, 1960–85)	-0.0176 (-1.867)	-0.0268 (-2.493)	-0.0177 (-1,906)
Number of assassinations (per million population per year, 1960–85)	-0.0055 (-1.526)	-0.0067 (-1.626)	-0.0033 (-0.920)
Absolute value of the deviation of the PPP value for the investment deflator (US=1) from the sample mean (1960)	-0.0086 (-1.093)	-0.0176 (-2.012)	-0.0063 (-0.810)
National household income distribution (bottom 40% to top 20%)	-0.0013 (-1.897)	-0.0018 (-2.406)	-0.0007 (-1.047)
Intercept	0.0418 (4.185)	0.0706 (7.871)	0.0330 (3.108)
R^2	0.5389	0.3574	0.4542
Number of observations	74	74	66

Note: Values of t-ratios are reported in parentheses beneath regression coefficients.

Source: Birdsall, Ross and Sabot (1995).

Figure 4.3: Simulated per capita GDP growth average economy, primary and secondary

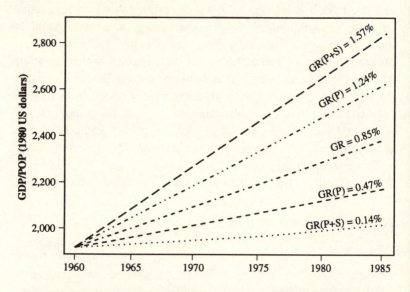

Note: GR represents growth path for average economy. GR(P) represents economy with one standard deviation in primary enrolment rates. GR(P+S) represents economy with one standard deviation in primary and secondary enrolment rates.

Barro regression to conduct counterfactual simulations that provide a basis for assessing the magnitude of the contribution of investment in human capital to rates of economic growth (table 4.1). Figure 4.3 shows the growth path of GDP per capita over 1960–85 for a country characterized by the average value of each of the variables in the Barro sample. It also shows the changes in growth and per capita GDP for that country, assuming it had achieved a 1960 primary enrollment rate or both a 1960 primary and secondary enrollment rate one-half standard deviation above (or below) the mean. There is a 0.7 per cent difference in the growth rate for the simulation that varies both primary enrollments and a 1.5 per cent difference in the growth rates for the simulation that varies both primary and secondary enrollments. The cumulative effect of these differences in growth rates on 1985 per capita GDP are large: 20 per cent and nearly 40 per cent, respectively.

In 1960 the Republic of Korea and Taiwan (province of China) had enrollment rates roughly one-half standard deviation above the mean, while Guatemala and Bolivia had rates roughly one-half standard deviation below the mean.[17] Moreover, our discussion of school quality suggests that the inter-regional gap in enrollment rates underestimates the gap in the output of schooling.

The impact on growth of educating girls

Substituting gender-specific, primary-school enrollment rates into the original Barro model, we find (results not shown) no significant difference between the coefficient values for boys and girls,[18] suggesting that increasing primary-school enrollments for girls will be just as effective in stimulating growth as increasing primary enrollments for boys.[19] This conclusion, based on cross-country data, is consistent with the microeconomic evidence summarized by Summers (1992), indicating that private rates of return to education among wage earners are roughly the same for women as for men.[20]

Of course, the rate of participation in the wage labour market is much lower for women than for men. But the economic payoff to educating girls is not confined to increases in the productivity of wage labour—it is also derived from changes in behaviour within households, such as fertility, which yield non-wage social benefits. Educated mothers have fewer children.[21] In east Asia the fertility rate for women with more than seven years of schooling is 54 per cent of the rate for uneducated women.[22] Closing a virtuous circle, the early fertility decline in east Asia that started in the mid-1960s resulted in a marked slowing of the growth of the school-age population in the 1970s. As I show below, this slowing contributed to the growth of public expenditures on basic education per eligible child, which was more rapid than elsewhere, permitting more rapid increases in the quantity, and improvements in the quality, of schooling provided.

While fertility rates in other developing regions have declined in the past two decades, their rates remain high relative to east Asian rates, particularly those in poorer countries. For example, in Bolivia, Guatemala, Honduras and Nicaragua the total fertility rate exceeds five children per mother, whereas in the Republic of Korea the total fertility rate is less than two children per mother. In many African countries the total fertility rate is still higher than six. There is high variance in total fertility in south Asia. In Pakistan, where the gender gap in schooling is large, the total fertility rate is above five, whereas in Sri Lanka, where women are better educated, the total fertility rate is less than three. High fertility has placed added stress on already strained resources for education—as noted, per-child spending on books, equipment and teacher training in regions other than east Asia has declined. While in the Republic of Korea the cohort entering primary school is shrinking, in the Philippines, where fertility remains high, the cohort has been increasing by roughly 500,000 children per year. Because of the decline in per-child spending, school quality has declined and high repetition and high dropout rates have continued.

Development strategy and the impact of education on growth

In short, both the microeconomic and cross-country evidence indicate that the difference between east Asia and other regions in growth rates has been due in part to inter-regional differences in educational performance. But differences in the supply of human capital are only part of the story of how education contributes to growth. The demand for human capital is also important. The import-substituting, capital-intensive strategies that primarily served the elite and labour insiders in regions other than east Asia

Table 4.2: Average annual percentage increases in the manufacturing sector wage bill, 1970–90

Country	Real earnings of labour	Wage employment	Real wage bill
Bolivia	-3.2	-0.50[d]	-3.68
India	1.9	1.77[a]	3.70
Indonesia	5.2	14.35[b]	20.30
Kenya	-2.0	7.74	5.59
Korea, Republic of	8.7	18.67	28.99
Mauritius	0.8	60.00	61.28
Singapore	4.0	11.37[a]	15.82
Venezuela	-0.2	4.27[c]	4.06
Zambia	0.0	1.39[a]	1.39

[a] 1970–89
[b] 1974–89
[c] 1970–84
[d] 1975–89

Source: Calculated from World Bank (1993b) and ILO.

did not generate strong demand for labour. By contrast, export-oriented strategies kept east Asia on a labour-demanding growth path. In the manufacturing sector real earnings, wage employment and the real wage bill increased at much faster rates in east Asia than in Latin America (table 4.2).[23] Moreover, the ratio of the growth of the real wage bill to the growth of GNP is also higher in east Asia, suggesting not only that aggregate growth is faster in east Asia, but that it is more labour-demanding as well.

Differences among countries in demand for skills have been neglected in cross-country assessments of education's contribution to growth. The resulting omitted variable bias may explain the substantial overprediction, by Barro-type growth functions, of rates of growth for some countries with higher-than-predicted rates of enrollment in primary and secondary schools in the 1960s. For example, weak demand for educated labour may help explain why countries such as Argentina, Egypt and Peru—which, like east Asia, had greater-than-predicted (for their initial levels of income) human capital endowments—have tended to underperform with respect to growth.

Figure 4.4 illustrates the link between the demand for skilled labour and education's contribution to growth, comparing east Asia and Latin America. S and D are, respectively, the skill supply and demand functions of the typical Latin American country; S' and D' are the skill supply and demand functions of the typical east Asian country.[24] S' is shifted to the right because of, for example, greater public commitment to basic education.[25] At any given rate of return to skills, skilled workers are in greater demand in east Asia than in the typical Latin American country.[26] As drawn, high demand for skills in east Asia have offset the tendency for educational expansion to induce diminishing returns to investment in human capital.

By contrast, while enrollment rates are higher in country X than in the typical Latin American country, the returns to education are lower—because X has the same human capital supply function as east Asia but the same skill demand function as the typical Latin American country. The net result of high supply of and demand for human capital is that skilled labour is more abundant in east Asia than in the typical Latin American country, while the rate of return to human capital investments is at least as high.

Figure 4.4: Demand shifts and the returns to human capital

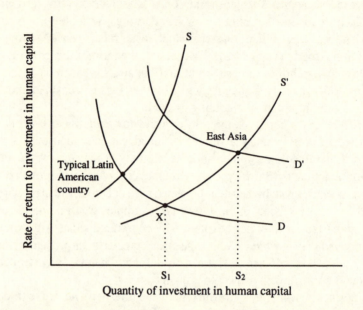

Birdsall, Ross and Sabot (1995) use the degree to which an economy is oriented towards manufactured exports as a proxy of demand for skills.[27] The hypothesis holds that in a standard growth rate function there is a positive interaction between education endowments in 1960 and an economy's orientation towards manufactured exports—that is, the more the economy is oriented towards manufactured exports, the greater will be the demand for skilled labour and the greater will be the impact of a given educational endowment on growth.

The results generally support this hypothesis, though not unambiguously.[28] Running the regression with the additional variables shows that the contribution of education to economic growth tends to be greater in countries in which exports as a proportion of GDP are higher. The stimulus that the greater supply of human capital has given to economic growth appears to have been augmented by the export orientation of the east Asian economies and the resulting labour- and skill-demanding growth paths they followed. Countries in other regions, which in general followed a more inward-looking, capital-intensive growth path, did not benefit from this positive interaction between human capital and the demand for skilled labour.

EDUCATION AND INEQUALITY

In high-income countries the inequality of pay accounts for two-thirds of total income inequality. In low-income countries, as the share of wage employment in total employment increases, so does the share of inequality of pay in total income inequality (Knight and Sabot, 1983; Knight and Sabot, 1991). As the relative abundance of educated workers increases, the scarcity rents that such educated workers earn are eroded. The resulting compression of the educational structure of wages may, in turn, reduce the inequality of pay. By reducing the inequality of pay, educational expansion may reduce total income inequality.[29]

The compression effect of educational expansion may, however, be counteracted by a disequalizing composition effect—brought about by the relatively rapid growth of the more educated, high productivity portion of the labour force.[30] Depending on whether the compression effect or the composition effect dominates, educational expansion will either raise or lower the inequality of pay. The compression effect tends to dominate. In a cross-section of more than 80 countries there is a strong, statistically significant, negative correlation between basic education enrollment rates and the level of income inequality as measured by the gini coefficient.[31]

A comparison of microeconomic data for Brazil and the Republic of Korea (Park, Ross and Sabot, 1992) confirms this negative correlation and suggests that differences in educational attainment contribute to the marked difference in inequality between east Asian countries and countries in other regions. Brazil and Korea have similar levels of per capita income. But as noted above, in Korea the share of income going to the top 20 per cent of income earners was only 8 times the share earned by the bottom 20 per cent (in 1976), while in Brazil that ratio was 26 (in 1983).

Again comparing Brazil and Korea,[32] between the mid-1970s and the mid-1980s the educational composition of the labour force in Korea changed markedly: the proportion of high school and post-

Development Strategy and Management of the Market Economy

Figure 4.5: Educational expansion and inequality in
Brazil and the Republic of Korea

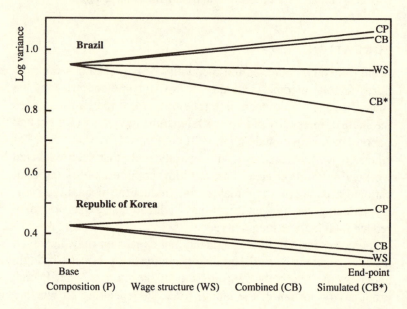

Base   End-point
Composition (P)   Wage structure (WS)   Combined (CB)   Simulated (CB*)

secondary graduates in the wage labour force sharply increased, and
the proportion of workers with elementary school or less education
declined to only 8 per cent (figure 4.5). Consistent with the competitive market prediction that the returns to a factor fall as its relative
supply increases, the wage premium earned by educated workers in
Korea declined. Standardizing for other predictors, in 1976 workers
with a high school education earned 47 per cent more than primary
school graduates, and by 1986 that premium had declined to
30 per cent (table 4.3). Similarly, the premium earned by workers
with a higher education declined from 97 to 66 per cent.

Figure 4.5 shows that, by itself, the compression of the educational
structure of wages would have reduced the inequality of pay in the
Republic of Korea.[33] And, by itself, the change in the educational
composition of the wage labour force would have increased the
inequality of pay. The compression effect, however, dominated the
composition effect. The net effect of educational expansion was to
reduce substantially, by 22 per cent, the log variance of wages.

Table 4.3: Male wage structure in Brazil and the Republic of Korea

	Brazil		Republic of Korea	
	1976	1985	1976	1985
Primary schooling	0.488	0.449	0.176	0.092
	(55.68)	(67.23)	(19.66)	(7.54)
Secondary schooling	0.958	0.886	0.473	0.296
	(85.70)	(110.53)	(48.19)	(23.40)
Tertiary schooling	1.593	1.508	0.969	0.655
	(100.22)	(127.40)	(71.48)	(42.06)
Employment experience	0.045	0.048	0.067	0.078
	(64.97)	(83.91)	(61.90)	(69.61)
Employment experience	-0.0006	-0.0007	-0.001	-0.001
	(61.41)	(79.27)	(39.13)	(50.27)
Constant	1.149	7.043	10.231	11.779
R^2	0.546	0.562	0.532	0.449
N	85,106	118,000	23,838	24,486
Mean log of wages	1.864	8.095	11.363	12.895

Note: Dummy variables were included to control for region, occupation, industry and head of household (Brazil only). T-statistics are in parentheses.

Source: Author's calculations.

In Brazil the proportion of workers with secondary or higher education increased as rapidly as in the Republic of Korea, but from a smaller base. Hence the absolute increment to the labour force of relatively well educated workers was so small that it did not take much of an increase in the demand for educated workers to offset any wage compression effect. Meanwhile, the educational structure of wages barely changed in Brazil (table 4.3). For example, the wage premium earned by university leavers was 159 per cent in 1976 and 151 per cent in 1985.[34]

Brazil did not benefit from a wage compression effect, and the impact on pay inequality of changes in the educational composition of the labour force was substantial (figure 4.5). By itself, the composition effect would have increased the log variance of wages by 8.1 per cent. The net effect of educational expansion in Brazil over the decade was an increase in the log variance of wages by roughly 4 per cent, in marked contrast to the 22 per cent decline in Korea. What would the inequality of pay in Brazil have been had educational policy resulted in educational attainment comparable to that in the Republic of Korea in the mid-1980s? Simulations (*CB** in figure 4.5) indicate that Brazil would have had a log variance of wages in the mid-1980s about 17 per cent lower than the actual. This 17 per cent reduction represents more than one-quarter of the gap in the log variance of wages between Brazil and the Republic of Korea.

WHY MIGHT LOW INEQUALITY STIMULATE GROWTH?

Rapid human capital accumulation contributes to low inequality. Does low inequality, in turn, stimulate growth? The conventional wisdom has long held that there is a tradeoff between augmenting growth and reducing inequality. There are two common explanations given for the view that an unequal distribution of income is necessary for, or the likely consequence of, rapid economic growth. First, following Kaldor (1978), since a high level of savings is a prerequisite for rapid growth, income must be concentrated in the hands of the rich, whose marginal propensity to save is relatively high.[35] Second, following Kuznets (1955), as labour shifts from a low productivity sector to a high productivity sector, aggregate inequality must first increase substantially and then, later, decrease.

Robinson (1976) observed that this pattern had "acquired the force of economic law". Few economists today would make so extreme a statement.[36] The recent experience of east Asia casts more doubt on the conventional wisdom. The countries of east Asia have had rapid growth over three decades, with relatively low levels of income inequality. And though evidence on the magnitude of the changes in income inequality is fragile, most east Asian countries have almost certainly achieved reductions in income inequality.[37]

The east Asian nations adopted productivity-enhancing policies, such as emphasizing basic education, that simultaneously reduced poverty and income inequality, and stimulated growth. By contrast, using income transfers, public ownership and regulation to reduce income inequality is not good for growth: transfers often result in the diversion of scarce savings from investment to the subsidization of consumption; the targeted group is often not the one that benefits from transfers, reducing the effectiveness of transfers as a means of raising the standard of living, and hence the saving and investment rates, of the poor; and transfers tend to distort incentives and reduce both allocative and x-efficiency. Similarly, the negative dynamic consequences of public ownership and heavy regulation are likely to outweigh any direct positive benefits reaped by the poor. Conversely, education and other policies that increase the productivity and earning capacity of the poor may be a different matter.

Consider four sets of hypotheses regarding the ways in which low inequality can stimulate growth.

Contributing to political and macroeconomic stability

Low inequality can, for example, reduce the government's tendency to sacrifice fiscal prudence for political expediency, discourage inappropriate exchange rate valuation and accelerate adjustment to macroeconomic shocks.[38, 39]

If the incomes of the elite increase rapidly, while the incomes of non-elites stagnate, a large proportion of the population may become politically alienated. Declining inequality implies that non-elites are sharing in the benefits of economic growth. This reduces the risk of their political alienation, legitimizes the government in the eyes of most of the population and helps build broad-based political support.

A more stable political environment is conducive to economic growth: investment is likely to be higher where the risk of economically disruptive political upheaval and the expropriation of private assets is reduced. The likelihood that policies will swing between the extreme of serving the narrowly defined, myopic interests of the elite[40] and an equally myopic populist extreme [41] is lower where there is broad-based political support for the government.[42]

Low inequality can also contribute to macroeconomic stability by strengthening resolve to avoid exchange rate overvaluation. A myopic, self-serving elite that is not concerned with the welfare of the poor will favour overvaluation of the exchange rate (Sachs, 1985). Overvaluation will reduce the price of imports, which the urban dwelling elite has a high propensity to consume, at the expense of agriculture, where the poor are concentrated, and other export-oriented sectors, thereby worsening the distribution of income.

In addition, overvaluation is likely to exacerbate external imbalance—a common cause of macroeconomic instability. A government that places high priority on raising the incomes of the poor is less likely to discriminate against agriculture and other exportables in this way. East Asian countries have avoided an appreciating real exchange rate so common in other regions.[43] Stable exchange rates eased the task of containing inflation and limiting internal and external debt to manageable proportions.

The ability to respond quickly to unanticipated shocks is another link between income distribution and macroeconomic stability. To respond quickly, a government must have the political legitimacy that comes from substantial popular support and, closely related, it must have enough power to act independently, not needing to gain approval for each major initiative.

Those in the bottom half of the distribution of income are more likely to be willing to share the burden of adjustment to a negative shock if the short-run consequence is a decline in the rate of growth of their incomes, rather than in the absolute level of their incomes.[44] Sharing the burden means that government will be better able to adjust domestic absorption by reducing consumption while protecting investment. If incomes of the poor are not rising or rising very slowly, a reduction of wages or subsidies as a means of reducing domestic absorption, even if to promote long-term growth, is more likely to provoke a strong negative reaction, which could lead to political and economic disruption.

Increasing the x-efficiency of low-income workers

Children from low-income households learn from experience that no matter how great their effort, in competing for rewards for academic excellence such as access to university places, they cannot compensate for the low quality of their schools and are thus unlikely to make an extra effort. By contrast, poor children in high-quality schools who see tangible rewards for effort are more likely to work hard.

Similarly, extra effort is unlikely to be forthcoming from low-income workers or farmers who, because of policy biases, face economic incentives that do not reward effort. They are more likely to shirk and to become resentful and alienated. By contrast, if economic incentives do reward effort, they are likely to respond.[45] Though difficult to quantify, the increases in productivity associated with low inequality may be large. The work ethic of east Asian children and adults is well known and may be less an exogenous cultural trait than an endogenous response to incentives that reward effort.

Raising rural incomes

Increasing rural incomes limits inter-sectoral income gaps and the rent-seeking associated with such gaps, and increases the domestic multiplier effects of a given increase in per capita income. As a result of policies that contribute to, rather than sap, the dynamism of the agricultural sector, societies with low income inequality will generally have a smaller gap between rural and urban income, and a relatively better-off rural population.[46] Hence, the pressure to generate make-work jobs in the high-wage urban public sector is reduced, as are the negative consequences for growth of an expanding "job sink".[47] The small rural-urban income gap also implies a relatively weak Kuznets effect—that is, the tendency for the inter-sectoral transfer of labour, which results from the rapid growth of output and employment in the sector manufacturing export goods, to induce greater income inequality is not as strong.

Higher income in the rural and agricultural sectors also means higher demand for agricultural inputs and consumer goods, which can then stimulate the growth of non-agricultural output and employment. In Taiwan (province of China), for example, in the 1950s and early 1960s agriculture, not manufacturing for export, was clearly the "leading sector", and roughly 60 per cent of the increment to aggregate demand was domestic. More generally, among Asian countries there is a strong positive correlation between the growth rate of the agricultural sector and the growth rate of the non-agricultural sector (Mellor, 1993). This relationship suggests that the multiplier effects of agricultural growth on manufacturing, construction and services are large: a 1 per cent increase in agricultural growth is associated with a 1.5 percentage point increase in the growth rate of the non-agricultural sector.[48]

Because the relatively simple manufactured inputs and consumer goods demanded by rural residents are generally more efficiently produced with labour-intensive techniques, the employment effects of these increases in demand are amplified.[49] By contrast, when the incomes of the urban elite increase, the tradeables on which they spend their increased income tend to be capital-intensive goods. Given high inequality, the domestic demand for labour-intensive goods tends to remain relatively weak. In east Asia, however, strong domestic demand may have given early manufacturers a competitive advantage in international markets by giving them the opportunity to test-market labour-intensive goods and achieve economies of scale.

Inducing large increases in the savings and investments of the poor

Liquidity constraints can keep the poor from investing even when expected returns are high. We see below how reducing inequality increases investment in education by easing such constraints. I am suggesting that the higher is the absolute income of the poor, the smaller is the negative impact that the capital market imperfection —which prohibits borrowing to finance investment in human capital —has on their investment rate. This implies that where income inequality is low, the positive association between income and saving rates may not be as strong as Kaldor presumed or national income data indicate. The data capture only savings channeled through financial intermediaries, not the increased investments in human capital that result from eased liquidity constraints.[50]

Let me elaborate on the savings linkage between low inequality and rapid growth. The key idea, as discussed by Birdsall, Pinckney and Sabot (1995), is that an improvement in the rate of return to investment opportunities for households that are unable to borrow can lead to decreased leisure, increased work effort, increased current income and the devotion of *all* of the increase in income to savings. Alternatively, given high returns to investment, an increase in the demand for, and returns to, labour can have the same effect. In addition, consumption will generally decline to help finance the investments. In effect, the marginal propensity to save from the increment in current income can be greater than 100 per cent.[51] This turns Kaldor's idea about the relative propensity to save of people at different income levels on its head: richer households who do not face borrowing constraints do not exhibit this behaviour. Such a response, if widespread among the poor, could form a substantial proportion of total domestic savings and simultaneously increase growth and reduce inequality. This phenomenon appears to have played a role in the equitable growth achieved in east Asia.

In analyzing savings and investment decisions made by households in industrial countries, economists typically distinguish between the determinants of savings and the determinants of investment. Financial intermediation enables households to finance current investments that exceed desired current savings, and to have net gains in interest-bearing financial assets in years that desired savings are greater than desired investments. These observations have led to the development of permanent income and life cycle models of savings behaviour, in which saving in any one year is influenced by current income—considered to be exogenous—but over the long run households save in productive years to provide income for future unproductive years.

The validity of life cycle and permanent income models is being questioned in high-income countries (Deaton, 1992b). They are less relevant still in developing countries. A large number of households in developing countries are multi-generational, and many of today's adults expect their children to support them when they grow older, just as they are supporting their parents (Deaton, 1990). Such households may have no need for "hump" or retirement savings, either as a vehicle for transferring income between high- and low-productivity phases of the life cycle or as a means of transferring wealth between generations. In this context the non-investment motivation for savings is that it acts as a buffer against stochastic decreases in income.

Deaton (1990, 1992a) develops a model that examines the savings behaviour of such households.[52] Deaton's model, however, does not consider the investment motivation for saving. In the absence of financial intermediation, savings must approximately equal investment at the household level—which implies that the expected returns to investment will be the "interest rate" relevant for determining savings (McKinnon, 1973). Thus in low-income countries, where the poor have no profitable opportunities for holding financial assets, an improvement in the opportunity for high-return investments will directly increase incentives for saving (as opposed to indirectly through increased demand for loanable funds and consequent increases in interest rates, as in industrial countries). Schultz (1964) makes this point in his classic volume on agriculture in order to explain the low savings rates observed in the absence of profitable investment opportunities.[53]

These poor households, however, can increase the share of present income that they allocate to savings only if they make substantial sacrifices. There are few luxuries to cut out of consumption bundles that are already scanty. Such considerations have led many long-time observers of development to conclude that substantial increases in savings will occur only among the highest income groups: the poor will consume any increments to their present income.

But although the poor are likely to have high rates of time preference given the pressing nature of their demands for cash, by definition, an investment with a rate of return higher than the rate of time preference will be attractive. A change in investment opportunities that results in a significantly higher return—which might arise from the development of a new agricultural technology, a new crop for the region, an improvement in the quality of local schools or an increase in the demand for educated labour—can lead a substantial number of households to perceive that the return to investment is higher than the rate of time preference. This realization consequently increases the need for savings. But given borrowing constraints and high demands for current consumption, what is the potential source of such savings?

Savings may come in part from decreased consumption and also from additional work effort, displacing leisure. Current income is then not an exogenous determinant of current savings, but a function of the perceived return to saving, which equals the perceived return to investment. This response has not been considered by other investigations of the impact of increases in investment opportunities. In such circumstances the marginal savings rate of the poor can be greater than one, and the percentage of all income saved, measured as a percentage of total income prior to the expansion of investment opportunities, can be exceptionally large.[54]

It is important to note, however, that the increase in income and the amount of investment will be large only if there are opportunities to increase current income by putting forth additional work effort. The marginal productivity of additional labour must decline slowly enough to allow for an increase in current income from decreased leisure. Increases in the demand for labour—hence in returns to labour—can thus enable large increases in savings and investment. On the other hand, if at the margin returns to labour decline rapidly, time devoted to labour will increase only slightly, necessitating that most of the increase in savings come from a decrease in current consumption. Given that for the poor small declines in consumption are likely to increase the marginal utility of consumption substantially, only small increases in savings would result from improvements in investment opportunities in such environments.

Examining inequality and growth: econometric results

Birdsall, Ross and Sabot (1995) assess econometrically the relationship between income distribution and economic growth in a cross-section of countries. That analysis builds on the results reported by Barro (1991). I review those results and, to illustrate the magnitude of the relationship, use those results to quantify the effect of Brazil's high level of income inequality on economic growth. Birdsall, Ross and Sabot assembled country observations from a variety of sources on the ratio of the income shares of the top 40 per cent and the bottom 20 per cent of the population. They chose the earliest available observation and dropped observations if the measure post-dated 1970. This procedure yielded a data set with 74 observations. The addition of the inequality measure to the basic Barro growth rate function (reported in equation 3 of table 4.1) does not change the parameter estimates substantially. The education variables remain significantly positive. The inequality variable is negative and significant (at the 10 per cent level). Thus controlling for other determinants of growth, inequality and subsequent economic growth are inversely related.[55]

How big a constraint on growth is high inequality? For the sample of low- and middle-income countries the average annual growth in per capita GDP between 1960 and 1985 was 1.8 per cent. A one standard deviation increase in primary and secondary education raises growth rates by 0.62 and 0.34 of a percentage point, respectively. A one standard deviation decrease in the level of income inequality raises the predicted growth rate by 0.32 of a percentage point. Although the impact on growth of a change in inequality is smaller than that of similar changes in enrollment rates, the effect of reducing inequality is still substantial. For example, ceteris paribus, after 25 years GDP per capita would be 8.2 per cent higher in a country with low inequality than in a country with inequality one standard deviation higher.

Moreover, as we will see below, the low enrollment rates in countries with high inequality were due in part to the constraint on the demand for schooling imposed by high inequality. The higher is inequality, the lower are enrollment rates likely to be, suggesting a still larger gross constraint of high inequality on economic growth. Crude though the data and methods may be, this evidence supports the hypothesis that low inequality in east Asia stimulated growth and that the impact was large.[56]

DETERMINANTS OF THE INTER-REGIONAL GAP IN EDUCATIONAL PERFORMANCE

The combination of a lower supply of and demand for educated workers contributed to slow growth in several regions. I focus on four factors that help explain why the performance of basic educational systems have been so much weaker in Latin America and, by implication, elsewhere than in east Asia.

The feedback from growth to human capital accumulation

In east Asia there was positive feedback from rapid growth and altered household behaviour to human capital accumulation. Elsewhere, this feedback was much weaker. Figure 4.4 illustrated one of the feedback mechanisms. Absent skill intensification of labour demand, diminishing returns result from educational expansion.

Households' investment in human capital is greater in east Asia than elsewhere partly because the demand for educated workers is greater, and, consequently, the returns to investment in schooling are higher.[57] Stronger demand for educated workers elicits a greater supply.

The other feedback mechanism is equally simple: in the ratio of public expenditures on basic education per school-age child, rapid economic growth in east Asia increased the numerator while declining fertility reduced the denominator. Neither in 1960 nor in 1989 were public expenditures on education as a percentage of GNP much higher in east Asia than in other regions. In 1960 the share was 2.2 per cent for all developing countries and 2.5 per cent for east Asia. Over the three decades all regions increased markedly the share of national output they invested in formal education—to 3.6 per cent for all developing countries and 3.7 per cent for east Asia.[58]

In short, it was not extraordinary government commitment that produced east Asia's extraordinary performance with respect to the provision of education.[59] By the same token, poor educational performance elsewhere can not be blamed solely on a lack of government commitment to education. It is obvious, however, that the more rapid is the growth of aggregate output, the more rapid is the growth of the constant share of GDP that goes to education. For example, from 1965 to 1980 GDP growth averaged 7.4 per cent in Malaysia and 3.4 per cent in Argentina. These figures imply that between 1965 and 1975, given that a constant share of GDP was allocated to education, the resources available to the education sector in Malaysia more than doubled, while in Argentina they increased by less than 50 per cent.[60]

In 1970 public expenditures on basic education per eligible child was not much higher in the Republic of Korea ($95 in 1987 dollars) than in Mexico ($68) (table 4.4).[61] But between 1970 and 1989 they more than quadrupled in Korea, to $433, whereas in Mexico they did not even double. As a consequence, in 1989 Mexican public expenditures on basic education per eligible child was only 26 per cent of Korean expenditures per eligible child. What accounts for this divergence? Again, it was not government commitment—public expenditures as a percentage of GNP during this period declined in

Table 4.4: Public expenditures on basic education per eligible child
and some determinants, 1970–89

Country	Expenditures on basic education	Public expenditure	Index	Number of eligible children (thousands)
Republic of Korea				
1970	95.3	3.1	100	10,274
1975	81.6	1.9	91	10,754
1985	357.1	3.8	388	10,420
1989	433.4	2.7	444	9,848
1970–89	354.7	-12.9		-2.2
Mexico				
1970	68.4	1.6	100	1,168
1975	124.9	2.6	222	19,746
1985	113.5	2.0	255	21,912
1989	111.9	2.0	259	26,649
1970–89	63.6	25.0		58.6
Kenya				
1970	38.6	4.0	100	3,814
1975				4,591
1985	46.6	4.9	220	6,973
1989	53.4	4.9	286	7,900
1970–89	38.3	22.5		107.1
Pakistan				
1970	7.9	1.1	100	20,983
1975	9.4	1.6	150	26,563
1985	13.4	1.6	277	34,414
1989				42,249
1970–89				101.1

Note: Absolute expenditures on basic education in real 1987 US dollars used to calculate indices for absolute expenditures on education. Number eligible for basic education calculated using enrollment rates and number of students in the first and second levels

Source: UNESCO, various years; World Bank, various years, for real gross national income figures.

Korea and rose in Mexico. The absolute level of expenditures on basic education rose much more rapidly in Korea because GNP was growing so much faster than in Mexico. Moreover, while in Mexico the number of children eligible for basic education increased by nearly 60 per cent, in Korea the school-age cohort was 2 per cent smaller in 1989 than in 1970.[62]

Inequality and the demand for schooling

Relatively low levels of educational attainment in regions other than east Asia contributed to above-average levels of income inequality.

There has also been a feedback effect, closing a vicious circle, from high inequality to low enrollment rates. High income inequality limits household demand for education and probably lowers public supply.

As discussed above, because of budgetary constraints and capital market imperfections, poor households often do not make human capital investments in their children even when returns are high. The pressing need to use income simply to subsist crowds out high-return investments and constrains the demand for education.

We can pair east Asian countries with others that have similar levels of average per capita income, but considerably higher levels of income inequality, hence considerably lower absolute incomes of the poor (table 4.5). For example, while the per capita income of Brazil (in 1983) slightly exceeded average income in Malaysia (in 1987), the bottom quintile of the Malaysian population received 4.6 per cent of total income and that of the Brazilian population only 2.4 per cent. The per capita income of the bottom quintile in Brazil was thus only 54 per cent of the income of households at the bottom of the income distribution in Malaysia. Given an income elasticity of demand for secondary education of 0.5 (a conservative figure), if the distribution of income was as equal in Brazil as in Malaysia, secondary enrollments among poor Brazilian children would be at least 40 per cent higher. There is some evidence that among the poor the income elasticity of demand for basic schooling exceeds 1.0, in

Table 4.5: Per capita income of the poor and secondary enrollment rates

Country	Year	Per capita income (dollars per annum)	Income share, bottom 20 per cent	Per capita income, bottom 20 per cent	Secondary school enrollment rate (per cent)
Indonesia	1976	240	6.6	79	21
Kenya	1976	240	2.6	31	17
Malaysia	1987	1810	4.6	416	59
Costa Rica	1986	1480	3.3	254	42
Brazil	1983	1880	2.4	226	35
Korea, Republic of	1976	670	5.7	191	88
Botswana	1986	840	2.5	115	31
Indonesia	1987	450	8.8	251	47
Philippines	1985	580	5.5	160	68

Source: World Bank, various years.

which case secondary enrollments among poor Brazilian children would be at least 80 per cent higher. Table 4.5 indicates that, in all cases but one, the country with lower inequality has higher secondary enrollment rates.

A variable measuring inequality in the distribution of income was added to an analysis of the determinants of differences in secondary enrollment rates among countries.[63] The income distribution variable had the predicted effect: more egalitarian societies had higher secondary school enrollment rates.[64] The estimated equation was used to decompose the difference in enrollment rates between Brazil and the Republic of Korea. The decomposition indicates that not any of the 27 percentage point difference can be explained by GNP per adult (table 4.6). Nor do less costly teachers contribute to the explanation, as teacher pay relative to GNP per capita was also lower in Brazil. The larger size of the school-age cohort in Brazil explains a small proportion of the gap.

Nearly all of the portion of the gap that can be explained is due to

Table 4.6: Why were commitments to secondary education so different in the Republic of Korea and Brazil in the early 1970s?

Variable	Mean value of variables for:		Difference in mean values (ΔX_j)	Regression coefficients $(\beta_{xj})^a$	Predicted impact of differences in means $(\beta_{xj}\Delta X_j)$
	Republic of Korea	Brazil			
Enrollment ratio	0.620	0.349	+0.271		
Log GNP per adult	6.800	6.904	-0.104	0.313 (2.379)	-0.033
Log relative price teachers	0.360	-0.538	+0.898	-0.457 (5.272)	-0.410
Urban ratio	0.494	0.582	-0.088	0.346 (0.608)	-0.030
School-age population ratio	0.149	0.159	-0.010	-1.860 (0.809)	+0.019
Bottom 40%/top 20%	0.373	0.105	+0.268	0.796 (1.234)	+0.213
'Culture' = Residual					+0.512

[a.] $R^2 = 0.831$; t-statistics in parentheses.

Source: Williamson (1993).

the greater inequality in income distribution in Brazil.[65] If income was distributed as equally in Brazil as in the Republic of Korea, instead of being 27 percentage points higher, Korea's secondary enrollment rate is predicted to be only 6 percentage points higher. The cross-country evidence is consistent with the microeconomic evidence: the impact of differences in income inequality on enrollment rates can be large.

The model of savings behaviour by the poor, discussed above, suggests some explanations, rooted in development strategy, of why enrollment rates are so high (and dropout and repetition rates so low) in the Republic of Korea, while enrollment rates are so low (and dropout and repetition rates so high) in Brazil. Korea's export-oriented, labour-demanding growth strategy raised the marginal return of the labour of the poor, making it attractive to increase time allocated to work to finance high-return investments in their children. Public policy also ensured high quality schooling, even in poor districts, thereby contributing to the high rates of return to investment in schooling. The labour-demanding growth path became increasingly skill-intensive over time—yet another factor contributing to high expected rates of return to schooling and hence strong household demand. In sum, in Korea there were strong incentives for the poor to invest in their children and to work more to finance that investment. It is reasonable to suppose that marginal savings rates among the poor were exceptionally high.[66]

By contrast, in Brazil the inward-looking growth strategy was not very labour-demanding and thus the returns to additional labour time allocated to work were quite low. In addition, school quality for the poor tended to be abysmal. Although the average returns to investment in schooling were high, for the poor returns to investment in schooling were low. Lack of dynamism in the demand for labour and skills also held down expected returns to investment in schooling. In sum, Brazilian public policy created incentives for high levels of leisure and low levels of saving among the poor.

High income inequality may have an influence on the supply side as well as the demand side of the market for education. For the government to provide subsidized basic education for a large segment of the school-age population when the distribution of income is highly unequal, the tax burden on the rich must be heavy. High-income families are likely to resist such measures and attempt to channel subsidies to higher education, where their children will be the beneficiaries. If incomes are more equally distributed, as in east Asia, the incidence of taxes to finance mass education need not be as concentrated, and resistance to such programmes by high-income families is likely to be weaker.

The allocation of public expenditures among education levels

While public expenditures on education as a share of GNP are not significantly lower in other regions compared with east Asia, the share of public expenditures on education allocated to basic education has been consistently lower, which helps to explain why opportunities for basic education are less abundant and of poorer quality in other regions. The lower share of public resources for education allocated to basic education may be a function of high inequality in the distribution of income.

The Republic of Korea and Venezuela are extreme examples. While in 1985 Venezuela allocated 43 per cent of its public education budget to higher education, Korea allocated only 10 per cent of its budget to post-secondary schooling (Birdsall and Sabot, 1993). Public expenditures on education as a percentage of GNP were actually higher in Venezuela (4.3) than in Korea (3.0). After subtracting the share going to higher education, however, public expenditures available for basic education as a percentage of GNP were considerably higher in Korea (2.5) than in Venezuela (1.3).

By giving priority to expanding quantity and improving quality at the base of the educational pyramid, east Asian governments stimulated the demand for higher education, while relying to a large extent on the private sector to satisfy that demand. In both east Asia and in other regions the probability of going to university is markedly higher for secondary school graduates from high- than from low-income families. Typically, government subsidization of university education is not related to need, implying that subsidies disproportionately benefit families with relatively high incomes who could afford to pay fees closer to the actual cost of schooling.

At the same time, in many countries, Brazil being a notable example, low public funding of secondary education forces poorly qualified children from low-income backgrounds into the private sector or entirely out of the education system. Because of the higher concentration of resources on basic education, in east Asia public funds for education are more likely to benefit children of low-income families who, otherwise, might have difficulty remaining in school. In east Asia large numbers of poor children benefit from public expenditures, whereas in other regions, small numbers of children from relatively high-income families benefit: the public cost of providing a student with instruction is roughly 50 times higher at the university than at the primary level (Schultz, 1988).

Administrative inefficiency

Expenditures per child in basic education are higher in east Asia than in other regions. In addition, administrative inefficiency is greater in other regions. Brazil provides a notable example of a country using resources inefficiently, thus undermining school quality. The main problem is overstaffing. In Brazil state education systems commonly employ nearly half of all state government employees—the recruitment of education staff is driven by patronage rather than efficiency. The ratio of non-teaching to teaching staff varies substantially across different state systems, and high ratios (a 2:1 ratio of non-teachers to teachers is not uncommon) are correlated with low completion and high repetition rates. In east Asia the objective of staffing decisions tends to be the improvement of student learning, whereas in Brazil maximizing public employment often appears to be the dominant goal (Birdsall, Bruns and Sabot, 1996).

CONCLUSIONS

Human capital accumulation has been an important dimension of development strategy in east Asia and a contributing factor to the difference in economic performance between east Asia and other regions. Over the last three-and-a-half decades east Asian nations have succeeded in simultaneously increasing the quantity of basic education provided to children and improving the quality of schooling. In other regions there has been a tradeoff: as enrollments have increased at a slower rate than in east Asia, the quality of schooling has eroded.

Assessments based on both microeconomic data and cross-country comparisons indicate that the difference in educational performance helps to explain why east Asia has grown so much faster than other regions. The labour force in east Asia is better endowed with productivity-enhancing cognitive skills than the labour force elsewhere and is better able to acquire technological capability. In east Asia the growth payoff to investments in education has been enhanced by the export-oriented, labour- and skill-demanding growth strategy, which has sustained returns to human capital even while educational systems have been expanding rapidly. Rapidly rising levels of educated women have changed household behaviour by, for example, reducing fertility, which has also stimulated growth. Development strategy in other regions has been less export-oriented and less labour- and skill-demanding—and the growth payoff to investments in education has been lower. The education of women has lagged, as have growth-augmenting changes in household behaviour.

Superior educational performance also contributes to the explanation of lower income inequality. Increases in the relative abundance of educated workers eroded the scarcity rents that they could command in the labour market. While the absolute wages of educated workers grew, the gap in wages between the more and less educated narrowed, contributing to substantial declines in the inequality of pay. Moreover, cross-country growth regressions suggest that lower income inequality was itself a stimulus to growth in east Asia, whereas elsewhere high inequality was frequently a constraint to growth.

East Asia's superior educational performance was not a function of a larger share of GNP spent on education. Rather, it appears to be due to the positive feedback from more rapid growth to larger expenditures on education, to the allocation of substantially larger shares of public expenditures on education to basic education, to markedly slower rates of growth of the school-age population and to the greater administrative efficiency of education systems. The positive feedback from low inequality to high rates of investment in human capital among the poor may have been a particularly important factor.

Human capital accumulation in east Asia offers important lessons for governments in other regions as they design policies to increase the growth payoff of investments in education. Simply raising the share of GNP allocated to public expenditures on education is unlikely to be sufficient to raise educational performance in other regions to the east Asian level. Indeed, in many countries where educational performance lags, public expenditures on education as a share of GNP are higher than in east Asia.

In many countries increased expenditures per pupil, particularly in schools attended predominantly by the poor, are essential for the improvement of school quality. But because of the complex relationships between inputs and outputs (learning) in schools, there is no master plan to follow to improve quality. Nevertheless, improvements in quality may save as much, or more, in recurrent expenditures, as they cost. Reallocating public resources devoted to education and increasing the efficiency of the educational system, while shifting to a more labour- and skill-demanding, inequality-reducing growth path are more likely to yield sustainable improvements in education performance than a simple commitment to raise the share of GNP devoted to educational expenditures.

NOTES

Presented at the Second Meeting of the United Nations High Level Group on Development Strategy and Management of the Market Economy held at the International Institute of Applied Systems Analysis, Laxenburg, Austria, April 20–22, 1995. I am grateful to participants in the meeting and to the referees for helpful comments. I am also grateful to Nancy Birdsall, David Ross and Coty Pinckney, co-authors of works on which I draw heavily in this chapter, and to Rebecca Foster for able assistance. The views expressed are those of the author.

1. African countries, too, are concentrated in the south-east quadrant. Diamond-rich Botswana, where both growth and inequality are high, is an exception. South Asian countries show low growth and low inequality. But the low inequality in these countries was achieved not by the market-oriented policies

adopted in east Asia, but by transfers, public ownership and regulation, and thus may not have had the same stimulative impact on growth.

2. The rapid growth in the east Asian region is unparalleled. Eight high-performing Asian economies not only outperformed the industrial economies since 1960 but also grew at rates higher than those that today's high-income countries experienced during their earlier periods of rapid growth. Since 1960 the gap in per capita income between a substantial majority of developing countries and the industrial nations has been increasing. By contrast, the east Asian economies are catching up, or converging. The decline in poverty and income inequality in east Asia has been equally remarkable. The percentage of people below the poverty line fell far more rapidly in east Asia than in other regions (see World Bank, 1993). While declines in inequality are more difficult to document, measures such as the gini coefficient show improvements in the distribution of income in each of the high-performing Asian economies between 1965 and 1990 (see World Bank, 1993).

3. The analysis I describe was conducted by Behrman and Schneider and presented in two papers, Behrman and Schneider (1991) and Behrman and Schneider (1992). The regressions control for average per capita income in the relevant year. Similar regressions were estimated with primary enrollment rates as the dependent variable, and similar results were obtained.

4. No African countries and only two south Asian countries were included in figure 4.2. However, numerous countries from those regions were included in the regressions.

5. While inequality of access by socioeconomic background is higher, inequality of access by gender is nearly as low in Latin America as in east Asia.

6. For a discussion of inefficiency and its impact on school quality in Brazil, see Birdsall and Sabot (1996).

7. The gap between the socioeconomic status of children who attended primary school in Latin America in the 1950s and the children who attended in the 1980s is large. It is not surprising that more, not fewer, inputs per child are needed to achieve the same level of cognitive achievement.

8. Of course, factors other than school quality will also influence the probability of dropping out. Most notably, as the opportunity cost of schooling rises with the age of the child, the incentive to continue to send the child to school declines, particularly for poor families.

9. Birdsall and Sabot (1996). The divergent trends in dropout rates could also be due to the fact that Korea's growth path was steeper and more labour- and skill-demanding than Brazil's. This difference generated higher rates of return to a given quality of schooling in Korea than in Brazil.

10. Spending per primary student in municipal systems in the rural north-east averages only $50 per year. In these schools there is typically money for only the teacher's salary, which is below the minimum wage. See Hanushek, Batista Gomes-Neto and Harbison (1996).

11. Behrman and Birdsall (1983) provide evidence of high external rates of return to investments in quality improvement in Brazil.

12. The characteristics of low-quality schools in rural Pakistan are similar to those in rural Brazil.

13. The estimates control for the selectivity of schooling and labour force participation, and the simultaneity of the human capital investment and labour force decisions.

14. Curriculum diversification into agricultural subjects at the primary level in Tanzania was one factor explaining why Tanzanian children acquired fewer cognitive skills than Kenyan children with the same ability and years of schooling. Language policy was another factor: in Kenya children were taught in one language throughout their school years; in Tanzania Swahili was the language of instruction in primary school and English in secondary school. See Knight and Sabot (1987).

15. Clark (1940) and Kuznets (1966) were pioneers in this effort. More recently, Chenery and Syrquin (1975) provided a comprehensive description of the structural changes that accompany the growth of developing countries.

16. See Barro (1991). He estimates equations to explain variation in the growth rate of real per capita income over 1960–85 in 98 countries. Among the explanatory variables, he includes the level of per capita GDP in 1960 and education enrollment rates in 1960, a crude proxy for the initial stock of human capital.

17. Similarly, if Korea had had Brazil's 1960 enrollment rate, its growth rate would have been 5.6 per cent rather than 6.1 per cent, resulting in a 1985 per capita GDP 11.1 per cent less than Korea actually attained.

18. There is substantial multicollinearity affecting the estimators of the primary-school enrollment coefficients in our models. Taken individually, the coefficients on the enrollment variables are indistinguishable from zero. However, a joint F-test rejects the null hypothesis that both primary-school enrollment coefficients are zero. The estimated equation differs from Barro's in that it drops the revolution and assassination variables and adds nine additional observations. All other coefficients are qualitatively unchanged.

19. Results are available on request. The relevant test statistics are $F_{2,101} = 8.16$ and $F_{1,101} = 0.001$, respectively. Barro and Lee (1993) have conducted a similar exercise. Their results show that the impact on growth of educating girls is smaller. Why their results differ from ours has yet to be determined.

20. See also Behrman (1991) and Schultz (1991) for detailed reviews of the evidence from developing countries. See Birdsall, Ross and Sabot (1992) and Sathar (1988) for evidence from rural Pakistan.

21. They are also more efficient users of health services for themselves and their children. They send children to school who are already better prepared to benefit from society's schooling investment, and they are more likely to send their own daughters to school. See Summers (1992).

22. There has been concern that Africa is different, that education of women does not have as great an impact on fertility there as elsewhere. However, Ainsworth, Beegle and Njamete (1996) have recently confirmed a strong negative relationship in 14 sub-Saharan countries.

23. Rapid growth of exports led to rapid growth of output from the manufacturing sector, which, in turn, stimulated demand for labour. In essence, as the labour demand curve shifted out, employment increased, and wages were pulled up. The rapid rise in wages was also a consequence of a slowdown in the rates of population and labour force growth (see Banerji, Campos and Sabot, 1996).

24. The horizontal axis measures the magnitude of human capital investment, as proxied, for example, by enrollment rates in basic education. The vertical axis

measures the rate of return to human capital investment (schooling) and, implicitly, for a given level of human capital investment, the contribution of investment to growth.

25. The supply function S' is more elastic because a more equal distribution of income, hence less absolute poverty, relative to the typical developing country enables families near the bottom of the distribution of income to be more responsive to increases in returns to human capital investments (see below).

26. Labour demand in east Asia has become increasingly skill-intensive, largely in response to the greater abundance of educated labour, and consequent declines in its relative price, and changes in comparative advantage. East Asian exporters shifted into more technologically sophisticated and more capital- and skill-intensive goods as rapidly rising wages of unskilled labour eroded international competitiveness in labour-intensive manufactured goods. As a share of wage employment, white collar and technical employment increased steadily during the 1970s and the 1980s, for example in the Republic of Korea from 29 per cent in 1980 to 36 per cent in 1990 or, in Taiwan (province of China) from 32 to 40 per cent over the same period. See Birdsall and Sabot (1993).

27. In doing so, they build on evidence that increases in the share of manufactured exports in output are associated not only with increases in the share of physical capital investment in GDP and the rate of economic growth, and hence in the derived demand for labour and skills, but also for a given rate of output growth with greater labour-and skill-intensity of production.

28. When the interaction term is added to the basic Barro growth regression, both the interaction variable and the educational attainment variable are significant and positive. When the average share of exports in GDP is added as a separate independent variable, the educational attainment variable remains positive and significant, but both the interaction term and the separate export share variable, though positive, are insignificant. However, there is a high degree of multicollinearity between the interaction term and the average ratio of manufactured exports to GDP, and an F-test rejects the null hypothesis that, taken jointly, the coefficients on the three variables (education, the interaction term and exports) are not significantly different from zero. Likewise, and more importantly, an F-test rejects the null hypothesis that, taken jointly, the coefficients on the interaction term and the export variable are not significantly different from zero.

29. The view that reduced inequality is a positive externality of investment in education is frequently used as a justification for government subsidization of basic education. See Knight and Sabot (1991).

30. The composition effect is analogous to the Kuznets (1955) effect, which results from the inter-sectoral transfer of labour.

31. See Birdsall and Sabot (1993). As I suggest below, the causality could run from low inequality to high enrollment rates.

32. Korea and Brazil have both achieved universal primary education. There has, however, been a large and widening gap between Brazil and Korea in secondary and tertiary enrollment rates.

33. Increases in the supply of educated workers outstripped increases in demand, despite the fact that demand for educated workers increased dramatically.

34. Because educational expansion compressed substantially the educational structure of wages in Korea but not in Brazil, the gap in premia between the two increased over the decade.

35. Kaldor assumed that a high proportion of profits and a low proportion of wages are saved.

36. Indeed, 20 years ago, prior to fulfillment of east Asia's remarkable potential, Ahluwalia (1974) concluded on the basis of the cross-country data then available, "there is no strong pattern relating changes in the distribution of income to the rate of growth of GNP,... This suggests that there is little firm empirical basis for the view that higher rates of growth inevitably generate greater inequality". Nearly all of the studies cited by Anand and Kanbur (1993) providing empirical evidence of an inverted *U*-shape relationship between inequality and per capita income were conducted in the 1970s. However, they demonstrate the sensitivity of the estimated relationship to changes in functional form and choice of observations.

37. Though controversial, the evidence suggests that unlike many other developing countries during this period, income distribution in east Asian countries either improved or, at the very least, did not worsen. See World Bank (1993).

38. By macroeconomic stability I mean that inflationary spending is kept under control, internal and external debt remain manageable and the macroeconomic crises that result from unanticipated shocks are quickly resolved.

39. Persson and Tabellini (1991) argue that where distributional conflict is greater, the incentives for individuals to accumulate knowledge are weakened. Alesina and Rodrik (1991) argue that democracies with a more unequal distribution of capital ownership will grow less rapidly than more egalitarian democracies, because the median voter has a relatively small endowment of capital when wealth is unequally distributed and thus favors high taxes on capital.

40. The substantial allocation of limited fiscal resources for tertiary education, so common in Latin America, is an example of a fiscal policy from which the children of the elite benefit disproportionately, but that contributes little to growth. The government, in essence, subsidizes the consumption of high-income families: since private returns to, and the resulting demand for, tertiary education are high, the elite would have undoubtedly been willing and able to pay to provide this schooling for their children in the absence of subsidies.

41. The provision by many governments of make-work jobs in the public sector in attempt to satisfy the excess demand for high-wage employment is an all-too-common example of populist policies. Because in these circumstances wages in the public sector are generally higher than the marginal product of labour, which may be zero or even negative, this excess employment is heavily subsidized and diverts scarce savings from high-return investments to consumption. See Gelb, Knight and Sabot (1991).

42. Such policy swings, much more common in regions other than east Asia, increase economic uncertainty and thereby reduce investment. Policies at each extreme also tend to divert scarce resources directly from high-return investments to consumption.

43. World Bank (1993, chapter 3). Why did east Asian governments avoid overvaluation while governments elsewhere were so much more prone to the problem? Sachs (1985) suggests that the greater political power of rural areas, which have a stake in a low exchange rate, was a factor. For example, he notes

that the proportion of the population living in urban areas in 1980 was markedly higher in Latin America, 72 per cent, than in east Asia, 31.5 per cent. See Birdsall and Sabot (1993). The political power of the rural population in east Asia was reinforced by the threat of communist insurgency.

44. Mazumdar (1993) notes that as part of the Republic of Korea's adjustment to the first oil shock "the unit cost of labor was reduced by a massive 25 percent", largely accounted for by currency devaluation. He goes on to observe that "even this amount of decline of the real share of labor did not imply a fall in the real wage. Rather, the wage increase in 1975 was held down to 1.4 percent compared with the annual wage increase in excess of 10 percent in 1966–73". By contrast, in Latin America adjustment generally entailed the erosion of real wages.

45. Timmer (1995), for example, argues that improving incentives to the agricultural sector has been shown to increase agricultural productivity because the rural poor respond with greater work effort and investment.

46. A larger share of public investment was allocated to rural areas in east Asia than in Latin America. Equally important, levels of direct and indirect taxation of agriculture were lower in east Asia. See World Bank (1993 pp. 32–7). More generally, Timmer (1994) notes that "it has been long established that, for a given level of per capita income, a higher share of GDP originating in agriculture contributes to a more equal distribution of income".

47. Similarly, lower inequality is likely to reduce the need for institutions, regulatory and otherwise, that are intended to benefit the poor, but which often instead reduce output and employment.

48. The relationship also implies that the faster agriculture grows, the faster its share of total output declines. Again, with the exception of the east Asian city-states, the Asian countries with the fastest rates of growth of agricultural output over the last 30 years have tended to experience the biggest declines in the share of agricultural output in GNP.

49. See Ranis and Stewart (1987). A detailed study of these backward and forward linkages in the Muda River region of Malaysia provides microeconomic confirmation of the magnitude of the inter-sectoral multiplier suggested by the cross-country relationship. See also Bell, Hazell and Slade (1982).

50. There may be a similar effect on other investments of the poor, for example, in agriculture or small enterprises, though this effect is more likely to be reflected in measured investment rates.

51. This argument does not imply that poor people are poor because they choose to be (that they could supply more labour but decide not to). Rather, it implies that poor people are poor because either the returns to labour at the margin are too low to justify additional effort or because the returns to investment are less than their discount rate.

52. Deaton's model also assumes that households cannot borrow because "at least for some households, borrowing restrictions are real and necessary to explain what we observe" (Deaton, 1990).

53. The rate of return on investments can have an impact on saving even if households can keep financial savings, earning positive nominal interest rates. Bevan, Collier and Gunning (1989) observe that during the coffee boom coffee farmers in Kenya had access to savings facilities through their cooperative societies. These facilities paid negative real interest rates, however, causing

farmers to hold savings in those accounts only until they were able to make a profitable investment.

54. The long-run dynamics of this behaviour can lead to virtuous circles of investment and increases in income through reductions in rates of time preference. Since the poor in general have a high rate of time preference, increasing their income through greater work effort should, over time, lower this rate. Other investment opportunities then become attractive to these households, which save and invest more in order to match savings to desired investment.

55. Of course, this assumes that any variables omitted from the growth equation are not correlated with the income distribution variable.

56. These results do not imply that using income transfers to reduce inequality will stimulate growth. Such transfers tend to be growth-constraining. Rather, Birdsall, Ross and Sabot (1995) suggest that growth would benefit from policies that reduce inequality by eliminating consumption subsidies for the rich and by increasing the productivity of the poor.

57. In figure 4.4, S_1–S_2 is the difference between the typical east Asian country and country X in the level of investment in human capital induced by greater demand for educated labour.

58. See Birdsall and Sabot (1993) for data sources. Government expenditures on education, expressed as a percentage of GNP, was used as an explanatory variable in a cross-country regression in which expected years of schooling of the school-age cohort (essentially an aggregate of enrollment rates) was the independent variable. For a sample of 15 Asian and Latin American countries the expenditure variable was insignificant. See Tan and Mingat (1992).

59. Nor were initial conditions—the colonial legacy—decisive in explaining why enrollment rates were so much higher in east Asia than elsewhere. While the Republic of Korea had much higher enrollment rates in 1950 than did most other developing countries, the roughly 50 and 70 percentage point increases since then in, respectively, primary and secondary enrollment rates, account for much of the current gap between Korea and other middle-income countries. Similar claims can be made for other east Asian countries.

60. Of course, rapid growth also raises the demand for labour, hence wages and, in particular, the wages of teachers. Because teachers' pay accounts for a large proportion of recurrent expenditures on education in low-income countries, the tendency for rising costs to reduce the benefits of rapid growth would be strong, except for an important mitigating factor. Rapid accumulation of human capital in one period increases the potential supply of teachers in the next, thereby reducing the relative earnings premium teachers command. While growth is inducing increases in average wages, the wages of more educated workers, including teachers, tend to rise at a slower rate.

61. In fact, in 1975 expenditures per eligible child were higher in Mexico than in Korea.

62. The difference in fertility rates, of which these diverging trends are a reflection, is in part due to differences in educational attainment, particularly the educational attainment of women.

63. See Williamson (1993), who builds on the analysis of Schultz (1988). The income distribution variable used was the ratio of the share of total income of the bottom 40 per cent of the population to the share of total income of the top 20 per cent. Among the other variables in the regression were GNP per capita,

a measure of teacher cost relative to GNP and the share of the population that is school-age.

[64.] In the equation in which expenditure per eligible child was the dependent variable, the income distribution variable was statistically significant. In the enrollment rate equation the *t*-statistic on the distribution variable was somewhat lower than that conventionally accepted for significance. See Williamson (1993).

[65.] Williamson attributes the unexplained portion of the enrollment rate gap, the residual, to a cultural bias against education in Brazil. Alternatively, it could be due to lower quality schooling in Brazil, hence lower expected returns and lower demand. Of course, any meaning attributed to the residual is speculative.

[66.] Data provided by Angus Deaton indicates that in Taiwan (province of China), where incentives for the poor to save were also strong, saving rates of the poorest quintile of households, as conventionally measured, rose from 12.9 per cent in 1977 to 33.8 per cent in 1990.

REFERENCES

Ahluwalia, M. 1974. "Income Inequality: Some Dimensions of The Problem." In H. Chenery, Montek Ahluwalia, Clive Bell, John Duloy and Richard Jolly, eds., *Redistribution With Growth*. New York: Oxford University Press.

Ainsworth, Martha, Kathleen Beegle and Andrew Nyamete. 1996. "The Impact of Women's Schooling on Fertility and Contraceptive Use: A Study of Fourteen Sub-Saharan Countries." *World Bank Economic Review* 10(1):85–122.

Alesina, Alberto and Dani Rodrik. 1991. "Distributive Politics and Economic Growth." NBER Working Paper 3668. Cambridge, Mass.

Anand, S. and R. Kanbur. 1993. "Inequality and Development: A Critique." *Journal of Development Economics* 41(3):19–43.

Banerji, A., E. Campos and R. Sabot. 1996. "The Political Economy of Pay and Employment in Developing Countries." In J. Edward Taylor, ed., *Development Strategy Employment and Migration*. Paris: OECD Development Center.

Barro, Robert J. 1991. "Economic Growth in a Cross-Section of Countries." *Quarterly Journal of Economics* 106(May):407–43.

Barro, Robert J. and Jong Wha-Lee. 1993. "International Comparisons of Educational Attainment." Paper presented at the conference "How Do National Policies Affect Long-run Growth?" World Bank, Washington, D.C., February.

Becker, Gary S. 1964. *Human Capital. A Theoretical and Empirical Analysis*. Princeton: Princeton University Press.

Becker, Gary S., Kevin M. Murphy and Robert Tamura. 1990. "Human Capital, Fertility, and Economic Growth." *Journal of Political Economy* 98(2): S12–S37.

Behrman, Jere. 1991. "Investing in Female Education for Development: Women in Development Strategy for the 1990s in Asia and the Near East." Working paper RM-129. Department of Economics, Williams College, Williamstown, Mass.

Behrman, Jere and Nancy Birdsall. 1983. "The Quality of Schooling: Quantity Alone is Misleading." *American Economic Review* 73 (December):228–46.

Behrman, Jere, David Ross, Richard Sabot and M. Tropp. 1994. "Improving the Quality Versus Increasing the Quantity of Schooling." Working paper RM-140. Department of Economics, Williams College, Williamstown, Mass. Processed.

Behrman, Jere and Ryan Schneider. 1991. "How Do Pakistani Schooling Investments Compare with Those of Other Developing Countries?" Department of Economics, Williams College, Williamstown, Mass. Processed.

____. 1992. "An International Perspective on Schooling Investments in the Last Quarter Century in Some Fast-Growing Eastern and Southeastern Countries." World Bank, Washington, D. C.

Bell, Clive, Peter Hazell and Roger Slade. 1982. *Project Evaluation in Regional Perspective*. Baltimore: Johns Hopkins University Press.

Berry, A. and W. Cline. 1979. *Agrarian Structure and Productivity in Developing Countries*. Baltimore: Johns Hopkins University Press.

Bevan, David, Paul Collier and Jan Willem Gunning. 1989. *Peasants and Governments: An Economic Analysis*. Oxford: Clarendon.

Birdsall, Nancy, Barbara Bruns and Richard Sabot. 1996. "Education Policy in Brazil: Playing a Bad Hand Badly." In Nancy Birdsall and Richard Sabot, eds., *Opportunity Foregone: Education in Brazil*. Baltimore: Johns Hopkins University Press.

Birdsall, Nancy, John Page Jr., David Ross and Richard Sabot. 1993. "Education and Economic Growth: Increasing Supply is Not Enough." World Bank, Washington, D.C.

Birdsall, Nancy, Thomas C. Pinckney and Richard Sabot. 1995. "Income Inequality, Savings and Growth." Department of Economics, Williams College, Williamstown, Mass.

Birdsall, Nancy, David Ross and Richard Sabot. 1992. "Underinvestment in Education: How Much Growth has Pakistan Foregone?" *The Pakistan Development Review* 3(4):18–35.

Birdsall, Nancy and Richard H. Sabot. 1993. *Virtuous Circles: Human Capital Growth and Equity in East Asia*. Washington, D.C.: World Bank.

____. 1995. "Inequality and Growth Reconsidered: Lessons from East Asia." *World Bank Economic Review* 9(3):477–508.

____. eds. 1996. *Opportunity Foregone: Education, in Brazil*. Baltimore: Johns Hopkins University Press.

Chenery, Hollis and Moises Syrquin. 1975. *Patterns of Development, 1950–1970*. New York: Oxford University Press.

Clark, Colin. 1940. *The Conditions of Economic Progress*. London: Macmillan Press.

Clarke, George. 1992. "More Evidence on Income Distribution and Growth." World Bank Working Paper Series 1064. Washington, D.C.

____. 1990. "Savings in Developing Countries: Theory and Review." In *Proceedings of the First Annual World Bank Conference on Development Economics*. World Bank: Washington, D.C.

Deaton, Angus. 1992a. "Household Savings in LDCs: Credit Markets, Insurance and Welfare." *Scandinavian Journal of Economics* 94(2):253–73.

____. 1992b. *Understanding Consumption*. Oxford: Clarendon.

Gelb, Alan, John Knight and Richard Sabot. 1991. "Public Sector Employment, Rent-Seeking and Economic Growth." *Economic Journal* 101(408):1186–99.

Hanushek, Eric. 1989. "The Impact of Differential Expenditures on School Perfor-
mance." *Educational Researcher* (May):45–52.
Hanushek, Eric, João Batista Gomes-Neto and Ralph Harbison. 1996. "Efficiency
Enhancing Investments in School Quality." In Nancy Birdsall and Richard Sabot,
eds., *Opportunity Foregone: Education in Brazil*. Baltimore: Johns Hopkins
University Press.
Hanushek, Eric, with Richard Freeman, Henry Levin, Richard Murnane, Richard
Sabot and Anita Summers. 1994. *Making Schools Work: Improving Performance
and Controlling Costs*. Washington D.C.: The Brookings Institution.
International Labour Office (ILO). Various years. *Yearbook of Labour Statistics*
(annual). Geneva: International Labour Office.
Kaldor, Nicholas. 1978. "Capital Accumulation and Economic Growth." In
Nicholas Kaldor, ed., *Further Essays on Economic Theory*. New York: Holmes
and Meier Publishers, Inc.
Knight, John and Richard Sabot. 1983. "Educational Expansion and the Kuznets
Effect." *American Economic Review* 73(5):1132–36.
_____. 1987. "Educational Policy and Labour Productivity: An Output Accounting
Exercise." *Economic Journal* 97(385):199–214.
_____. 1991. *Education, Productivity, and Inequality*. New York: Oxford University
Press.
Kuznets, Simon. 1955. "Economic Growth and Income Inequality." *American
Economic Review* 45(March):1–28.
_____. 1966. *Modern Economic Growth*. New Haven: Yale University Press.
Levine, Ross and David Renelt. 1991. "A Sensitivity Analysis of Cross-Country
Growth Regressions." World Bank Working Paper Series 609, Washington, D.C.
Lucas, Robert E. Jr. 1988. "On the Mechanics of Development Planning." *Journal
of Monetary Economics* 22(2):3–42.
Mazumdar, Dipak. 1993. "Labour Markets and Adjustment in Open Economies:
The Republic of Korea and Malaysia." *World Bank Economic Review* 7(3).
McKinnon, Ronald L. 1973. *Money and Capital in Economic Development*.
Washington, D.C.: The Brookings Institution.
Mellor, John, ed. 1993. "Agriculture on the Road to Industrialization." International
Food Policy Research Institute, Washington, D.C.
Nelson, Richard and Edmund Phelps. 1966. "Investment in Humans, Technological
Diffusion, and Economic Growth." *American Economic Review* 56(1):69–75.
Park, Young-Bum, David Ross and Richard Sabot. 1992. "Educational Expansion
and the Inequality of Pay in Brazil and Korea." Working Paper RM-146.
Department of Economics, Williams College, Williamstown, Mass.
Persson, Torsten and Guido Tabellini. 1991. "Is Inequality Harmful for Growth?
Theory and Evidence." NBER Working Paper 3599. Cambridge, Mass.
Ranis, Gustav and Frances Stewart. 1987. "Rural Linkages in the Philippines and
Taiwan." In Frances Stewart, ed., *Macro-Policies for Appropriate Technology in
Developing Countries*. Boulder: Westview Press.
Robinson, Sherman. 1976. "A Note on the *U*-Hypothesis." *American Economic
Review* 66(3):437–40.
Romer, Paul. 1990. "Endogenous Technological Change." *Journal of Political
Economy* 98(3): S71–S102.
Sachs, Jeffrey. 1985. "External Debt and Macroeconomic Performance in Latin
America and East Asia." *Brookings Papers on Economic Activity*. 93–121.

Sathar, Zeba, et al. 1988. "Women's Status and Fertility Change in Pakistan." *Population and Development Review* 14(1):415–32.

Schultz, T. Paul. 1988. "Education Investment and Returns." In Hollis B. Chenery and T. N. Srinivasan, eds., *Handbook of Development Economics*. Amsterdam: North Holland Publishing Company.

____. 1991. "Returns to Women's Education." In E.M. King and M.A. Hill, eds., *Women's Education in Developing Countries*. Baltimore: Johns Hopkins University Press.

Schultz, T.W. 1961. "Investment in Human Capital." *American Economic Review* 51(1):1–17.

____. 1964. *Transforming Traditional Agriculture*. New Haven: Yale University Press.

Squire, Lyn. 1981. *Employment Policy in Developing Countries: A Survey of Issues and Evidence*. New York: Oxford University Press.

Summers, Lawrence H. 1992. "Investing in All the People." World Bank, Washington D.C.

Tan, Jee-Peng and Alain Mingat. 1992. *Education in Asia: A Comparative Study of Cost and Financing*. Washington, D.C.: World Bank.

Timmer, C. Peter. 1994. "Population, Poverty and Policies." *American Economic Review* 84(2):12–20.

____. 1995. "Getting Agriculture Moving: Do Markets Provide the Right Signals?" *Food Policy* 20(5):455–72.

United Nations Educational, Scientific and Cultural Organization (UNESCO). Various years. *Statistical Yearbook* (annual). Paris: UNESCO.

Williamson, J. 1993. "Human Capital Deepening, Inequality and Demographic Events along the Asia-Pacific Rim." In Naohiro Ogawa, Gavin W. Jones, and Jeffrey Williamson, eds., *Human Resources in Development along the Asia-Pacific Rim*. Singapore: Oxford University Press.

World Bank. Various years. *World Tables* (annual). Washington, D.C.: World Bank.

____. 1993. *The East Asian Miracle*. New York: Oxford University Press.

5

Some Thoughts on Equitable Development

GERT ROSENTHAL

During the first meeting of the United Nations High Level Group on Development Strategy and Management of the Market Economy its members decided that their future work should address initially issues of economic planning and policy at the national level, and that it would focus on eight interrelated clusters of issues. I was asked to prepare a brief analytical chapter on one of those clusters—the one dealing with the possibility of increased inequality and aggravated social exclusion in economies that are growing rapidly, using open, market-friendly policies. The implementation of policies aimed at promoting better social integration was grouped under the heading "participatory development".

As the Secretariat of the United Nations was reminded during the preparatory work for the World Summit for Social Development, the general concern for achieving more equitable and participatory development—the fashionable term today is "people-centred development"—opens up a wide array of topics, and thus spills over into the other clusters of issues identified by the Group. It therefore raised the question of how to address such a broad subject in a brief chapter meant to enrich the Group's discussion. One possibility was to focus on the participatory approach based on empowerment of excluded social groups, which has given rise to a large body of literature in the past decade (Ghai, 1988; Wignaraja and others, 1991; Schneider, 1995). But because the main thrust of the Group's inquiry relates to the blend of state and market, the following remarks are centered more on highlighting the issues concerning the attempt of government policies and institutions to blend equity (distributional) and efficiency (growth) objectives in the development process.

THE THEORETICAL EVOLUTION OF GROWTH AND EQUITY

The links between income growth and income distribution have been the subject of inquiry since the time of Adam Smith and David Ricardo. Then, no distinction was made, of course, between developing and industrial countries. But the classical tradition was followed by authors who took that distinction into account, notably Sir Arthur Lewis (1954). The stylized parameters of the classical analytical framework are as follows. Economic growth requires capital accumulation and savings. Only the upper-income groups are capable of saving, and inequitable income distribution is therefore necessary to generate higher levels of saving, investment and growth. Growth spurred by capital formation and technical progress results mostly in higher profits (rather than in higher wages, given the "unlimited supply of labour", as argued by Lewis), thus perpetuating the income-concentrating effects of growth. As the economy grows and there are more goods to distribute, and as surplus labour is gradually exhausted, wages begin to rise and everyone benefits (the "trickle-down" effect).

This line of reasoning led to the idea that a lopsided income distribution and a high incidence of poverty were more or less inevitable in the development process. In fact, inequality was perceived to be a "good thing", because it was thought to be necessary to generate higher levels of saving and capital accumulation—and thus greater growth. Economists were led to believe that there were trade-offs between achieving optimum growth and improving income distribution. But there was a light at the end of the tunnel: if economic growth was allowed to proceed untrammelled, in the end everyone would be better off. That, at least, had been the experience of the now-wealthy countries from the industrial revolution through the 1960s (Kuznets, 1966).

The Keynesian and then the post-Keynesian revolutions (or, rather, the revolution and the counter-revolution), introduced many refinements into the classical analytical framework. New models explaining the process of growth were concerned with not only the amount of capital accumulated but also the type of capital accumulated. Moreover, economists recognized that innovation and organizational capacity have played increasingly important roles in explaining that process (Denison, 1985; Leibenstein, 1987; Olson, 1988). Today we think of growth not only as the expansion of productive capacity through investment in physical capital, but also in terms of production functions, market imperfections, institutional restrictions and the impact of international economic relations on economic performance. We recognize that investment in human capital (especially education) is a crucial element in explaining both efficiency and patterns of income distribution (Schultz, 1961, 1981).

After World War II economists further recognized that the dynamics of income distribution in industrial and developing countries were very different—meaning that the degree of people's participation in the economy varied significantly. Some of the important distinctions between and within these groups of countries were found in the degree of organization of workers (reflected in the possibility of undertaking collective bargaining for wages), the distribution of assets (especially land), the structure of industrial and agrarian economies, the empowerment of different groups in society, the forms of political interaction in democratic and authoritarian societies, the capacity of public institutions to translate policy objectives into concrete actions, the population's level of education and awareness, and demographic patterns.

Still, the suspicion lingers among some economists that there is some kind of fundamental trade-off between efficiency and equity. On the other hand, many economists have questioned the conceptual framework itself, arguing that equity and efficiency can be achieved simultaneously. Recently, some authors have tried to demonstrate that, at least in the case of industrial countries with democratic political systems, inequality is actually harmful to growth (Persson and Tabellini, 1994). In the case of developing countries the premise that worsening income distribution inevitably accompanies sustained economic growth has also been questioned (Chenery and others, 1974; World Bank, 1990; ECLAC, 1992). Thus, the interaction of economic growth and income distribution opens up a host of conceptual and practical issues.

A FOCUS ON GROWTH WITH EQUITY

Discussions over whether or not it is desirable to achieve growth and improve income distribution simultaneously gradually faded—to the point where the development literature of the 1960s insisted that growth was not enough to generate "development". Qualitative changes in the structure of the economy and improvements in income distribution were equally important. In the 1980s these arguments were taken one step further. The focus shifted to the realization of human potential, expressed in terms such as "human dignity", "self-respect", "social emancipation" and "enhancement of moral, intellectual and technical capabilities". (This broader definition of development is compatible with the participatory approach). This focus sets development issues squarely in the arena of policy-making, since distributional goals affect the content and scope of economic and social policies.

Some defend this focus on ethical, moral and political grounds, while others, as already mentioned, argue that greater equality actually leads to greater growth, and vice versa. Many call for deliberate policies to mitigate the potentially regressive effects of economic growth. They include land reform and progressive taxation and public expenditure, especially in the provision of health care and education. In the 1970s targeting expenditure towards the poor—to meet basic needs—received much attention (Streeten, 1984, 1989). More recently, the strategy of choice has been to further the creation of employment opportunities for the poor in conjunction with the provision of basic social services and the promotion of their participation in political and economic decision-making (World Bank, 1990; ECLAC, 1992).

This rather heterogeneous set of results is the basis of a major debate in the realm of public policy (Oman and Wignaraja, 1991). Is the popular premise that "the market has no social conscience" true?[1] Do specific public policies mitigate the possible regressive effects of market-oriented growth? Or is it the other way around: do public policies actually reinforce those regressive effects, unintentionally or otherwise? And even if some public policies do mitigate those regressive effects, what is their cost in terms of potential growth forgone? These are some of the issues that have been debated over the past 40 years, without reaching definitive answers (although revealing some important clues). They clearly fall into the arena of defining the role of public action.

In fact, equity considerations were a main justification to "tamper" with the market, even in industrial economies. Since the classical framework showed a strong regressive bias in market-led growth, interventions were considered to be the antidote. During the first three decades after World War II increasing reliance was placed on policy-making—especially in the field of public finance—as an effective way to achieve distributional objectives, among others. The idea persisted that the more countries relied on market signals to allocate resources and to guide the actions of firms and individuals, the higher was the probability that income distribution would deteriorate.

EMPIRICAL EVIDENCE ON GROWTH AND
INCOME DISTRIBUTION

Today, there is a wealth of empirical evidence on patterns of growth and income distribution. But despite the abundant literature relating the incidence of taxation to income distribution, doubts persist as to the causal relationships between different sets of policies and outcomes in terms of efficiency and equity. Many countries bear out the classical prediction that the distribution of income tends to become more concentrated in the early stages of development. Many countries also bear out the prediction that as growth continues, its benefits are spread more widely. In fact, by the mid–1970s there was enough empirical evidence to support almost any argument, depending on the group of countries and the time-span selected for analysis. In some developing economies that were growing, the poor received little benefit, while in others the opposite was true (Chenery and others, 1974).

Empirical evidence has continued to mount in the past decade— during which market orientation and openness have overshadowed the interventionist practices of the past. For example, considerable evidence has accumulated since the 1970s that there has been a secular deterioration in income distribution in the United States and in the United Kingdom, apparently aggravated by the market-friendly policies promoted by President Ronald Reagan and Prime Minister Margaret Thatcher (Krugman, 1990; Thurow, 1980; Johnson and Webb, 1993). In the United States the share of the richest 25 per cent of the population in total national income increased from 48.2 per cent to 51.3 per cent between 1980 and 1992, while the share of the poorest 25 per cent dropped from 7.6 per cent to 6.5 per cent. In fact, the real per capita income of the poorest 25 per cent actually declined by almost 7 per cent during this period (United States Council of Economic Advisers, 1989, 1994). In the United Kingdom the gap between the richest and poorest also widened significantly during the 1980s, but the real income of the poorest 20 per cent of the population did not decline (*The Economist,* September 12, 1992, p. 63).

Similar observations have been made in numerous Latin American and African countries, especially those that applied "open and market-friendly policies" in an effort to adjust to a rapidly changing international environment (World Bank, 1990; ECLAC, 1993, 1994a; UNDP, 1994). But it is difficult to determine whether these policies increased inequality or created a higher incidence of poverty, or whether these conditions were the (predictable) result of a profound and protracted recession.

Of the 10 Latin American countries that offer comparable indicators for the early and late 1980s, income inequality increased in eight (the exceptions were Colombia and Uruguay). In all of these countries the relative share of national income of the poorest quartile of households went down, while the relative share of the richest 10 per cent of households went up (ECLAC, 1994a, table 18, pp. 152–3).

Further, the incidence of absolute poverty rose between 1980 and 1990 after having decreased in the previous decade. This trend was observed in most countries, especially during the first half of the 1980s. Again, Colombia and Uruguay and, to a lesser degree, Costa Rica and Chile were the exceptions among 14 countries. In the aggregate the incidence of poverty in Latin America increased from 41 per cent in 1980 (136 million people) to 46 per cent in 1990 (196 million people) (ECLAC, 1993, table 20, p. 100). It is interesting to note that since the early 1990s, with resumed economic growth, these trends appear to be reversing.

But there are other regions in which a large group of countries simultaneously achieved rapid economic growth, declining income inequality and reduced poverty—and, to boot, high levels of investment and saving—over a protracted period of time. There is some justification for the World Bank's characterizing this feat as "the making of a miracle" (World Bank, 1993). It is probably the performance of these countries that accounts for the World Bank's relatively optimistic assessment that "the 1980s—often called the 'lost decade' for the poor—did not, in fact, reverse the overall trend of progress. The incomes of most of the world's poor went on rising, and ... other social indicators also continued to improve" (World Bank, 1990, p. 1).

LESSONS FROM THE PAST

Thus the most fascinating task in analyzing the empirical evidence is to try to isolate those factors that have helped to enhance or, conversely, to obstruct relatively more participatory patterns of development. Some of the lessons of the past decades include the following.

A stable macroeconomic context is a precondition, though not a guarantee, of growth (Fisher, 1991). Moreover, there is ample evidence that excessively unequal income distribution retards progress and accentuates social and political instability, adversely affecting investment and growth (Larraín and Vergara, 1992). Economic and political stability has come to be seen as a central component of the development process, meaning that social equity must be suitably incorporated into economic policy and development options. This calls for an integrated approach to economic and social policies that emphasizes, in the first, those instruments and measures that are most compatible with social equity, and, in the second, not only social development in and of itself but also its contribution to efficiency and growth.

The capacity of nations to shape their own destiny is largely associated with the *choice of sound policies*. The ability to distinguish good policies from bad ones, regardless of ideological differences, probably represents one of the advances towards consensus in that field (Williamson, 1993). Of the various areas requiring sound macroeconomic management, experience has demonstrated the decisive importance of sustainable fiscal balances and realistic exchange rates (Fishlow and others, 1994; Summers and Thomas, 1993).

The proper *blend of state and market* in the economy remains a decisive factor in development, and successful countries have employed a pragmatic combination of the two that makes the most of their complementarities and the specific advantages of each. Development of the market requires state action to strengthen markets (Streeten, 1993), to foster competition, to substitute for markets where they are not operative and to "complete" markets that are underdeveloped (ECLAC, 1994b). The state must also support distributional objectives through public expenditures, including some targeting of said expenditures to benefit vulnerable groups (Cornia, Jolly and Stewart, 1987).

In this respect the central issue is not a question of intervention versus laissez faire, but rather a question of the *proper division of responsibilities* between the state and market, and of efficiency. Consider that one of the keys to successful government intervention has been the discipline imposed by international competition (Summers and Thomas, 1993).

Public policies can contribute to more equitable growth both at the macroeconomic and the microeconomic levels. At the macroeconomic level probably the main contribution of public policies, together with promoting a stable environment that attracts investment, lies in *fostering investment in human capital and physical* infrastructure, which have positive externalities and for which private investment is inadequate. Market failure—negative spillovers, pollution, congestion, overuse of natural resources—justifies intervention, but intervention must be guided by market-friendly criteria and must carefully consider "government failure" (Datta-Chaudhuri, 1990). Orienting growth towards the external sector, with low levels of protection and the elimination of anti-export biases, enables countries to profit from economies of scale, technological externalities, access to better-quality factors of production and higher levels of foreign investment—all of which translate into optimal conditions for increasing total factor productivity.

At the microeconomic level, *selective interventions to support higher levels of productivity*—such as through facilities for training, the development of infrastructure, access to credit and technical assistance—while unpopular with proponents of "the market", still play a useful role, especially where small and medium-size enterprises are concerned.

Increased productivity is, in effect, the key to the differences in income growth between countries and is related to the central role of *disseminating technical progress* in productive activities. Technical progress does not take place in an institutional void, nor is it exogenous to growth—it involves a learning process that can be stimulated by appropriate policies and institutions (Lucas, 1988; Stiglitz, 1987).

Successful experiences are marked by the *development of institutional capacities* that promote growth. This process includes improving the functioning of the market, modernizing public institutions and establishing institutional mechanisms to promote consensus-building and medium-term agreement among different agents, thereby reducing uncertainties.

Competitiveness can be promoted with institutional arrangements that foster consensus-building among different actors which paves the way for innovation and the establishment of cooperative relations in business and between public and private agents. The current debate on economic development highlights the important role of institutions in that process (Williamson, 1994; Doeringer and Streeten, 1990). An efficiently-run state, competitive markets, secure property rights and stable rules of the game form the basic institutional framework for strengthening competitiveness. These institutional arrangements can also lead to institutional innovations for cooperating and competing, such as the promotion of business associations for productive development, alliances between large and small firms, subcontracting and linkages within enterprises and between the private and public sector. This debate also reflects the ideas on organizational change and the new industrial paradigm that appear in studies on the behaviour of firms (Porter, 1980; Lawrence and Dyer, 1983); economies of scale or of scope (Chandler, 1977; Elbaum and Lazonick, 1986); business strategies (Bluestone and Harrison, 1982; Piore and Sabel, 1984); the product cycle (Norton, 1986); and the working environment (Kieschnick, 1981; Wheaton, 1979).

Economic growth models since the 1960s have conceived of *innovation* as a public good that can be stimulated with appropriate policies and institutions (Arrow, 1962). This idea is in line with studies on technological change and labour relations in industrial economics, which note that the main obstacle to innovation is non-cooperative relations within firms (Solow, Dertouzos and Lester, 1989). These studies also highlight that a well-qualified, flexible and motivated workforce is a critical input for technological innovation—that is, firms must create a climate of cooperation and openness to participation and innovation. This feature will increasingly become crucial to competitive performance.

There is ample scope for promoting growth and equity at the *grass-roots level*, meaning scope for promoting a participatory approach based on empowerment and self-reliance of excluded social groups. Appropriate policy measures include decentralizing governmental machinery by transferring decision-making powers to lower-level organs or to the community (Hirschman, 1984). Such measures include extending credit to the poor (the Grameen Bank of Bangladesh is the most cited example), organizing the rural and urban poor (for example, home-based workers and casual labourers into trade-union-type associations), promoting peasant groups and rural workers' organizations and implementing land reform.

Finally, public policies must prevent or correct *damage to the environment*. This implies an inalienable public responsibility to adopt policies that build on the positive links between development and the environment, as well as policies that target specific problems requiring regulations and incentives to incorporate environmental variables into economic decision-making. The prices of goods and services must reflect their effective social cost, including the negative externalities of environmental pollution or degradation. Environmental sustainability is more compatible with competitiveness when it incorporates technologies that combine the preservation of the environment and take advantage of opportunities to market and export environmental technologies.

CONCLUSION

In summary, the current thinking on development is placing renewed emphasis on issues such as growth in the context of a stable market economy open to international trade; technological change and innovation, as pillars of competitiveness; investment in human resources—education, training and dissemination of knowledge—as the cornerstone of growth, equity and competitiveness; increased participation at the grass-roots level in the context of more open and democratic societies; and political stability, manifested in long-term social compacts that promote governance and social consensus-building among the main agents of development and environmentally sustainable development.

From this perspective social integration or cohesiveness and social consensus-building among different actors takes on more relevance and represents an endogenous means of promoting development. This view reflects traditional considerations of political stability, but also the fact that participation reduces uncertainty and stimulates investment; is in line with recent developments in the theory of economic growth, which emphasize learning and technological innovation and conceive of them as public goods that generate externalities and require a climate of cooperation among the agents of development; promotes the decentralization of power and the targeting of social policies; contributes to economic growth by enhancing governance and social consensus-building; and contributes to development not only by establishing stable rules of the game but also by furthering progress towards medium-term agreements and stimulating institutionalized cooperation among various actors.

NOTE

[1.] "It is no coincidence that the biggest increases in income inequalities have occurred in economies such as those of America, Britain and New Zealand, where free-market economic policies have been pursued most zealously. The collapse of communism may have proved Adam Smith's invisible hand to be a superior economic engine, but it is one that is still morally suspect to many who worry that economic rewards are not being shared adequately. For the market economy has no moral sensibility: income inequalities arise from the independent actions of individuals with different skills and assets who are rewarded according to what consumers and producers are prepared to pay." *The Economist* November 5, 1994, p. 19.

REFERENCES

Arrow, K. 1962. "The Economic Implications of Learning by Doing." *Review of Economic Studies,* 29(3):155–73.

Bluestone, B. and B. Harrison. 1982. *The Deindustrialization of America: Plant Closings, Community Abandonment and the Dismantling of Basic Industry.* New York: Basic Books, Inc.

Chandler, A.D., Jr. 1977. *The Visible Hand: The Managerial Revolution in American Business.* Cambridge, Mass.: MIT Press.

Chenery, H., S. Ahluwalia, C.L.G. Bell, J. Duloy and R. Jolly. 1974. *Redistribution with Growth.* New York: Oxford University Press.

Cornia, A., R. Jolly and F. Stewart, eds. 1987. *Adjustment with a Human Face: Protecting the Vulnerable and Promoting Growth.* Oxford: Clarendon Press.

Datta-Chaudhuri, M. 1990. "Market Failure and Government Failure." *Journal of Economic Perspectives* 4(3):25–39.

Denison, E.F. 1985. *Trends in American Economic Growth: 1929–1982.* Washington, D.C.: The Brookings Institution.

Doeringer, P. and P. Streeten. 1990. "How Economic Institutions Affect Economic Performance in Industrialized Countries: Lessons for Development." *World Development* 18(9):1249–54.

ECLAC (Economic Commission for Latin America and the Caribbean). 1992. *Social Equity and Changing Production Patterns: An Integrated Approach.* Santiago.

____. 1993. *Social Panorama of Latin America 1993.* Santiago.

____. 1994a. *Social Panorama of Latin America 1994* LC/G.1844. Santiago.

____. 1994b. *Latin America and the Caribbean: Policies to Improve Linkages with the Global Economy.* LC/G.1800 (SES.25/3). Santiago.

Elbaum, B.L. and W. Lazonik. 1986. *The Decline of the British Economy.* Oxford: Oxford University Press.

Fishlow, A., Catherine Gwin, Stephan Haggard, Dani Rodrik and Robert Wade. 1994. "Miracle or Design? Lessons from the East Asian Experience." Policy Essay 11, Overseas Development Council, Washington, D.C.

Fisher, S. 1991. "Macroeconomics, Development, and Growth." *NBER Macroeconomics Annual, 1991.* Cambridge, Mass.: National Bureau of Economic Research (NBER).

Ghai, D. 1988. "Participatory Development: Some Perspectives from Grass-Roots Experiences." Discussion Paper 5, United Nations Research Institute for Social Development, New York.

Johnson, P. and Steven Webb. 1993. "Explaining the Growth in UK Income Inequality: 1979–1988." *The Economic Journal* 103(March):429–35.

Hirschman, A. 1984. *Getting Ahead Collectively: Grassroots Experiences in Latin America.* New York: Pergamon Press.

Kieschnick, M. 1981. *Taxes and Growth: Business Incentives and Economic Development.* Washington, D.C.: Council of State Planning Agencies.

Krugman, P. 1990. *The Age of Diminished Expectations. US Economic Policy in the 1990s.* Cambridge, Mass.: MIT Press.

Kuznets, S. 1966. *Modern Economic Growth.* New Haven: Yale University Press.

Larraín, F. and R. Vergara. 1992. "Distribución del ingreso, inversión y crecimiento." *Cuadernos de economía.* Series 87. Pontificia Universidad Católica de Chile. Santiago:207–28.

Lawrence, P.R. and D. Dyer. 1983. *Renewing American Industry.* New York: The Free Press.

Leibenstein, H. 1987. *Inside the Firm.* Cambridge, Mass.: Harvard University Press.

Lewis, W.A. 1954. "Economic Development with Unlimited Supplies of Labour." *The Manchester School* 22(2):139–91.

Lucas, R. 1988. "On the Mechanics of Economic Development." *Journal of Monetary Economics* 22(1):3–42.

Norton, R.D. 1986. "Industrial Policy and American Renewal." *Journal of Economic Literature* 24(1):1–40.

Olson, M. 1988. "The Productivity Slowdown, the Oil Shocks, and the Real Cycle." *Journal of Economic Perspectives* 2(4):43–69.

Oman, C. and G. Wignaraja. 1991. *The Postwar Evolution of Development Thinking.* London: Macmillan Press.

Persson, T. and Tabellini, G. 1994. "Is Inequality Harmful for Growth?" *American Economic Review* 84(3):600–21.

Piore, M.J. and C. Sabel. 1984. *The Second Industrial Divide. Possibilities for Prosperity.* New York: Basic Books, Inc.

Porter, M.E. 1980. *Competitive Advantage.* New York: The Free Press.

Schneider, H. 1995. *Participatory Development: from Advocacy to Action.* Paris: OECD Development Centre.

Shultz, T. 1961. "Investment in Human Capital." *American Economic Review* 51(1):1–17.

_____. 1981. *Investing in People: The Economics of Population Quality*. Berkeley: University of California Press.

Solow, R., M.L. Dertouzos and R.K. Lester. 1989. *Made in America: Regaining the Productive Edge*. Cambridge, Mass.: MIT Press.

Stiglitz, J. 1987. "Learning to Learn, Localized Learning and Technological Progress." In P. Dasgupta and P. Storeman, eds., *Economic Performance and Technological Change*. Cambridge, Mass.: Centre for Economic Policy Research, Cambridge University Press.

Streeten, P. 1984. "Basic Needs: Some Unsettled Questions." *World Development* 12(9):973–8.

_____. 1989. "Poverty: Concepts and Measurement." Discussion Paper Series 26. Institute for Economic Development, Boston University, Boston, Mass.

_____. 1993. "Markets and States: Against Minimalism." *World Development* 21(8):1281–98.

Summers, L. and V. Thomas. 1993. "Recent Lessons of Development." *The World Bank Research Observer* 8(2):239–54.

Thurow, L.C. 1980. *The Zero Sum Society*. New York: Basic Books, Inc.

UNDP (United Nations Development Programme). 1994. *Human Development Report 1994*. Oxford: Oxford University Press.

United States Council of Economic Advisers. 1989. *Economic Report of the President 1989*. Washington, D.C.: United States Government Printing Office.

_____. 1994. *Economic Report of the President 1994*. Washington, D.C.: United States Government Printing Office.

Wheaton, W.C. 1979. "Metropolitan Growth, Unemployment, and Interregional Mobility." In *Interregional Movements and Regional Growth*. Washington, D.C.: The Urban Institute.

Wignaraja, P., A. Hussain, H. Sethi and G. Mignaraja. 1991. *Participatory Development: Learning from South Asia*. Oxford: Oxford University Press.

Williamson, J. 1993. "Democracy and the Washington Consensus." *World Development* 21(8):1329–36.

Williamson, O. 1994. "Institutions and Economic Organization: the Governance Perspective." *Proceedings of the World Bank Annual Conference on Development Economics*. Washington, D.C.: World Bank.

World Bank. 1990. *World Development Report 1990: Poverty*. New York: Oxford University Press.

_____. 1993. *The East Asian Miracle. Economic Growth and Public Policy*. New York: Oxford University Press.

PART THREE

INSTITUTIONS

6

The Role of Institutions in Economic Development

Y V E S B E R T H E L O T

It is now widely recognized that the determinants of economic growth cannot be reduced to the accumulation of production factors and technological progress. Over the past two decades researchers have sought to identify and analyze the "intangible" sources of growth, which are essentially institutional and organizational in nature. They include the regulatory environment, incentive schemes, the provision of public goods and policy-making within the public sphere, and, within the firm, labour management and business strategies that respond to the need for adapting managerial practices, skills and attitudes to technological change and to changes in the structure and scope of markets. This work has shown that institutional inefficiencies and organizational failures may be as damaging to growth as inefficient price structures or other forms of market failure (Doeringer and Streeten, 1990). Furthermore, as evidenced by the comparative historical research conducted by Morris and Adelman (1988), institutions play an important part in shaping the development process, because they play a crucial role in promoting growth and disseminating its benefits.

In practice, market orientation, globalization and deregulation partly overshadowed the importance of institutions in determining the direction and structure of economic development—and particularly the role of the state. But perceptions changed in the early 1990s as a result of several developments: the persistence of chronic problems in some developing countries, such as deficits, inflation, debt, deterioration of the civil service; continuing unemployment and increased poverty in some countries, despite the success of structural adjustment programmes in others; the difficulties encountered by eastern European countries in their transition to market economies; and, finally, the coexistence of highly productive economies and ever-greater social problems in industrial countries.

The need to cope with these problems has encouraged further thinking on the role of institutions and their effective functioning. Such thinking has to some extent crystallized around the concept of "good governance", which emerged in 1990. This concept highlights the need to establish an organic relationship between the market economy, the state and civil society in order to generate a sustainable process of growth with equity. This approach calls for institutional changes leading to a competitive market economy, a well-managed state and a democratic civil society. Currently, all countries are experiencing rapid institutional changes, either through ongoing adjustments or through profound mutations. In all cases the interdependence of economies, the demands of competitiveness, the spread of democratization and the growing mobility of people, goods and capital are destabilizing existing institutions, altering their roles and respective weights and forcing new institutions to emerge through the impetus of a dual movement of globalization and decentralization.

This chapter will first present a general approach to institutions, reviewing their characteristics and types. It will then examine the main objectives and functions of institutions in the context of a changing environment—which increases uncertainty, heightens social concerns and makes economic forecasting both more difficult and more necessary. Finally, making a particular reference to economies in transition, it will examine the obstacles encountered in implementing institutional reforms and undertaking adjustments or other approaches to reaching an "equilibrium point" between market dynamics and the preservation of social ties.

THE NATURE OF INSTITUTIONS

Regardless of the form institutions take, they can be defined by two basic characteristics. On one hand, they govern relations between individuals or between groups either through constraints or, on the basis of a commitment to shared objectives and values, through mechanisms that allow for negotiation and compromise. On the other hand, institutions endow those relations with some degree of predictability and stability.

According to the different schools of thought institutions can be viewed either from a "behavioural perspective" (Uphoff, 1986) or from a "rules perspective" (Ruttan and Hayami, 1984). Viewed from a behavioural perspective, the informal approach is favoured: institutions rely on codes of conduct or complexes of behavioural norms that persist over time and serve collectively valued purposes. From the rules perspective the formal approach prevails: institutions lay out rules and laws that define a framework for cooperation among individuals or organizations and that enable the reconciliation of divergent interests.

In fact, the two views are not contradictory. They coexist, albeit in varying proportions, in both formal and informal institutions. In informal institutions, constraints are internalized and values, tradition and culture—such as nation, family, or ethnic or religious community—hold sway. In formal institutions constraints are explicit and the objectives and modes of functioning—such as rules of the state or another institution governing relations within the institution itself (statutes) or with the outside world (laws and contractual arrangements)—are explicitly defined. Among formal institutions the state is unique in that it makes and reinforces laws and regulations that apply to all individuals or organizations. Accordingly, it possesses the authority to establish a coercive system and corresponding enforcement mechanisms, including sanctions.

There is a dynamic connection between formal and informal institutions. The breakdown of traditional systems of solidarity within the village, community or extended family results in exclusion that can be countered only by replacing those systems with welfare systems or social safety nets based on laws and regulations. With the proliferation of rules on commercial enterprises and contracts, the amount of informal productive activity has decreased considerably in a number of countries, being replaced by formal activities. But transaction costs linked to those increasingly numerous and complicated regulations, overtaxation and competitive pressure may frustrate people and lead them to pursue survival strategies and informal activities. Other practices also take place outside the laws and regulations laid down by formal institutions. These include restrictive business practices related to the globalization and monopolistic structure of markets or the emergence of free rider or opportunistic behaviour, linked to either deregulation or to diminished control and sanction systems in the case of non-compliance with trade and financial regulations. In sum, what matters is that the development of institutions proceeds in step with the increase in complexity of the economy: discrepancies create problems.

The state has primary responsibility for fostering the development process and limiting these discrepancies. Depending on economic changes and related changes in norms of behaviour, it must adjust its role over time. In countries with a low degree of productivity and openness to outside markets, informal institutions dominate. An important role of the state, then, is to initiate or support activities that stimulate production, both upstream—training, dissemination of technology, provision of inputs—and downstream—trade and marketing. At this stage of development the state may even have a role in production by creating "growth poles" in the economy as a whole. Successful examples may be drawn from Japan, the Republic of Korea and Taiwan (province of China), as well as Côte d'Ivoire, where publicly owned and managed palm oil plantations and processing plants stimulated the productivity and encouraged the entrepreneurship of the people living around the plantations. The risk is that privatization may come late. As production becomes diversified and the levels of technology and productivity increase, the state should withdraw from production, establish a framework for competitiveness, open the economy and diversify incentives for production activities. Then, formal institutions become predominant in both the public and private sectors. Over time, the state must define its optimal role in managing the relationships between these spheres, which are decisive in increasing the level of economic development.

In general, the growing complexity of economies and societies, and the mobility of actors and their individualization give rise to institutional regulation based more on law, incentives and coercion than on commitment to stable, commonly accepted values and norms of behaviour. This development implies that increasingly systematic enforcement mechanisms will be established. They will be counterbalanced by concerns for freedom of action and economic efficiency, which demand the reduction of formal regulations. Also, whatever are the rules and enforcement mechanisms, every society needs institutions whose values are shared by all its members in order to ensure their cohesion.

THE OBJECTIVES OF PUBLIC INSTITUTIONS

It follows that institutional regulation through the combination of rules and behavioural changes, as well as the dynamic link between these two poles over time, is essential for ensuring trade-offs between order and movement, freedom and control, efficiency and solidarity. Public institutions have the greatest responsibility for attending to these trade-offs. They act formally, through regulations, or informally, through their influence on values and behaviour, to ensure a framework for dialogue and cooperation.

Their ultimate role is thus to build consensus on a vision of society that is based on shared values and that allows each individual, group or organization to place itself within that society. This vision is based on the principle of integration, which is essential for ensuring the self-regulation of society. It encourages individuals and organized groups to mobilize themselves by highlighting their common or mutual interests—positive-sum games. This sense of interest and of belonging to a society with a shared value system allows one to extend responsibility and actions directed towards oneself or one's immediate relations to a larger community. Building consensus on a global vision of development should stimulate not only synchronic integration but diachronic integration as well by highlighting the interests of future generations and short-term behaviour or actions that risk thwarting those interests.

The legitimacy of public institutions lies in their ability to forge a cohesiveness in society and maintain it over time. But, because of their regulatory and coercive powers, these institutions can digress from their fundamental role by creating advantages for specific individuals or population groups. Some of these advantages are not justified but are based sheerly on positions of influence or dominance. Others may be economically or socially justified at a given time but become unfair at a later stage of development. In all cases, they lead to rent creation and the consolidation of vested interests. Furthermore, in any monopoly—be it in the public or the private sector—there is a tendency to discard mechanisms that question undue or obsolete advantages and status. The establishment of appropriate institutions and procedures is therefore indispensable to counter this tendency. In the public sphere these institutions comprise primarily independently functioning executive, judiciary and legislative powers; the regular organization of elections; systems of accountability and transparency in public administration; and strict management of basic macroeconomic and budgetary balances, as budgetary constraints help to identify undue advantages. It is within this framework that public institutions can play their role fully in achieving two complementary objectives: economic prosperity and social equity.

The role of public institutions in growth

Public institutions influence decisively several key factors of economic growth, such as the evolution of property rights, the reduction of transaction costs, the development of new market institutions and the increased mobility of human, financial and technological resources. North and Thomas (1973) went so far as to explain economic growth in western Europe between the tenth and eighteenth centuries in terms of innovation in the institutional rules that governed property rights.

In market economies property rights to land, industrial and financial capital, and technological innovation have evolved considerably, in line with two main trends: growing privatization, along with the maintenance, to varying degrees, of communal, cooperative or public forms of ownership, and increasingly complex systems of ownership, illustrated by the evolution of corporate law. These changes have been powerful incentives for accumulation and growth. And they have been accompanied by other institutional changes that are equally important for increasing the efficiency of market economies: the establishment and development of laws, regulations and mechanisms that govern the negotiation of contracts and their enforcement; the proliferation and spread of market institutions—labour, monetary and financial markets or specialized markets, such as commodity markets; legislation and regulation on taxation, accounting and banking; policies enabling industrial restructuring and encouraging investment; policies encouraging the movement of goods and the growth of exchange, such as the development of infrastructure, the removal of trade barriers and the establishment of measures for facilitating trade; and, finally, health and education policies aimed at improving the human resource base.

This brief overview shows clearly that economic efficiency cannot be attributed only to changes in property rights—complementary policies serving the same objective have been established and have subsequently evolved. Thus privatization in transition economies can succeed only if it is included in the framework of broader institutional changes.

The role of public institutions in redistribution

We must make a distinction between redistributive transfers aimed at providing minimum income and social welfare to the poorest members of the population and policies designed to increase the productivity of the poor. Richard Sabot, in his contribution to this volume, argues convincingly that such policies, particularly educational policies, are effective in increasing the income and savings of the poor and, consequently, total national savings. It should be added that, as demonstrated by Morris and Adelman (1988), strenghtening market institutions alone will worsen the distribution of income (in countries that start with a high degree of concentration of land, capital and human resources).

In other words, policy emphasis on markets will have a favourable impact on most of the population as long as institutions develop policies that ensure the broadest possible access to productive resources—land, capital goods, financial capital (credit, bonds, stock), technology and skills. These policies can be global in scope, such as agrarian reform or provision of basic education. They can be differentiated according to the empowerment of population groups—organized or not—within society, for example, training systems aimed at specific categories of workers or credit schemes for micro- or small-scale enterprises.

Growth-with-equity therefore depends, in the first place, on a broader distribution of productive assets. But too egalitarian an approach in this respect is impossible without extremely coercive systems, which would damage economic efficiency. However successfully a country involves its citizens in the production process, there will remain households for which sickness, age, family situation or disability make it impossible for them to earn sufficient income from work. Such households will have to rely on income distributed through social welfare mechanisms—more so as traditional solidarity channels weaken with urbanization and development.

In order to secure minimum incomes and to involve the poor in the production process, public institutions must ensure some income redistribution and the enjoyment of basic social rights through appropriate fiscal and welfare policies—taxes, transfers, social insurance systems and safety nets—and through the redistribution of assets and capacity-building.

The magnitude of such policies varies among market economies. Differences in the extent and nature of welfare systems are main reasons for the existence of varieties of capitalism. They depend on basic values shared by the population of a given country, as well as on changes in power relationships between social and political forces. The attempt to combine allocative efficiency, mainly through market forces, and a concern for equity and social justice has been driven by democracy in western countries and by a social consensus on a vision of "shared growth" in a number of south-east Asian countries (World Bank, 1993). The former socialist countries guaranteed universal access to basic social rights. This was a major component of their value system. They now face the challenge of redesigning social policies to be compatible with economic performance and market rules. In a newly democratic system such policies are crucial to preserving social stability, which, in turn, is required for popular acceptance and implementation of economic reforms.

FUNCTIONS OF PUBLIC INSTITUTIONS

Public institutions carry out five main functions in order to achieve the above-mentioned objectives: regulation, provision of public goods, mediation, information dissemination and planning.

Public institutions as regulators

Public institutions must perform a regulatory function to ensure the security of citizens, enforce the respect of fundamental rights, ensure that market institutions function properly and encourage compromise in the case of divergent interests and conflicts. The regulatory framework is established through recourse to two types of instruments: constraining regulations and incentives. Constraining regulations establish the rules of the game in civil, political, economic and social fields, and prohibit any type of behaviour or action that is contrary to the general interest. Incentives influence individuals or organizations to select policy options considered to be priorities by public authorities—such as incentives to increase savings, bolster employment, respect the environment and so on.

Public institutions as providers of public goods

Public institutions have an organizational function linked to the provision of public goods: physical infrastructure, social services that are a part of welfare policies, services of general interest, information and technological knowledge that is in the public domain. Public institutions have the greatest responsibility for guaranteeing access to these collective goods or services, with a view to ensuring equal opportunities. They must also ensure that these goods and services are provided efficiently. The questions of service delivery and cost effectiveness are now being widely debated (World Bank, 1994). This debate focuses in particular on the privatization of some services or infrastructures, as well as the transfer of responsibility for social activities from the state to associations within civil society. Reconciling the principle of equal access to basic goods and services (or public goods and services) with the need for efficiency in production and distribution is one of the most important dimensions of current thinking on the respective roles of the state, the private sector and civil society, as well as on the relationships they must maintain with one another.

Public institutions as mediators

Public institutions serve as mediators between different interest groups. They can provide a framework for negotiation or play a catalytic role in collective bargaining processes. They can intervene more directly in social conflicts, proposing, and if necessary imposing, arbitration. In addition, they can reject or accept the claims of interest groups, whether those groups are seeking to protect a rent derived from a position of dominance or unjustified advantage, or to obtain justifiable compensation on the basis of an economically or socially weak position. These interventions must operate on the basis of equity and a search for social peace. Once again they raise the question, though from a different standpoint, of the relations between public institutions and the representatives of economic and social forces within the private sector and civil society.

Public institutions as disseminators of information

Proper information is the basic requirement for the functioning of market economies, as it helps economic agents to both identify their options and, by reducing uncertainty, make decisions. Because information is a good that has a market value, to enquire about the role of institutions in ensuring its dissemination is to attempt to answer three questions: which information should be considered a public good, which institutions are best placed to disseminate that information and do the answers to these two questions evolve over time in accordance with the degree of diversification and development of the country's institutions?

Information is a good that can be produced and exchanged, or consumed within the enterprise that possesses it. A priori, that enterprise has no incentive to share information free of charge. But incomplete or asymmetric information can generate transaction costs and result in adverse selection or market failure. At the microeconomic level the suggestion has been made that "incentive mechanisms capable of overcoming them, such as appropriate forms of contract" should be developed in order to avoid opportunistic behaviours on the part of the possessor of the information, as well as acquisition costs by the party that does not possess it (Nabli and Nugent, 1989, p. 1337).

At the macroeconomic level the first question is to determine whether some information should be considered a public good and made available to all economic agents—rendering the entire system more efficient. A priori, there are three possibilities: such information is produced naturally by the public sector; it is produced better by the public sector or it is too difficult for most actors to access and its possession would provide rents to those with the easiest means of access. At least three types of information correspond to at least one of these criteria: information on laws, rules and public bodies. But citizens are poorly acquainted with the law and are unaware of their rights and duties, as well as of how institutions function. This is, in part, a matter of education—public bodies must provide information about themselves. In addition, there are also complex operations that involve central and local administrations and for which there are specific provisions for reducing costs. For example, studies have shown that two obstacles to foreign investment are the complexity of administrative procedures and the lack of clear regulations, which facilitate corruption, thus generating excessive costs or discouraging investment. For that reason it has often been recommended that a single office govern all the formalities. Other examples could be cited as to the costs incurred by a lack of familiarity with institutions and regulations and as to what administrations can do about the situation.

A number of countries have established public institutions to gather and disseminate information on technologies. The most famous example is undoubtedly Japan's Ministry of International Trade and Industry (MITI), which has succeeded in gathering available information on technologies from publications, organizing the information and making it available to enterprises through various channels without attempting to influence the use to which the information is put or to limit its dissemination. It has thus created a forum for the free exchange of information and for dialogue and cooperation among actors interested in the same economic activities. MITI has also promoted joint research by ensuring the impartial distribution of findings among interested parties, again without attempting to influence how the findings are used. Critiscisms about the erroneous directions that research has sometimes taken in this context must be weighed against the disadvantages resulting from less transparent forms of enterprises' research subsidized by the state.

Thus far, we have considered the dissemination of information on technologies from the user's viewpoint. From the standpoint of the producer of information, the desirability of disseminating research depends on how one conceives of the stimuli for research. Incentives can come from the dissemination of technologies, pushing enterprises to develop new research in order to preserve their competitive edge. The draft International Code of Conduct on the Transfer of Technology, prepared within the framework of the United Nations Conference on Trade and Development, was based on this approach. But the project was dropped as countries rallied around another approach during the second half of the 1980s, favouring rent as an incentive for developing resesarch: this led to the negotiations on intellectual property as part of the Uruguay Round.

Aside from the supposed neutrality of a public body, the legitimacy of entrusting such a body with the jobs of promoting and disseminating information can depend on how developed a country's institutions are. MITI was indisputably efficient during the industrial development period in Japan. Today, however, there are multiple channels for gaining information on technology, and one might ask whether it is still necessary to have a central informational body. The answer is not always clear, unless it can be demonstrated that such a body provides newcomers with access to information at the least possible cost, thereby increasing opportunities.

Public institutions as planners

Edmond Malinvaud also asks about the planning function in his contribution to volume I. He concludes: "In most countries, information will be better processed and the results of prospective studies will be better known and examined if a central institution, with recognized public standing, is involved." The purpose of a plan is not to offer a "global market survey", as was envisioned in France during the 1960s, nor to be an authoritarian instrument for allocating resources, but to minimize the negative impact of uncertainties by identifying them and initiating discussion on the strategies needed to cope with them (Masse, 1965). Also, national planning was designed to introduce elements into the parameters of decision-making that had not been highlighted by the market, such as the environment.

The French plan played this role by bringing together social partners—and MITI or the office of the Korean plan by involving enterprises—in debates on macroeconomic trends and sectoral developments. In some developing countries, by providing an encompassing and plausible vision of the future, the plans facilitated investment decisions by private companies, even though their investment differed from that envisaged in the plans. Furtado (1987) conveys the idea that the plan must not be a substitute for decision-making by public and private actors, but must share a vision of possibilities and influence expectations.

In the paragraphs above I emphasized the role of public institutions without discussing their limits or the risks of inefficiency. Without entering into this recurrent debate, which in recent years has tended to be influenced by a positive view of the role of the state, we might stress the fact that activities of public institutions need not preclude activities of private institutions. On the contrary, competition of this sort can lead to a better division of labour and greater flexibility in adapting to change.

INSTITUTIONAL CHANGES IN TRANSITION ECONOMIES

Development thinking on economies in transition during the 1980s and 1990s has greatly enriched the understanding of the difficulties and slow pace of institutional change, as well as of the desirable sequence of reforms.

Obstacles to change

Institutions, even if they are poorly adapted and inefficient, can endure for a long period of time. They can simply be taken for granted, no one questioning their efficiency (Nabli and Nugent, 1989). Alternatively, the lack of information on alternative forms of institutions can lead to the maintenance of the status quo.

Even if the need for change is recognized, there are many obstacles. When Macchiavelli declared that "there is nothing more difficult to take in hand, more perilous to conduct, or more uncertain in its success than to take the lead in the introduction of a new order of things", he identified two reasons for failure: determined resistance of those benefiting from the status quo and lukewarm support from those benefiting from the reform. The weak support of the latter was due in part to fears of the hostility of those favoring the status quo and in part to uncertainty about the results of the new order. "If individuals are uncertain as to whether they will benefit from a reform, there may be a bias against the change, even if it is certain that the majority will benefit. Individual uncertainty can therefore distort the aggregate vote—the majority might vote against itself" (ECE, 1993).

In transition economies these difficulties are compounded by the scale and complexity of the reforms being undertaken simultaneously—the likely negative impact on the majority in the short run and the uncertainty surrounding the time required to produce the promised benefits may lead governments to electoral defeat. This happened in most of the central and eastern European countries during the past two years, but without significantly affecting the path of reform. Primarily, it brought the need to develop appropriate safety net mechanisms to the forefront of governmental concerns.

As stressed by the Austrian school, institutions and behaviour develop over extended periods. In a legal sense institutions can be easily replicated, but the development of institutional effectiveness is a much slower process of learning and adaptation. This is particularly relevant in countries in transition, which cannot be "shocked" into market economies (ECE, 1993). That system was so consistent and had produced such deeply entrenched behaviours and habits that changes remained blocked, that in western economies would be spontaneous reactions to the prevalent incentive system (Boyer, 1992; Buchanan, 1992).

The process of change

Some of the foregoing remarks were inspired by observations of the reform process in eastern Europe and countries of the former Soviet Union. Those remarks stress the importance of the amount of time required for the new institutions to become operational and the importance of the sequence of reforms. The first point is reinforced—as demonstrated by the observable differences between the eastern European countries and those of the former Soviet Union—by the weight of collective memory: 40 years of central planning for the first and 70 years of central planning for the second.

In the reform process the government plays a key role in constructing institutions and setting formal rules of competitive behaviour, and in reducing the uncertainties that impede reforms. The government must be able to define a clear set of objectives, to demonstrate a clear understanding of what is required to achieve those objectives and to convince economic agents and the electorate at large that it possesses—or will soon acquire—the necessary economic instruments to implement its programme (ECE, 1992).

The drive towards a market economy must therefore be spelled out in terms of a series of intermediate objectives (institutional reforms, for example), and the interdependencies between them set out in a transparent and comprehensible manner. This issue is related to that of sequencing. The literature on sequencing shows the fact that the probability of success in achieving a given objective may be increased by following one sequence of measures rather than another—in the worst case an incorrect sequencing would destroy all chance of success. This insight is useful, but the theory does not provide operational formulae for policy-makers in transition economies.

In practice, correct sequencings will rely on pragmatic judgement, made in light of each country's particular circumstances. But there may be a few general rules derived from experience. For example, the experience of some transition economies suggests that it may be unwise to opt for rapid price liberalization if authorities do not possess effective instruments of monetary control (ECE, 1993).

The privatization of large enterprises—which entails abandoning social functions, education, housing, recreation and employment guarantees, and which risks accelerating unemployment—is slowed by the absence of an adequate social security system. Likewise, the lack of resources to finance investment in a sustainable way has highlighted the weaknesses of an insufficiently diversified banking system and encumbered bad loans that had piled up from the start of the reforms due to a lack of satisfactory regulations on reserves and a staff poorly adapted to market rules.

The literature on sequencing may also be misleading insofar as it suggests alternative, linear sequences of policy actions. The transition process, with economic and political programmes of reform intertwined, is highly complex and will frequently require simultaneous action on a number of interdependent issues for significant progress to be made. The task is therefore to identify key sets of interdependencies that in turn would help to identify those subsets or menus of reform that should be given priority in the transition programme.

Because different elements of reform have their own subset of requirements, a set of reforms must be simultaneously completed rather than simultaneously begun.

On that basis it is not possible to propose any optimum sequencing of reforms, but only to indicate some domains that must be considered in an inter-related manner: price and trade liberalization, instruments and policies to maintain macroèconomic stability, privatization, property rights and social safety nets, labour laws, competition laws, enforcement instruments and procedures, and a diversified financial system.

It may be useful to recall that it is much more appealing to imitate an institution if it is well established in several other countries even if it is not the institution best adapted to the situation or culture of the adopting country. One wonders if the "lock-in" phenomenon for technologies and institutions noted by Bardhan (1989) can be transposed to economic systems. One might also ask, along with Boyer (1992), about the make up of a mixed economy that would be best adapted to central Europe or the Commonwealth of Independent States (CIS).

CONCLUSIONS

In western economies the construction of the legal and institutional network has developed through successive adjustments resulting from ongoing interaction between economic and technical changes on the one hand, and evolutions in social behaviour and values on the other. This process is highly complex, combining an array of legal and financial institutions, formal and informal rules and shared values and traditional modes of behaviour—all of which are rooted in a country's political and social institutions.

In transition economies, far more than in developing countries, the old command system collapsed before the new coordinating mechanisms of a market economy could be put in place. Furthermore, that disruption has thrown the value system into turmoil, resulting in anxiety and disorientation, which impede the process of change and the coherence of reforms.

The ability to continue the transition process in an orderly, evolutionary manner will therefore depend largely on the rate at which the underlying structure of moral and social values can respond and adapt to the need to solve new problems and meet new challenges.

This raises the question of the relationship between democracy and development. History shows that in highly industrialized countries, certain stages of economic development led to democratization: organized demands for respecting civil, political and social rights intensify over time, and democratization itself becomes necessary for the continuation of the development process. Since the end of the Cold War a large majority of countries have opted for democratic systems, although a number of them are democracies more in name than in deed. The basic issue for such countries is to make democratization and development mutually reinforcing. For that to occur, democratization must be effective enough to lead to the decentralization of decision-making power, the promotion of the right of association and the free expression of social demands.

Finally, in all countries public institutions, in constant interaction with civil society, have a central role to play in managing change in an orderly fashion. As this chapter has demonstrated, their main responsibility is to combine consensus-building with the design of a coherent set of incentives, rules, policies and effective enforcement mechanisms that must be adjusted over time, thereby providing an essential continuity in the progress towards economic and social well-being.

REFERENCES

Bardhan, P. 1989. "The New Institutional Economics and Development Theory: a Brief Critical Assessment." *World Development* 17 (9):1389–95.
Boyer, R. 1992. "La grande transformation de l'Europe de l'Est: une lecture régulationniste." Paper presented at the ARCII seminar on "The Major Transformation in Eastern Europe." June.
Buchanan, J. 1992. "The Role of Economics in Post-Socialist Reform." Address to the Eighteenth Annual Conference of the Eastern Economic Association. New York. March.
Doeringer, P. and P. Streeten. 1990. "How Economic Institutions Affect Economic Performance in Industrialized Countries: Lessons for Development." *World Development* 18 (9):1249–53.
ECE (United Nations Economic Commission for Europe). 1992. *Economic Bulletin for Europe* 44. New York and Geneva
____. 1993. *Economic Survey of Europe*. 1992–93. New York and Geneva.
Furtado, C. 1987. "La Fantaisie organisée: le développement est-il possible?" Paris, Publisud.
Massé, P. 1965. *Le Plan ou l'Anti-Hasard*. Paris: NRF.
Malinvaud, E. 1997. "The Future of Planning in Market Economies." In Edmond Malinvaud et al., eds., *Development Strategy and Management of the Market Economy*, Volume I. Oxford: Clarendon Press.
Morris, C.T. and I. Adelman. 1988. *Comparative Patterns of Economic Development 1850–1914*. Baltimore: Johns Hopkins University Press.
Nabli, M.K. and J.B. Nugent. 1989. "The New Institutional Economics and Its Applicability to Development" *World Development,* 17 (9):1333–47.
North, D. and R. Thomas. 1973. *The Rise of the Western World*. Cambridge: Cambridge University Press.
Ruttan, V.M. and Y. Hayami. 1984. "Towards a Theory of Induced Institutional Innovation" *Journal of Development Studies* 20 (July 1984):203–23.
Uphoff, N. 1986. *Local Institutional Development*. West Hartford: Kumarian Press.
World Bank. 1993. *The East Asian Miracle: Economic Growth and Public Policy.* New York: Oxford University Press.
____. 1994. *World Development Report 1994: Infrastructure for Development.* New York: Oxford University Press.

7

Planning: Between Mitigating Market and Government Failures

MUSTAPHA K. NABLI

The role of institutions in explaining variations in economic performance and growth rates has been a focus in recent literature on growth and development. Many of these institutions can be seen essentially as arrangements or mechanisms devised to deal with market failures and to improve the performance of government. In this chapter I develop the idea that planning can be viewed as a valuable institutional arrangement for managing market economies. I suggest that we can interpret the experience of planning—in countries where it has played a significant role—as an institutional framework for dealing with market failures and, even more significantly, with government failures. An institutional structure or process is involved in public planning if it is concerned with enhancing the efficiency of decentralized economic processes. Overall, these functions aim essentially at mitigating market failures or government failures, or both.

It is surprising that the recent World Bank report on the "East Asian Miracle" (World Bank, 1993) did not address the role of planning. The report was largely interested in institutions that contributed to the economic success of these countries—institutions that improved the performance of both market and government intervention. This was despite the fact that most of these countries had planning institutions that were strongly involved.[1] This omission may be due to the disrepute that has befallen planning in the last two decades—a time when liberalization and markets have taken center stage. It has been easy to deny any role for planning in a market economy.

In order to assess the relevance and content of planning, I assume that we are dealing with a *mixed economic system* in which both the market and the government play a major and significant role in resource allocation. The role of the government is reflected in a number of given parameters, such as its size, the extent of public intervention and the extent of public ownership. In such an economy the government is a participant, and the role of public planning should be viewed as part of the overall institutional set-up for managing the economy.

Planning as an instrument or institutional framework for managing economies concerns essentially the national level and in an accessory way the regional level. It is with respect to issues that have a national dimension that the term planning is mostly used.

Also, it should be emphasized that planning should not be equated with government intervention. As we will discuss extensively below, planning is a valuable vehicle for improving the performance of government activities, but many aspects of government intervention and policies should not be considered planning. Only when these policies are embedded in an overall national perspective that takes into account interactions with other sectors and considers the implications for the overall performance of the economy should they be considered planning activities. On the other hand, some planning activities, such as the provision of information to the private sector, are not government interventions.

For individual projects and when using cost-benefit analysis, for instance, planning is relevant and important if there is a need to maintain coherency across various projects on a number of forecasts or parameters used, such as the discount rate, expected remuneration rates and so on. Planning activities are also relevant at the sectoral level when they involve issues and interactions of a national character, which are often complex and relate to many subsectors, agencies and institutions. This would apply, for instance, to the many sectors in which government intervention is extensive, such as education, health, transportation, infrastructure, telecommunications, water resources and agriculture.

PLANNING AND MARKET FAILURES

Most of the debate about planning has centred on the question of whether such an institutional set-up can improve the efficiency of a decentralized market mechanism. It is assumed in such discussions that agents participate in the market according to incentives typical of a competitive environment. If there are public firms, they are assumed to respond to market incentives and not have monopoly or dominant positions. The implications of having such dominant public sector firms are discussed in the next section. The theory of development planning has been concerned with a decentralized market mechanism and its failure to achieve efficiency. From this concern developed a large body of planning models designed to help governments overcome these failures.

Theoretical foundations

The theory of development planning as it evolved in the 1950s and 1960s has been constructed on two major premises: the existence of market failures and the inadequacy of price-based mechanisms for dealing with them. A good account of these theoretical arguments is given by Chakravarty (1973) and an appraisal by Chakravarty (1991).

Three types of market failures have received attention in this context. The first one relates to the Rosenstein-Rodan (1943) argument, claiming the existence of non-convexities, due to indivisibilities and economies of scale, and of pecuniary externalities in the Scitovsky (1954) sense, or aggregate demand spillovers. Under such conditions a price-guided mechanism does not necessarily produce efficient outcomes, and hence a coordinated effort—the "big push"—may help to achieve a better equilibrium. This type of argument was formalized recently by Murphy, Shleifer and Vishny (1989) and readdressed by Krugman (1992). Both papers showed that the joint presence of economies of scale and pecuniary externalities can generate multiple equilibria. The existence of "strategic complementarities" in this sense leaves room for coordinated investment programmes that improve efficiency. Closely related are the backward and forward linkages arguments of Hirshman (1958), which are also based on economies of scale and pecuniary externalities. A review of recent contributions related to these issues is given by Rodríguez-Clare (1997).

The second argument concerns incomplete markets in the face of uncertainty. The existence of incomplete futures markets and the difficulty of forecasting future prices may lead to inefficient investment outcomes. In its interpretation in the development literature (such as in Chakravarty, 1973) this argument is in fact part of the preceding one, since it involves the existence of pecuniary externalities. But the issue has been addressed more clearly in the context of the theory of indicative planning in industrial economies. The approach is concerned with reaching coordinated and consistent long-term forecasts in order to reduce uncertainty and better use resources. Another concern is about raising demand expectations in order to create a virtuous circle in the growth process.[2]

The third argument is based on the existence of consumption externalities—which generate differences between market and social discount rates. This difference, in turn, may result in suboptimal saving and an excessive orientation towards projects with short-term pay-offs and therefore lower growth rates.

The other premise of the theory of development planning, most forcefully advocated by Chakravarty (1973), is that price-based mechanisms for dealing with these market failures are inadequate. When multiple equilibria arise, the question of whether the market left to itself would lead to the better solution remains open. The internalization of externalities is presumed to be difficult because of high transaction costs, precluding the development of appropriate markets or institutions. Overcoming externalities may also require restrictions on property rights—and difficulty implementing these changes are notorious. The implementation of Pigovian taxes and subsidies to correct some of these failures is also thought to be problematic because of computational difficulties and the complexity of their administration in developing countries.

The structuralist literature also adds that significant rigidities in the market system makes it too slow to achieve desired allocations through price signals.

In development planning, as it has actually evolved, these considerations of market failures were used as a basis for a planning process concerned with the determination of quantity-based directives for investment allocation. From there a quantum jump was made towards the use of economy-wide quantitative models to formulate investment plans. My aim is to assess the extent to which the theoretical arguments of market failures were used as a justification for economy-wide planning models and the extent to which the models deal effectively with the presumed market failures. I will then discuss issues of emphasis and implementation of solutions.

The justification of economy-wide planning models

That there is an unwarranted jump from theoretical arguments to the practical use of economy-wide models for investment allocation can be seen by examining these arguments more closely. First, some market failures do not call for the government to directly affect investment decisions. The arguments used in the indicative planning type of analysis call for coordination among agents to produce coherent forecasts. The coordinated solution would be self-implemented by the agents in the decentralized market process. The government may help organize the coordination process and provide technical support for the production of consistent forecasts. But this role would require only forecasting models that ensure consistency.

Second, the existence of economies of scale, externalities and information imperfections may call for direct government intervention, as discussed by Stiglitz (1997). But such intervention may take a variety of forms, such as price incentives or the design of appropriate institutional structures. They generally do not involve a clear role for planning, such as in the infant-industry argument, even though they may affect the nation's industrial structure.[3] But the arguments based on strategic complementarities among industries that involve inter-sectoral allocations identify an obvious role for planning. The problem that remains, however, concerns which type of planning and which type of instruments are appropriate for this purpose. I will discuss this issue in the next section.

Third, the empirical knowledge about market failures was extremely limited, making modeling these problems quantitatively very difficult, if not impossible. It would have been necessary, for instance, to know which activities were associated with externalities, what the origins of these externalities were and what the characteristics of these industries were. Even today such knowledge is not available.

Market failures in planning models

I turn now to the issue of the extent to which economy-wide planning models deal effectively with market failures, making the traditional distinction between consistency and optimization models.

Consistency models

An array of aggregate consistency models of the Harrod-Domar and two-gap type have been used in developing countries to test alternative scenarios for growth. The analysis is usually about the feasibility of future growth paths and their consistency with basic parameters, such as saving rates, capital-output ratios and the import content of investment. These models are not based in any meaningful way on market failures, except for incorporating price rigidity, which makes the analysis essentially macro-analytic.

The other models that had great success and were used extensively in development planning are input-output-based consistency models.[4] Whether static or dynamic, they have been used widely in the preparation of plans in most developing countries because of their simplicity and, often, the ready availability of data. They appeared to be the most appropriate instrument for producing coherent forecasts and coordinating inter-dependent activities with strategic complementarities. They are also used as pricing models to calculate consistent cost-based price systems.

But for capturing strategic complementarities (which are rooted in the existence of economies of scale and indivisibilities, and pecuniary externalities), linear input-output models are inappropriate. The choice of the level of some activities or investments known to exhibit economies of scale can be made exogenously, taking into account its consistency with other activities. But there is no way to test the efficiency of such a choice and whether the model solution is superior to a market-determined one. The models are able to capture only the linkages between sectors—which are only part of the story.

Consistency models can be useful as a framework for producing forecasts to coordinate private sector investment. For this purpose input-output models are rich in the specification of technology and inter-industry linkages. But they are deficient in the specification of behavioural and institutional issues. The rigidities of the linear system, the use of historical experience to estimate parameters and the lack of behavioural specifications make the models ill-suited to forecast future changes in a market system characterized by technological change, dynamic behaviour and permanent adjustment.[5] Finally, the type of closure rule for the models[6] and the choice of terminal conditions for dynamic models, which are mostly ad-hoc, make the value of the produced forecasts subject to much uncertainty.

Optimizing models

Planning models of optimization were the most intellectually prominent tool in development planning theory and modeling during the 1960s and early 1970s. They were considered to be the appropriate tool for analyzing policies and helping to design development strategies that overcame the limitations of the market mechanism. They are designed to allow replication of a Walrasian competitive allocative mechanism, but are constructed so as to eliminate the effects of efficiency-reducing distortions and imperfections that are widespread in developing countries. They were concerned mostly with the sectoral allocation of investment—that is, with growth and structural change in production and international trade—and with the size and timing of required domestic and foreign investment.[7]

Static linear programming models were developed first and were the most widely used, because they were extensions of linear input-output models and solution techniques were not costly and were readily available. Dynamic linear models and non-linear models were developed later. The objectives of those models were ambitious, including assessment of the feasibility and consistency of solutions, given the specified constraints and inter-linkages, and identification of equilibria that markets would not achieve. Particular attention was given to the shadow price system that the models produced. Those systems were interpreted as prices not subject to distortions and imperfections, and therefore a better guide for resource allocation than market prices.

Two arguments underlie the optimization models. The first is the "big push" argument, whereby a coordinated effort can lead to higher output than an uncoordinated effort, hence the search for allocations that maximize desired outcomes subject to the feasibility and consistency conditions. The second, present in dynamic models based on optimal growth theory and well-articulated by Chakravarty (1969), is the non-optimality of market-determined saving rates. Differences between private and social discount rates lead to the under-supply of savings. Optimization models are used to calculate alternative optimal paths of consumption and saving.

Like the consistency models on which they are based, optimizing models are rich in technology specifications but poor in behavioural and institutional specifications. Saving and consumption behaviour are determined by the planner's choice of objective function. The solutions are sensitive to the specification of the objective function, particularly to the values of the parameters attached to the consumption variables and the value attached to future capital stock. There are no behavioural relationships among economic agents and no explicit treatment of the supposed externalities in consumption and saving that motivate use of the models. In fact, in many instances model solutions generate saving rates that are too high, compared with what historical observations deem reasonable, leading to problems of interpretation and implementation.

In all but a few cases[8] economies of scale are absent from those models. The linearity of production technology is typical. There is no analysis of the activities exhibiting scale economies and the attendant pecuniary externalities. And thus policies or strategies for dealing with these problems cannot be suggested from these models.

Issues of coordinating expectations for investment decisions are dealt with only in the sense of obtaining consistent solutions. Such solutions are often of limited value, given that exogenous rules or forecasts are used for investment decisions, without including behavioural content.

Because microeconomic behaviour is not specified in the models, macroeconomic considerations, such as constraints on foreign exchange and savings, have predominated. The linearity in most applications leads to unrealistic specialization and solutions that behave erratically. These problems were solved by the addition of various types of constraints. But their addition results in difficulties with the interpretation of shadow prices, which also became unstable and thus useless as a guide for allocating resources, such as in cost-benefit analysis.

Optimizing models, like consistency models, have not been subjected to empirical tests of their predictive power as compared, for instance, to other relevant alternative models.[9] It was almost impossible to appreciate the empirical relevance of the models and of the calculated solutions.

These limitations added to the lack of success among policy-makers with these optimizing models, and led to their abandonment and withering away from the development literature since the mid-1970s.[10] This period witnessed, however, the increasing use of computable general equilibrium models. These models were found to be more useful for analyzing policy issues, having more relevance to development problems in market economies, even with the presence of many distortions and imperfections (which the models could take into consideration).

Emphasis and relevance of planning models

According to Chakravarty (1973) planning is used to determine optimal levels of investment for each sector or optimal choices of technology as a first step in a more general theory involving choice over institutions. This emphasis on capital accumulation was in accordance with the then prevailing views in the economic development literature. But planning models did not go beyond this first step—which itself came to be questioned.

One aspect that was questioned is the dependence of most models and analyses on the assumption of a closed economy. The argument of strategic complementarities, which itself is based on economies of scale, is not valid in the context of an open economy. When trade is possible, economies of scale can be realized independently of the development of other activities in the country. The argument may remain valid only for non-tradables with economies of scale or tradables with high transportation costs. The argument of the consistency and coordination of future expectations of economic agents in indicative planning also loses its validity in the context of an open economy, though retains some interest for non-tradables. The emphasis on the closed economy assumption and the orientation towards import substitution have played a major role in discrediting development planning once the importance of outward orientation and export growth were recognized.

Developments in economic growth theory have also shown the importance of productivity growth, technical progress, learning by doing and so on. These issues are typically not found in development planning models. The role of human capital has also been recognized as a fundamental factor in development. And this subject did not receive any attention in development planning models. The same can be said of infrastructure. It is surprising how much these models emphasize the productive sectors and how little human capital and infrastructure—areas in which arguments for government intervention and planning can be more readily developed.

The multiplicity of objectives that cannot be easily introduced into a formal framework has been another limitation in planning models. The objective functions of optimizing models have emphasized consumption and output growth. Other important issues of government policy, like employment, poverty reduction, inter-regional equity and so on are difficult to introduce formally. They are sometimes introduced as additional constraints, which does not enable policy analysis and choice.

Implementation of planning models

The planning models I have discussed lack incentive compatibility characteristics, because they do not capture market mechanisms, and the solutions obtained do not relate to any incentive instruments according to which decisions are made in market economies. Thus countries differed widely in the mechanisms they used to implement their investment plans.[11] The mix varied according to a country's overall policies and orientation, but the general features of strong and far-reaching state control and quantity-based instruments prevailed in most developing countries. They have come to be associated with development planning. Licensing and control of investment by the private sector, whether national or foreign, were widely used. They were often accompanied by restrictions to entry, assured markets and protection from imports—all of which resulted in poor incentives to reduce costs and make technical progress. Prices were controlled in a variety of ways. The financial sector was highly regulated with a basic credit allocation mechanism to assure coherency with investment licensing. Since the private sector could not be relied on to carry out the desired investment programme, direct investment programmes by state-owned enterprises developed as an easy alternative. And this alternative was made easier when the banking sector itself was under government control. This was the era of the ever-expanding public sector, with its well-known characteristics of captive markets, soft budget constraints, a multiplicity of objectives and consequent low efficiency. Trade policy was used mainly as an instrument for import substitution, and direct quantity controls were prevalent.

Price incentives were also used in the form of investment codes with fiscal and monetary instruments, but they were rarely based on the analysis of planning models. They were most often used to mitigate the limitations of the quantity-based planning process.

In fact, implementation of the plan was subject to political economy constraints concerning which groups were affected, which instruments were used and how these interests were balanced. All of these quantity-based interventions gave rise to rent-seeking behaviour. In his reappraisal of planning Chakravarty (1991) recognized the need to take into account political and administrative constraints in the implementation of plans, as well as the need to use a mixture of price and quantity instruments.

The preceding discussion shows clearly that planning models, and planning more generally, had little success in helping developing countries deal with market failures. The instruments used for economy-wide policy-making were not effective for the design of policies and institutions intended to improve the workings of decentralized market mechanisms. The reliance on quantity-based instru-

242 Development Strategy and Management of the Market Economy

ments that were linked to planning models was not associated with successful development policies.

These arguments do not preclude any role for planning in helping to deal with market failures. But they clearly show the inadequacy of the traditional planning models and their associated policies. Such a role must be closely related to the type and extent of government intervention in the market. Planning must include the appropriate mechanisms and instruments for implementing government intervention most effectively, whether through information exchange and diffusion or coordination. But this prescription leads to the role of planning in improving the performance of government and the need to deal with the associated failures of government intervention.

PLANNING AND GOVERNMENT FAILURES

The practice of development planning, in contrast to the theory, has been concerned mostly with government activity. An early observer and insightful analyst of development planning, Lewis (1966) was clearly aware of this fact. He states that "the first task of a Development Plan is to bring order, priority and foresight into Government expenditure" (p. 22). Other main tasks are also essentially about government involvement, such as providing infrastructure, training and education; helping to create more and better markets; and improving the institutional framework. The "fundamental task of planning in the private sector is to remove the obstacles in the way of legitimate private initiative by increasing the knowledge of resources and their potential utilization, and by improving infrastructure and the institutional framework of economic activity" (p. 274). Promoting entrepreneurship, supporting scientific research and offering inducements to promote better use of resources should also be considered.

Given the range of government activity, the concerns of planning in the context of mitigating government failures are three: the efficiency of decentralized non-market processes, the feasibility and sustainability of policies, and the enhancement of credibility of such policies.

The efficiency of decentralized non-market processes

In any modern economy and in any developing country a significant chunk of resources is allocated by the government, not by market mechanisms. Such resources typically make up between one-quarter and one-half of GDP. Given the importance of these government activities, they are decentralized through a myriad of institutions, including various ministries and departments, agencies, regional centers, public firms and so on. But their essential characteristic is that decisions made and resources allocated within this public sector are carried out in accordance with bureaucratic and political processes. I would say that a planning institution is the part of bureaucracy that is concerned with guarding the principles of economic efficiency, particularly in the public sector.

It is well known that the allocation of resources, regulation and policy-making in the public sector are subject to government failures, that is, to rent seeking, to non-optimizing behaviour and various forms of non-market exchange. The theories of bureaucracy and public choice describe a large array of situations in which economic efficiency criteria are often not the main determinants of decisions made in the public domain. It is thus important, if not essential, that within the government bureaucracy there be an institutional structure or process that is concerned with efficiency.

I am not suggesting that a planning institution replace the political process or become a central-decision-maker within the bureaucracy. That set-up would bring us back to the failures of centralized planning. Rather, I think that a planning organization can be a useful vehicle within the bureaucracy to promote and support efficient outcomes, decisions and policies. Not directly part of the political process but part of the bureaucracy and clearly in charge of efficiency-enhancing activities, it can play an important role in mitigating government failures through three main activities: coordination and coherency, optimization of collective choices and insulation from specific interests.

Coordination and coherency

While the debate about the usefulness of coordination and cooperation among agents acting in a competitive market is inconclusive, it seems clear that there is scope for such activities when public agents are not subject to market discipline and incentives for profit maximization. This role becomes more important when there are strong interactions between the various units undertaking government activities. Crémer and Crémer (1993) show that theoretical support for these functions can be found from the theory of teams, whereby homogenization of the information set between different public agencies can lead to more efficient outcomes. It can also be found from game theory that coordination and cooperation may lead to more efficient outcomes than uncoordinated Nash equilibrium solutions. We can illustrate the scope for such coordination by looking at a number of aspects of public sector activities.

Within government analysis and decision-making activities there is wide scope for assuring the coordination and consistency of public investment programmes, especially in the absence of markets and in a medium- to long-term framework. Primary and secondary education investment programmes should be coordinated with those in higher education and in vocational training. Investment programmes in transport infrastructure must be coordinated with those of productive activities, urban development and protection of the environment. The importance of land planning arises here, when multiple claims are made on a given zone: urban development, agriculture and other productive activities, preservation of the environment. For the development of a tourism or industrial zone investment programmes in infrastructure and supply of utilities (such as water, electricity, telecommunications and transportation, which are often carried out by public agencies) must be fully coordinated. In most of these cases markets do not exist or are not developed enough to allocate resources efficiently.

More generally, public policies relating to different sectors and activities—such as industrial and trade policies, investment and price policies, environmental and land planning, health and education, transportation and regional policies—must be consistent in their objectives and instruments.

In the last two decades structural adjustment and liberalization reforms have been the subject of much attention and debate in developing countries. Planning ministries are often in charge of managing reforms, that is, they are responsible for the design, coordination and supervision of implementing reform programmes. The issues of consistency, timing and sequencing of liberalization programmes are at the center of this preoccupation—the objective being the minimization of adjustment costs and the generation of most benefits from the reforms. These reforms are generally very comprehensive, running from external liberalization to liberalization of domestic prices, investment, credit and the financial sector. The strong interactions among these reforms necessitate a proper design for their implementation. Planning organizations may be the institutions to help manage this process.

The optimization and efficiency of collective choices

In view of our discussion about planning models it may seem awkward to assign planning an optimization role, but I believe that it is an important aspect of a planning institution's activities. I am not suggesting that this role be carried out or conceived based on mathematical optimization and programming at the national level. All of the issues about the quality of information, economic knowledge, uncertainty and the complexity of human behaviour and society are well known. They show clearly that concern with optimization in this sense is not a function of planning.

But one can make a strong case that planning processes should be part of national mechanisms for revealing collective choices. In the wide area of public intervention, particularly that of provision of public goods, the problem of optimal provision in the presence of competing claims is at the heart of planning. It is not sufficient to ensure that public investment programmes are consistent—society must strive towards optimizing collective choices. The usual problems facing planners concern the amount of resources to allocate to education, health, infrastructure, poverty reduction and so on. Society must be able to allocate public resources so that social marginal rates of return are equalized. Planners deal with such questions as whether it is acceptable to allocate 5 per cent or 7 per cent of GDP to health compared with 3 per cent or 5 per cent for vocational training, or to allocate 2 per cent for rural roads compared with 4 per cent for improving roads in the cities. No mathematical programming models have been found that can solve these problems formally and simply, and precise cost-benefit analysis is seldom feasible. But the process of planning, which involves intensive discussions and consultations among national actors, should help to make the chosen allocations tend towards a social optimum or at least to aim for acceptable social choices. This process involves comparing projects within and across sectors. For example, a planner must address the question of whether it is more efficient at a given time to invest in a dam that costs $200 million or to build an airport. But neither the agriculture department nor the transport department is likely to worry about such an issue. Representatives of specific departments are expected to push for their projects, aiming at the maximization of their share of government expenditures. In accordance with the "maximizing of budgets" principle, which is a common bureaucratic objective, projects are pushed through the budgetary process so as to increase the share of the department or agency. Studies or cost-benefit analyses of projects are designed by these parties with the intent of justifying them. There is strong need in the bureaucracy to control and check these studies in order to make better choices.

Insulation from specific interests

The theories of rent seeking and public choice show that decisions and policies are not necessarily efficiency-oriented. Through the political market, interest groups play a significant role in the allocation of resources and in the design of regulations and policies. Trade or industrial policies, regulations relating to competition or the environment, and other types of policies are subject to continuous pressure for change to appease specific interests. It has been observed that regulators often become captive to the regulated, and that politicians get locked in their support for these specific interests. Even with exchange rate and monetary policies there is scope for influence by specific interest groups.[12]

In open and democratic societies it is natural for such influences to exist and for specific interest groups to exert political pressure. Society has, however, a stake in promoting general welfare and should strive to avoid policies becoming hostage to such interests. Its institutional structure must contain safeguards against such excessive negative influence. Planning institutions can be part of this institutional set-up, which works at arm's length from these interest groups. This part of the bureaucracy should play a role in monitoring and limiting harmful influences on national welfare. Suzumura (1997) stresses this point in his assessment of the implementability of justifiable industrial policies, and points out the role of professional expertise and personal sincerity of government bureaucrats. World Bank (1993) documents that one of the factors explaining the success of the east Asian countries has been their ability to insulate decision-making and government intervention from excessive interest group influence. This relates to various parts of the bureaucracy, but planning institutions are certainly a prominent institution.

Long-term feasibility and sustainability

One role of a planning organization is to be concerned with the feasibility of outcomes and the sustainability of policies and programmes in the long-run. This concern is more important when markets are non-existent or imperfect and some actors are not present to participate in decision-making.

A major preoccupation of a planning institution is the sustainability of macroeconomic policies as related to public debt and foreign debt accumulation. Activities related to long-term forecasting and explorations of debt, including that of public social security programmes, are important from the point of view of management of the public sector itself. They are also useful information for the private sector. They may be part of the domain of any ministry of finance or treasury, but the perspective of a planning institution on these issues is unique in the sense that it would deal with inter-temporal choice and arbitrage between generations.

Planning institutions usually carry out exercises on the sustainability and feasibility of policies. Whether it is public and balance of payments deficits and their sustainability, or future employment and growth prospects as relating to ongoing policies, planning organizations can play a significant role in identifying challenges, and helping to resolve conflicts and bring about policy changes.[13] This explains why planning ministries have been the main initiators of reforms in many developing countries. The management of shocks[14] is another area in which planning institutions usually play a significant role, given the widely felt and inter-related issues involved that pose problems of sustainability, feasibility and long-term adjustment.

Another similar issue is that of the environment and the extent to which a society at a given level of development should invest in environmental protection and restoration activities, which are costly to the present generation and to growth. Future generations, which are the main beneficiaries of environmental improvement and preservation activities, are not participants in the above-mentioned processes of social choice. A society's institutional framework must contain institutions that help defend the interests of these generations, ensuring that decisions are not biased excessively towards the present.

Enhancement of public policy credibility

Planning may play a role in helping to enhance the credibility of public policies in a variety of ways. First, it is a useful framework for announcing the government's long-term policies, especially those concerning the setting-up of fundamentals of public policy. World Bank (1993), for example, lists six such areas that may constitute basic issues in planning: ensuring low inflation and competitive exchange rates, building human capital, creating effective and secure financial systems, limiting price distortions, absorbing foreign technology and limiting the bias against agriculture. Other issues may also be of interest.

Second, planning could achieve more credibility if policies and choices were subject to "concertation"[15] with the private sector and validated by a political process, such as a parliamentary ratification. This is particularly important in the case of fundamental reforms that have a medium- and long-term character. When the planning process contains procedures for consensus-building in the context of an open political debate, it enhances significantly the credibility of public policies and reforms, reduces their costs and increases their effectiveness.

Of course, enhancing the credibility of policies through planning should not mean that such policies become rigid or no longer subject to continuing debate. The aim is to mitigate the tendency of the political process to focus on short-term considerations and contingencies that may lead to damaging reversals and changes of policies. A point is often made as to why one should expect policy-makers to accept a planning framework that limits their discretionary power and commits them over the medium-term. But constraints on policy-makers that impose medium- and long-term commitments may be a choice that society makes, as through a constitution, whose objective is to improve the management of society.

PLANNING'S MECHANISMS, INSTRUMENTS AND INSTITUTIONAL FRAMEWORK

Planning, in the role and functions described above, is carried out through a number of mechanisms and instruments and requires an appropriate institutional framework. Within the public sector, a planning organization should be involved in the screening of investment projects—through evaluations and reviews of cost-benefit analyses and any other studies related to proposed projects—and in the budget decision-making process. A planning institution is also usually involved in evaluating public policies to determine if they are effective, if their results conform with the stated objectives and how important any deviations and side effects might be.

Another set of planning instruments includes modeling and preparing studies to make projections, which exhibit different policy options and scenarios.[16] Of course, the sophistication and range of such studies will vary according to the country and issue, but their basic character concerns medium- and long-run tendencies, changes and challenges. Macroeconomic models and computable general equilibrium models with microeconomic features would be useful.

A mechanism that is increasingly recognized to be useful is that of concertation and consensus-building in the planning process. Whether it is through harmonization and exchange of information, the clarification and discussion of collective choice issues, or the debate about policies and their implications, the planning process can help build "social capital", improve decision-making and enhance the credibility of the policies. Concertation and consultation involve all groups and parties in development: the government and the various parts of the public sector, the business sector, the banking sector, labour unions and any other relevant groups. The usefulness of concertation has long been discussed in the context of French indicative planning as a mechanism to improve the flow of information between business and government. It has also been discussed in the context of the east Asian experience, particularly with respect to industrial policy, in which deliberation councils have been used to improve the flow of information, to coordinate firms and to assess performance. But consensus building through nation-wide planning extends beyond these limited exercises and helps improve the coherency of public policy, social decision-making and economic performance.

In the preceding discussion I purposely avoided using the word "plan" to emphasize that planning should not be associated exclusively with the elaboration of periodic plans and to suggest that there is room and a role for planning even without adopting "plans" as the foremost instrument or vehicle for planning. In fact, the institutional set-up of planning involves three aspects that I have used somewhat interchangeably: the process of planning, the planning institution and the plan. These aspects are discussed extensively in Malinvaud and Nabli (1997), who show that the process and institutional set-up involve a mixture of periodic planning and continuous assessment, evaluation and adjustment. But the main thrust is to focus on efficiency-enhancing activities, always with a long-term perspective.

CONCLUSION: WHAT'S IN A NAME?

In this chapter I described the important activities that should be carried out by planning institutions. Such activities, as they relate to information exchange, coordination, consensus building, the rationalization and efficiency of public policies and programmes, and the improvement of private sector performance, are varied and complex.

It is relevant to ask whether the term "planning" is an appropriate designation for these activities, since that term has been subject to much use and misuse. At least three meanings have been given to the term in the literature. It has often been used to mean general government intervention in economic activity. It has been more widely used to designate a programme of investment or a blueprint of economic growth and resource allocation over the long run. It has also sometimes been applied to techniques to analyze methods of government intervention.

Some terminology should clearly be avoided, such as "central planning bureau", which conveys the idea of central command. But it is not clear what a new designation for such activities should be. Without a reasonable alternative we might as well maintain the term planning. In my country, Tunisia, it was found awkward to continue using the term "planning ministry" in the context of liberalization and development of a market economy—but no satisfactory alternative has been found.[17] In addition, development plans are still used and are found to be useful. Some countries, such as Morocco, have abandoned planning and development plans. But authorities now seem to be preoccupied by the lack of a long-term framework for policy analysis and guidance. The contest to find the appropriate terminology is open.

NOTES

Useful discussions with members of the United Nations High-Level Group on Development Strategy and Management of the Market Economy are gratefully acknowledged. I am also indebted to comments and suggestions from Lod Berlage, Paul de Grauwe and Jeffrey Nugent. Some of the research was made during a visit to the Centrum voor Economische Studien at the Catholic University at Louvain, Belgium.

1. This was strongly argued and documented, for instance, by Wade (1990).
2. See Turner and Collis (1977) for a review of these arguments.
3. See Suzumura (1997).
4. Surveys are given by Manne (1974), Clark (1975) and Bulmer-Thomas (1982).
5. See Datta-Chaudhuri (1990).
6. A closure rule is the manner in which equilibrium is achieved between aggregates for some macro-balance, such as between savings and investment.
7. A survey of the literature as of the mid-1970s is given in Taylor (1975). The high point of state of the art in this literature can be seen in Chenery (1971) and Blitzer, Clark and Taylor (1975).
8. Such as Westphal (1971, 1975).
9. A demonstration of a possible testing procedure for a linear programming model was developed by Nugent (1970), but such an approach was not followed. The procedure is based on the possibility of explaining the deviations of the

calculated solution from the actual one by underlying market imperfections. For input-output models Bulmer-Thomas (1982) has also developed some tests.

10. It is telling that such models do not appear in the recent *Handbook on Development Economics*, Chenery and Srinivasan (1988, 1989) and Behrman and Srinivasan (1995).

11. See Datta-Chaudhuri (1990).

12. Ranis and Mahmood (1992) study these issues extensively, trying to explain their role in policy changes in developing countries.

13. It is shown using models of political economy that unsustainable policies may be pursued for some time, even when they are known to be so, because of political bargaining over distributional consequences. See, for instance, Alesina and Drazen (1991).

14. On this, see the discussion by Milleron (1997).

15. A term used in French planning, broadly meaning an exchange of views and information.

16. These techniques are discussed in some detail by Malinvaud and Nabli (1997).

17. The title Ministry of Economic Development was used.

REFERENCES

Alesina, Alberto and Allan Drazen. 1991. "Why Are Stabilizations Delayed?" *American Economic Review* 81(5):1170–88.

Behrman, Jere and T.N. Srinivasan. 1995. *Handbook of Development Economics.* Volumes IIIA and IIIB. Amsterdam: Elsevier Science B.V.

Blitzer, Charles R., Peter B. Clark and Lance Taylor, eds. 1975. *Economy-Wide Models and Development Planning.* Oxford: Oxford University Press.

Bulmer-Thomas, Victor. 1982. *Input-Output Analysis in Developing Countries: Sources, Methods and Applications.* Chichester, New York: Wiley.

Chakravarty, Sukhamoy. 1969. *Capital and Economic Development.* Cambridge, Mass.: MIT Press.

____. 1973. "Theory of Development Planning." In H.C. Bos, H. Linnemann and P. de Wolf, eds., *Economic Structure and Development: Essays in Honor of J. Tinbergen.* Amsterdam: North Holland.

____. 1991. "Development Planning: A Reappraisal." *Cambridge Journal of Economics* 15(1):5–20.

Chenery, Hollis B., ed. 1971. *Studies in Development Planning.* Cambridge, Mass.: Harvard University Press.

Chenery, Hollis B. and T.N. Srinivasan. 1988 and 1989. *Handbook of Development Economics.* Volumes I and II. Amsterdam: Elsevier Science.

Clark, Peter B. 1975. "Inter-Sectoral Consistency and Macro-Economic Planning." In Charles R. Blitzer, Peter B. Clark and Lance Taylor, eds., *Economy-Wide Models and Development Planning.* Oxford: Oxford University Press.

Crémer, Helmuth and Jacques Crémer. 1993. "L'apport des Théories Economiques à la Planification Indicative." *Revue Economique*, N°. Hors Série, 44.

Datta-Chaudhuri, Mrinal. 1990. "Market Failures and Government Failures." *Journal of Economic Perspectives* 4(3):25–39.

Hirshman, Albert O. 1958. *The Strategy of Economic Development*. New Haven: Yale University Press.

Krugman, Paul. 1992. "Toward a Counter-Revolution in Development Theory." *Proceedings of the Annual World Bank Conference on Development Economics*. Washington, D.C.: World Bank.

Lewis, Arthur W. 1966. *Development Planning: The Essentials of Economic Policy*. George Allen and Unwin.

Malinvaud, Edmond and Mustapha K. Nabli. 1997. "The Future of Planning in Market Economies." In Edmond Malinvaud et al., eds., *Development Strategy and Management of the Market Economy*, Volume I. Oxford: Clarendon Press.

Manne, Alan S. 1974. "Multi-Sector Models for Development Planning." *Journal of Development Economics* 1(1):43–69.

Milleron, Jean-Claude. 1997. "Global Aspects of a Development Strategy." In Edmond Malinvaud et al., eds., *Development Strategy and Management of the Market Economy*, Volume I. Oxford: Clarendon Press.

Murphy, K.M., A. Shleifer and R. Vishny. 1989. "Industrialization and the Big Push." *Journal of Political Economy* 97(October):1003–26.

Nugent, Jeffrey B. 1970. "Linear Programming Models for National Planning: Demonstration of a Testing Procedure." *Econometrica* 38(November):831–55.

Ranis, Gustav and Syed Akhtar Mahmood. 1992. *The Political Economy of Development Policy Change*. Cambridge, Mass. and Oxford: Basil Blackwell.

Rodríguez-Clare, Andrés. 1997. "Positive Feedback Mechanisms in Economic Development: A Review of Recent Contributions." In Richard Sabot and István P. Székely, eds., *Development Strategy and Management of the Market Economy*, Volume II. Oxford: Clarendon Press.

Rosenstein-Rodan, P.N. 1943. "Problems of Industrialization in Eastern and Southern Europe." *The Economic Journal* 53:202–11.

Scitovsky, Tibor. 1954. "Two Concepts of External Economies." *Journal of Political Economy* 62:143–51.

Stiglitz, Joseph. 1997. "The Role of Government in the Economy of Developing Countries." In Edmond Malinvaud et al., eds., *Development Strategy and Management of the Market Economy*, Volume I. Oxford: Clarendon Press.

Suzumura, Kotaro. 1997. "Industrial Policy in the Developing Market Economy." In Edmond Malinvaud et al., eds., *Development Strategy and Management of the Market Economy*, Volume I. Oxford: Clarendon Press.

Taylor, Lance. 1975. "Theoretical Foundations and Technical Implications." In Charles R. Blitzer, Peter B. Clark and Lance Taylor, eds., *Economy-Wide Models and Development Planning*. Oxford: Oxford University Press.

Turner, R. Kerny and Clive Collis. 1977. *The Economics of Planning*. Macmillan Studies in Economics, Macmillan Press.

Wade, Robert. 1990. *Governing the Market: Economic Theory and the Role of Government in East Asian Industrialization*. Princeton, N.J.: Princeton University Press.

Westphal, Larry E. 1971. "An Intertemporal Planning Model Featuring Economies of Scale." In Hollis B. Chenery, ed. *Studies in Development Planning*. Cambridge, Mass.: Harvard University Press.

____. 1975. "Planning with Economies of Scale." In Charles R. Blitzer, Peter B. Clark and Lance Taylor, eds., *Economy-Wide Models and Development Planning*. Oxford: Oxford University Press.

World Bank. 1993. *The East Asian Miracle: Economic Growth and Public Policy.* New York: Oxford University Press.

8

The Role of the State in Post–chaos Situations

VITO TANZI

There is now an extensive literature on the role of the state for groups of countries that share common characteristics—groups such as industrial, developing, transition, newly industrialized and very poor countries. Researchers have reached several important normative conclusions about that role in countries with well-functioning markets and with poorly functioning markets. In the first the role of the state should be largely to correct the market's shortcomings; in the second it should be to supplement market activities.[1] But much of this literature is of limited use for defining how the government should behave in post-chaos circumstances, which have arisen with unfortunate frequency in recent years.

Many countries or territories have recently experienced chaotic situations, during which the government largely stopped functioning and many economic institutions were destroyed. Countries that have undergone, or are still undergoing, such experiences are Angola, Cambodia, Liberia, Mozambique, Rwanda and Somalia.[2] Other countries or territories that could be added to this group are some of the former Soviet economies, Bosnia and the West Bank and Gaza Strip. In this latter group the post-chaos situation was less the result of war or revolution than of the sudden birth of new political entities—which needed to create the institutions that would make them viable economies.

Whether a situation is chaotic or not is, of course, a matter of judgment. Chaos comes in many forms and degrees so that it may be difficult to distinguish between a situation that is truly post-chaotic and one in which extreme poverty or poor economic policies have created disastrous economic conditions. Rather than discussing possible cases, I will assume here that a country (or a territory) is post-chaotic if it has emerged from a destructive (civil) war or another calamity that has fundamentally changed the character of the country and its economy. Much of the physical and social infrastructure has been destroyed, and the country has operated temporarily without a government.[3]

As the name implies, the post-chaos situation assumes that some semblance of stability has returned in that widespread destruction or fighting has ended; that at least a minimal authority has been established, which is capable of enforcing some degree of law and order on a significant part of the national territory; and that such authority has been recognized by the international community as representing the particular country. This last condition is important, because in its absence the country will not be able to draw on foreign assistance for financial and technical resources.[4]

CREATING A BASIC POLICY FRAMEWORK

Because it lacks resources, the government will be forced to select a minimal set of policies and institutions in post-chaos situations. It will not have the financial means, the personnel or the ability to do more than take care of the most immediate needs. Attempts to exceed that minimal structure are likely to fail: financial resources will be extremely scarce and, especially at the beginning, will be limited largely to foreign assistance. The personnel available will generally be low quality, because the civil strife eliminated the skilled personnel—they emigrated, were killed or simply disappeared. At the same time there may be strong pressures to give the few government jobs to former combatants, even though they do not have the skills for these jobs. The integration of these demobilized former combatants in the official economy is essential. However key jobs should be reserved for individuals with some minimum expertise.

Most of the essential institutions that allow a government to function, such as the tax administration, customs, the central bank and administrative offices, may have been destroyed or badly damaged and may have been inoperative for years. For a while, at least, the post-chaos government will not be able to recreate all the needed institutions. It will thus have to focus on rebuilding, or creating from scratch, the most essential ones.[5] Thus building basic institutions will be the government's most urgent and essential task in the post-chaos period. In addition, the government should make a clear statement of the policies that it intends to follow over the medium and long run once the essential institutions are in place. This statement will provide the road map for future developments and should explain to potential domestic and foreign investors the role that the government wishes to allocate to the public sector in the medium and long run. This statement should be seen as an important building block in establishing the credibility of the government.[6]

Because the control that the government has on the country may still be tenuous, for a while its main activities may have to be concentrated on the capital city and on the better-controlled or accessible territories. Furthermore, the urgency of the situation will require that the government act immediately and will largely determine the areas to which the government should give most of its attention. Some government functions that would be considered important in more normal times may have to be neglected.

The role of the state is generally expressed or specified through laws and through rules or regulations. For example, the government sets speed limits and regulates traffic. It enforces contracts and regulates economic and social behaviour. It taxes some individuals and subsidizes others. The government enacts laws and introduces rules, but it requires institutions that will enforce or administer these laws and rules. For example, the enactment of a tax law by itself does nothing to ensure that the government will receive any tax revenue. To achieve that objective, the government will need to create a tax administration.

In stable and more developed countries laws and rules can be complex, because they meet several objectives and the institutions that enforce them are sophisticated. In post-chaos situations laws and rules must be simple so that embryonic and unsophisticated institutions can cope with them. The government must thus search for laws that are relatively simple, enforceable and can be adapted quickly—and for institutions that can operate with limited means.

If a country has a past—if the country existed, in an administrative or political sense, before the chaos set in, or if it was part of a larger jurisdiction—it is likely that some of the old laws and rules can be borrowed and adopted to the new conditions. But borrowing must be selective and limited to only those laws and rules that are simple enough to be administered and enforced under present conditions. For example, the West Bank and Gaza Strip has found it convenient to adopt some of the tax laws that had been introduced by the Israeli administration.

The acceptance of some pre-chaos laws and rules may create some problems by revealing old claims. For example, if tax records still exist and past tax laws are adopted, unpaid tax bills from the pre-chaos situation may create government claims against some individuals who may not have the means to settle them. Another example: relying on past rules and contracts may create claims arising from unpaid loans to banks or to other institutions. Furthermore, recognizing ownership rights from the pre-chaos period will enable past owners to make claims on properties occupied by others during the period of chaos. These problems of overhang have introduced uncertainty about claims and property rights, which have discouraged investment or other beneficial economic actions. The government thus must be careful in recognizing past obligations and using past laws.

The government's early adoption of a clear policy stance or policy framework would help to accelerate the transition from a post-chaos situation to a more normal one. This framework should state in broad but clear terms the views of the government on the relative role of the state and the market in the newly evolving economy. For example, decisions on privatization, property rights and the economic freedom of individuals should be made and announced at this time. It is important to reiterate that the announced policy framework must be simple, clear and transparent and must be seen as an honest declaration of intention on the part of the political forces in power.[7]

Transparency will be particularly important because post-chaos situations (just like the situations created in the restructuring of transition economies) create many opportunities for the groups in power, or for those who have access to them, to accumulate wealth through corrupt practices or various forms of rent seeking.[8] A demonstration of absolute honesty and objectivity on the part of political leaders will be essential if good governance is going to characterize economic policy in the future. Good or bad habits developed at this time, and poor policies are likely to become ingrained and have lasting effects. Uganda is a country that after undergoing a period of near chaos set clear goals and attempted to eradicate or, at least, sharply reduce corruption. Its example should be instructive for other countries.[9]

CREATING A MINIMAL INSTITUTIONAL CAPACITY

Institutions are needed to administer the specific policies that give substance to the general policy framework. As indicated above, these institutions must be simple and transparent and must not require more resources (financial and human) than the country can afford. And they must allow the country's authorities to pursue their most basic and urgent goals.

Fiscal institutions

Any organized society must create institutions that mobilize public resources and use them to promote social goals. Therefore, a first and most essential institution is the ministry of finance. This ministry will have the double responsibility of raising public resources and using them for the most urgent and essential public uses.[10]

The ministry of finance must have two branches: a budget and treasury office, and a revenue mobilization office. The budget and treasury office must register all the revenue received and all the expenditures made. It must authorize all spending and record the amount spent and the use to which the money is put. It will be important to create a single account that registers all revenue and all expenditures. The creation of extra-budgetary accounts is discouraged unless there are strong reasons for such accounts. In the post-chaos period, when the management of public spending is in its infancy, misclassification of uses and the under-recording of spending may be common problems. These problems may lead to misuse of public funds. Another problem may be the tendency for cash spending to lag behind spending measured by commitments. This tendency will lead to the creation of arrears and contingent liabilities, and will begin to obfuscate future fiscal policy. Because the basic conditions for running an efficient treasury system will not be in place, it will be important to put the most able and honest individuals in charge of the treasury. These individuals must have the power to deny requests for spending that will inevitably come from people with strong political power.

Because of the scarcity of funds to carry out the main activities that the government would like to undertake, there may be strong pressures to engage in quasi-fiscal actions. These are regulations that have the objective of replacing taxing and spending while broadly aiming for a particular objective. For example, the cost of medicine might be reduced not through direct subsidies to users but by allowing the importation of medicine at an overvalued exchange rate. Another example would be to guarantee some forms of borrowing so that the interest cost is reduced.[11] Quasi-fiscal activities may appear costless at the time they are created, but they often create future problems. The governments of post-chaos countries must resist the urge to engage in these activities.

The budget and treasury office must introduce public expenditure planning. Planning for spending will be difficult because much needed information will not be available, economic conditions will be changing rapidly, the course of future revenue will be uncertain and necessary staff and essential equipment, such as computers, will be scarce.

While the essentially political effort on the part of the government to establish a basic policy framework cannot be easily helped from outside the country, the effort to create the institutions that will enable the implementation of the basic policy framework can draw on outside help—because the decisions made in this context will be more technical than political. Technical assistance available from various international institutions, such as the United Nations, the IMF, the World Bank and the European Community, and from individual countries can be helpful. This assistance can provide scarce and essential resources and skills, and can facilitate the process of institution creation.

But some basic rules must be followed when relying on external resources. First, the organizations providing technical assistance must ensure that the experts that they send are professionals with wide, international experience and not experts who have worked only in their own country and are thus unfamiliar with the constraints in countries with different environments. These "national" experts might advise policy-makers of the post-chaos countries to reproduce the institutions of their own country—which would be too complex and too resource-intensive for the situation at hand. This problem has been common in many countries.

Second, the assisting organizations must coordinate their actions and advice to ensure that they do not confuse the receiving countries with too much or with conflicting advice. Third, the organizations providing technical assistance must help the post-chaos country to create needed institutions—they must not do the work themselves. If they create institutions without involving local personnel, they will provide little or no training to those who will eventually run the institutions and may create alien and ineffective institutions.

The scarce resources available for government spending must be used with extreme care and with the aim of converting the post-chaos situation into a more normal situation. A fast return to normalcy should be the most immediate objective. Some spending may be required to increase the country's security—for the most urgent defense or police needs. Some spending will be needed to resettle soldiers and misplaced civilians, and some to put the damaged physical infrastructure into minimum working condition. For example, the most important roads and bridges must be repaired. Some buildings must be fixed to house the new government institutions.

Some funds must be spent for essential health care, such as for vaccinations or for medicines for the sick or wounded. In the early period the focus should be in restoring whatever is left of the past social and physical infrastructure rather than engaging in new investments. Operation and maintenance spending should prevail over investment spending.[12] Sectors that will become important later may have to be ignored initially. For example, much educational spending can be put off until the country resumes normalcy.

The other branch of the ministry of finance is the revenue mobilization branch. Initially a substantial portion of total resources available to the government will come from foreign grants. Thus accountability for these external funds will be very important, because the size of the foreign grants will be influenced by the perception of whether or not the funds are put to good use. As time passes, foreign assistance will become less important or will dry up given the greater needs of the country and the likely reduction in the size of grants as the country's situation stabilizes. It is thus important to focus on the tax system so as to make it productive in the medium run—it will have to replace foreign assistance as the main source of revenue. But creating a productive tax system from scratch is no easy task. Short cuts have to be taken to speed the process.

It would be helpful to rely, to the extent possible, on aspects of the system that existed before the chaos. With modifications, some old taxes may still be usable and could be supplemented by new, simple taxes. Excises on some products should be the first taxes relied on. Fees and charges can also be levied. These can be made to reflect presumptive tax bases. Most taxes will be imposed on visible or tangible bases (cars, houses, cigarettes, gasoline) rather than on invisible ones (income, value added).[13] Imports will provide an important tax base, especially if the bulk is channelled through a few easily controllable entry points.[14] In sum, the government will have relatively few "tax handles", and these will need to be used fully, keeping in mind that effective tax rates should not become so high that they discourage incipient activities or encourage smuggling and the development of an underground economy. The policy framework might include an implicit tax constitution in the sense that the government must make an explicit commitment not to raise tax rates above some reasonable level.[15]

Monetary institutions

During periods of chaos barter (and use of some foreign exchange) replaces national money in the conduct of economic exchanges. Some use of barter is likely to continue, especially during the early part of the post-chaos period. But the absence of a liquid means of exchange can be a substantial impediment to the revival of the economy. A continuation of the extended use of barter would thus become an obstacle to establishing a viable economy. Barter also increases the difficulty of raising taxes. Therefore, as the country emerges from chaos, it will be necessary to create liquidity for transactions. It will also be necessary to create the institutions that allow payments to be made and received by parties who are not in direct physical contact.

An alternative to a national currency would be to use, or continue to use, the currency of another country. The problem with this alternative is that foreign currency is very scarce. Furthermore, in post-chaos countries, as economic conditions improve, there will be an increasing need for money because economic exchanges that use money will replace barter.[16] Thus the use of foreign currency requires that a substantial share of foreign currency obtained from exports or from foreign aid goes to satisfy this liquidity need rather than be used to import badly needed foreign goods. In sum, the use of a foreign currency as the means for domestic transactions would impose an excessive cost on the country. A better alternative is to use a national currency.

If stocks of national currency are available from the past, these stocks can be put to immediate use. If stocks are not available, but printing plates are, these can be used to produce liquidity relatively quickly. If neither stocks nor plates are available, the process of generating a new, national currency can take years and can be costlier. The need to make these decisions calls for the immediate creation of a monetary authority (which I will call the central bank).

The central bank will perform several essential functions. It will provide a national currency and by controlling supply, ensure that it keeps its relative value over time. It will provide guidance on the reopening of some banks and regulate their activity afterwards. It will establish a system for making payments within the economy. It will also decide on the exchange rate and convert foreign aid or grants into national currency. Spending institutions will thus receive domestic currency instead of foreign currency.[17]

The use of a national currency in a period when the demand for money is growing will provide the government with some seigniorage revenue. This revenue, added to the grants that the country gets from abroad and to the (still-limited) tax revenue, will provide the government with the non-inflationary resources on which to base its spending. There will be a rather rigid limit on spending, because at this stage there will be little or no possibility of financing a fiscal deficit domestically, except through inflationary finance. This implies that fiscal authorities have to be extremely careful in conducting their affairs and that the exchange rate should be either fixed or managed in a way that keeps its real value relatively constant.

Some post-chaos policy-makers have seen the creation of a central bank as providing some relaxation of the budget constraint. However, the use of inflationary finance for financing public expenditure imposes many distortions and costs on an economy. In particular, new economies that are trying to attract foreign resources and to stimulate domestic private sector activities should resist the temptation to use inflationary finance.

The establishment of a national currency and its increasing use in the economy brings to the fore the need to pay attention to the payments system. Banks are the institutions that permit payments to be made among economic agents who may not come into physical contact and do not exchange cash. They allow for deposits, foreign exchange transactions, associated payments services and some intermediation between surplus units and deficit units. Banks allow economic units with current surpluses to lend to economic units with current deficits without the need for these individuals to meet. Once non-cash payments become insignificant, payment systems become important, and clearing facilities must be in place to serve each region, performing their clearing function daily or at least frequently.

This function must be developed because it is likely to have disappeared during the period of chaos. It is closely tied to the soundness and the efficiency of the banking system. Thus the role of the monetary authorities in reopening banks, in regulating them and in trying to restructure their assets will be very important.

CONCLUSIONS

This short chapter has attempted to highlight some of the issues related to the role that governments of post-chaos countries should play immediately after the widespread fighting or destruction has ended. The chapter has emphasized the role of essential institutions. Often, institutions are taken for granted and little thought is given to their fundamental role. It is only when they disappear or become badly damaged that their true importance becomes obvious. We forget that institutions are the vehicles that carry out policies. In post-chaos countries in which institutions have been largely destroyed, the most fundamental role of the government is to recreate them.

Once basic institutions have been recreated and the economy has started to function, the attention of the government can move from building institutions to pursuing optimal policies. These policies should be consistent with the policy framework announced during the immediate post-chaos period.

NOTES

1. For a recent contribution to the debate, see Stiglitz (1994).
2. In other countries civil strife created very bad economic conditions but some semblance of government always remained in place.
3. The example of Somalia indicates that a country can operate for some time without a proper government.
4. However, such a country may still be able to draw on the resources of non-governmental organizations (NGOs).
5. As countries grow and become more advanced, the number of institutions will grow to deal with the economy's increasing complexity. But only few of these institutions are truly essential.
6. Institution building and a clear statement of government policies are also important to satisfy the economic and political conditions of donors in the short

run. More and more donors make their assistance conditional on good governance and accountability.

7. Post-chaos countries will have the benefit of starting the process without the heavy baggage of past rules and regulations that often slow down the growth of countries. They can thus take advantage of the opportunity to start with a clean slate.

8. There will be strong pressures on the part of some groups to promote policies (say, protection from imports) that will provide them with rents in the future.

9. See Ruzindana (1996). For a discussion of general issues related to post-chaos situations see Mooney (1995) and Bernarder, and others (1995).

10. The country can do without other ministries except those related to foreign affairs and, perhaps, defense and internal security. Gandhi (1994) suggests that five ministries would be needed. These are finance, internal and external security, foreign affairs, economy, and education, health and social welfare.

11. For various examples see Tanzi (1995).

12. Thus the principal goal should be capital restoration rather than capital accumulation.

13. See Tanzi (1994).

14. A customs office may need to be established.

15. The level could be determined on the basis of international practices. Gandhi (1994) lists the laws, institutions and information required by a post-chaos country.

16. Also, more precautionary balances may be held in money rather than in goods.

17. For more details on some of these aspects, see IMF (1995).

REFERENCES

Bernarder, Bernt, Joel Charney, Marita Eastmond, Claes Lindahl and Joakim Ögendal. 1995. *Facing a Complex Emergency: An Evaluation of Swedish* Support to Emergency Aid to Cambodia. Stockholm: SIDA Evaluation Report.

Gandhi, Ved P. 1994. "The Architecture of a Minimal Fiscal Structure for Countries in Post-Chaos/Post-Conflict Situations." IMF, Fiscal Affairs Department, Washington, D.C.

IMF (International Monetary Fund). 1995. "The Design of a Minimal Monetary and Exchange Structure for Countries in Post-Chaos/Post-Conflict Situations." Washington, D.C.: Monetary and Exchange Affairs Department IMF.

Mooney, Terrance Lorne, ed. 1995. *The Challenge of Development within Conflict Zones.* Paris: Development Centre of the OECD.

Ruzindana, Augustine. 1996. "The Importance of Attitude of the Leadership in Flighting Corruption in Uganda." Paper presented at the Institute for International Economics, Washington, D.C., April 17.

Stiglitz, Joseph E. 1994. *Whither Socialism?* Cambridge, Mass.: MIT Press.

Tanzi, Vito. 1995. "The Role of Government and the Efficiency of Fiscal Instruments." IMF Working Paper 95/100, Washington, D.C.

Tanzi, Vito. 1994. "Taxation and Economic Structure." *Public Choice Studies.* Twentyfourth issue 24(12):35–4.

PART FOUR

FINANCE

9

Financial Sector Development Policy: The Importance of Reputational Capital and Governance

THOMAS HELLMANN AND KEVIN MURDOCK

The performance and effectiveness of financial institutions are important considerations for policy-makers concerned about economic growth. Growth, after all, is heavily dependent on investment, and a significant fraction of all investment flows through financial institutions. Furthermore, incidences of financial instability in some countries have shown that poor financial policies can have serious consequences. For example, when the Southern Cone countries liberalized financial markets before achieving macroeconomic stability and low inflation, banks in those countries performed disastrously. In the United States the partial deregulation of the savings and loans (S&L) industry invited a great deal of gambling and looting of depositors' funds, ultimately costing taxpayers hundreds of billions of dollars.

Partly because the financial sector of the east Asian high-growth economies grew substantially, financial development has received special attention recently in several developing countries. King and Levine (1993a, 1993b) demonstrated in a broad cross-country study that financial deepening had strong explanatory power for differential growth performance. If financial stability and financial deepening are worthy goals, what are the mechanisms that policy-makers can employ to achieve such goals?

Policy-makers are faced with a vast array of options. They can affect interest rates, they can decide which financial institutions will be allowed to operate and they can devise a regulatory framework for financial intermediaries. Policy-makers must decide which type of financial system they would ultimately like to develop. In the former socialist economies, for example, policy-makers must decide whether they should look to the west for a US-style market-based financial system, or whether they should look to the east for a Japanese-style relationship-based financial system.

Here, we will propose a conceptual framework for thinking about these issues, emphasizing how theoretical concepts can be applied to the fundamental questions that underlie financial policy formulation. The reader should be aware that the views established here are not necessarily shared by all people. Moreover, we argue that the theory of financial markets and policy has developed rapidly over the past 20 years—and the empirical evidence is lagging behind. We will therefore make only cursory reference to empirical work.

We begin at the very nucleus of the financial system: the individual financial transaction. How does a financial transaction, say the disbursement of a loan, differ from a standard economic transaction, like purchasing a good with cash? The financial transaction is fundamentally different—it is the exchange of a real asset for a promise. The borrower promises to make a payment at some time in the future. The value of the transaction to the lender thus depends critically on the quality of the promise, which is in turn dependent on a number of characteristics, such as the reputation of the borrower, the ability of the lender to monitor and control the borrower and the consequences of default for the borrower. This simple observation implies that policy-makers should focus on two key characteristics of the financial system—the *reputational capital* possessed by private agents and the *governance mechanisms* of financial institutions.

By reputational capital we mean the incremental profits that accrue to borrowers when they have good reputations. Each period, borrowers have an incentive to maintain this reputation because if the reputation is ruined, borrowers lose these excess profits in all subsequent periods. Thus, possessors of reputational capital have powerful incentives preventing them from engaging in predatory behaviour designed to extract value from creditors—borrowers must trade-off the one-period gain against the ongoing loss of profits from a ruined reputation. By governance mechanisms we mean both monitoring (ex ante, interim and ex post), through which lenders influence the behaviour of borrowers, and the credible enforcement and discipline mechanisms used to punish those who deviate from good investment behaviour. In this chapter we argue that reputational capital and governance mechanisms form the common thread that helps to unify the analysis of financial markets and policies.

We begin this chapter with a brief review of the thinking on market failures and government failures. Rather than attempting to define whether policy-makers should rely on the government or on markets, we recognize that each institution has comparative strengths and weaknesses. For example, most economists accept the role of the government in creating a legal infrastructure that facilitates efficient contracting. And for the allocation of commodity-like products, markets are definitely superior institutions. Policy should thus consider the comparative advantages and disadvantages of each institution.

Our discussion of financial markets in the second section begins with a restatement of their role in the economy. In addition to the well-recognized role of allocating capital—mobilizing, aggregating and distributing funds for investment—we emphasize the role of financial markets in exercising governance control, that is, the assurance that funds are used well.

Recognizing that different financial systems have different degrees of governance control, we identify a simple two-by-two matrix that describes four combinations of ownership and governance (see figure 9.1). Soft-budgeting banking (S-banking) is characterized by government ownership and low governance, in particular the lack of discipline imposed ex-post on borrowers that do not live up to their promises. The financial institutions in China provide an example. Hard-budgeting banking (H-banking) is characterized by government ownership and strong governance control, especially in terms of ex-ante selection criteria and ex-post enforcement mechanisms. The Republic of Korea is an example of this model. Relationship-based banking (R-banking) is characterized by private financial institutions that exercise strong governance control, in terms of monitoring relationships. The main bank system in Japan is an example. Finally, arm's-length banking (A-banking) is characterized by private financial institutions and low governance. Different agents specialize in different monitoring functions, and no one agent is able to exercise significant control. The US financial system fits this description.

Which system is desirable? The answer depends critically on a country's stage of financial development. First, we consider private ownership a desirable property. We argue, however, that there is a steep "cliff" between S-banking and A-banking: a country cannot simply privatize an ill-managed financial sector and expect specialized monitoring institutions to function properly. Instead, we argue that *a feasible transition path must include a period of high governance* (an R-banking system, preceded possibly by an H-banking system), in which sound financial institutions are allowed to develop reputational capital. Whether an economy should move closer to A-banking or remain closer to R-banking in the long run is an open question.

If we agree that an R-banking system should be the goal of financial development, we must identify the policies that allow for development of reputational capital and good governance controls. In doing so, we will be able to put into perspective some of the policy issues that are now being debated in the context of financial development. We will lay out the key arguments that others have brought to the various debates and then analyze these arguments within our framework.

In the third section we show that interest rate controls, while typically chosen for the wrong reasons, can have beneficial effects on the behaviour of banks. We advocate an integrated analysis of interest rate controls and prudential regulation. We show that the effectiveness of prudential regulation is mainly a function of governance and, in particular, the discipline that can be imposed on bank managers. As for deposit insurance, we argue that it is socially useful and that it will not undermine the soundness of the banking system as long as prudential regulation is successfully implemented.

A very different question is that of the role of securities markets. We argue that policy-makers should not push for the development of securities markets before reputational capital and good governance are deeply ingrained in financial institutions. Banks should be allowed to participate in these markets, that is, the government should allow for universal banks. A final topic of discussion is the role of directed credits. Here, we argue that extreme caution should be exercised. Directed credits are not a financial policy, but an industrial policy that uses financial markets to distribute subsidies. Such policies should never be implemented at the expense of creating inflationary pressures or undermining the franchise value of banking institutions. If, however, directed credit policies are subjected to an appropriate governance structure, they may become a powerful tool for industrial policy.

What do all of these policies amount to? Policy-makers are looking for a paradigm, a few powerful ideas, on which to base policy. As we will see in the first section, economic theory can no longer provide a simple formula for the role of government. We therefore believe that there is a need to search for a new framework. In an earlier paper (Hellmann, Murdock and Stiglitz, 1996b) we attempted to develop the outlines of a new paradigm for financial development, which we called *financial restraint*. The underlying philosophy is that government can complement markets using a small number of well-targeted policies. These policies—modest deposit rate controls and restrictions on competition—create rents in the banking sector that can be captured only by the continued operation of the institution. Thus the government, through financial restraint, can exogenously create reputational capital. These policies should give private agents incentives to refrain from opportunistic behaviour that may otherwise occur in private markets. The development of reputational capital and governance structures are key stepping stones towards that purpose. The essence of these policies is that they give banks an interest in their long-term operation, rather than in the extraction of value from their current assets.

Successful implementation of financial restraint requires several important constraints on government actions. First, even though the government places a ceiling on the deposit rate, this rate must always be positive in real terms. This requirement, in turn, demands that the government maintain macroeconomic stability and a low inflation rate. A government running large budget deficits or practicing inflationary monetary policy will be unable to successfully implement this policy regime. Second, as the economy matures, private sector financial institutions and firms will endogenously develop reputational capital, which will reduce and ultimately eliminate the need for government intervention. Thus, the government should gradually free entry and increase the deposit rate ceiling. The policies of financial restraint are thus designed to promote the transition from a low state to a high state of financial development, rather than to be used to maintain a steady-state position.

When a government effectively practices financial restraint, the banking sector will contain institutions whose incentives are aligned with creating social value and that can focus their interests on the long-term success of the firms they finance. The banking sector can thus become the cornerstone of the development process, facilitating the economy's transition to a more efficient state.

COMPARING MARKET FAILURES AND GOVERNMENT FAILURES

The Lange-Lerner-Taylor theorem stated that there would be no difference between a central planning system and a free market system as long as planners set quantities appropriately.[1] This result probably constitutes an all-time low in economists' understanding of the differences between markets and government. Given the tremendous importance of that understanding and despite the temptation for ideological polarization, economists have made significant headway. Most economists now agree that old-fashioned central planning has failed. The other polar belief, that free markets are always good and that there is no role for government in the economy, has been slower to recede—mostly due to what we would call blind-sighted adherence to neoclassical economics. The first and second welfare theorems of Arrow and Debreu state that under perfect information, complete markets, perfect competition, "well-behaved" consumer preferences and technology, and no externalities, free markets are always Pareto-efficient, and every Pareto-efficient allocation can be achieved by free markets given an appropriate choice of initial endowments. Greenwald and Stiglitz (1986) derive a general result showing that virtually any departure from the assumptions of Arrow and Debreu void the first and second welfare theorems.

Today, most economists admit that the government has some role in the economy. For example, they accept that there are public goods, such as maintaining a legal system. Not surprisingly, most current debates therefore focus on specific questions: Should the government run education? Should the government regulate health care? How should the government regulate financial markets?

In answering these questions, economists typically begin with the ideal of an efficient market and then ask what deviations from the ideal apply to a particular problem. This approach has been the basis for a large literature on market failures arising from imperfect competition, public goods and externalities, incomplete markets or imperfect information (Stiglitz 1988). A temptation in that literature is to identify a market failure and then demonstrate that a cognizant and benevolent government policy could solve it. Although this methodology has some merit, it is important to recognize that the assumption of a cognizant and benevolent government policy may differ as much from reality as Arrow and Debreu's assumption of perfect competition. In other words, any serious policy analysis should attempt to trade-off market failures and government failures.

What are some of the recurrent themes that arise in discussions of market versus government failures? Stiglitz (1989, 1993a) discusses this issue at great length. He argues that governments have a number of fundamental advantages and disadvantages compared with the market. The government has three fundamental advantages: it has the ability to tax, the ability to punish and the ability to prohibit.[2] It is easy to see that these are three potentially very powerful tools that could be used to increase the efficiency of private markets, as well as to extract rents from the private sector. Stiglitz argues that this ambiguity sits at the root of the government's disadvantages. Because the government can use powerful instruments, society must place significant constraints on their exercise. As a result we observe very detailed and often contradictory rules and restrictions applied to government agencies. It may also explain common observations, such as that, relative to markets, the government may have less access to information, a weaker ability to price-discriminate or greater difficulty in transferring property rights. Stiglitz (1989) provides numerous examples of how these arguments can be applied to specific trade-offs between market and government failures. The point of the exercise is to identify exactly where government action can increase economic efficiency, given its capabilities and limitations.

It is also important to realize that government actions are often complementary to, rather than a substitution for, the market. That certain markets are imperfect does not imply that the government should take over those markets. Instead, the government should take actions to make markets more efficient. This is the essence of regulation. A recurrent theme in this chapter will be that the government can intervene in the economy by affecting the transfer of rents among private agents without capturing any of those rents itself: the rents should be used to alter the incentives of private agents so that private marginal incentives approach social marginal incentives, thereby improving social returns to private decisions.

This last point emphasizes the need to move away from a dichotomous view of government and markets. This need becomes even more evident when government and private business cooperate to make markets and regulation more efficient. Good government-business relations (as witnessed, for example, in the Republic of Korea) can lead to more efficient outcomes than either the government or free markets functioning alone can achieve.

Another interesting question is whether different countries face different trade-offs. Here, we emphasize the importance of institutions and path dependence. A country's institutions affect the feasibility of different policies. A country with good accounting standards, for example, will find it easier to implement capital requirements than a country that has no effective accounting. Once we recognize that institutions matter, path dependence is also likely to be important. A country with a tradition of efficient bureaucracies will find it easier to implement capital requirements: if banks believe that regulators will check their books, many banks will conform with regulations. And if most banks conform with regulations, regulators will find it much easier to supervise banks' books, as they can focus on a much smaller set of problem cases. History can thus influence expectations that determine the equilibrium behaviour in the economy.

The distinguishing feature of financial markets—the promise

We begin our analysis by considering a particularly important feature that distinguishes financial market transactions from other kinds of transactions: in a financial transaction a real good is exchanged for a promise of payment sometime in the future. In analyzing the value of this promise, a number of important aspects must be considered. First, the value of a promise depends on who makes it. Promises from the US government have much more value than promises made by a street-corner vendor. Second, the value of a promise depends on the credibility of the counter-party's behaviour. This is the moral hazard problem that arises from limited liability—the counter-party does not have as strong an incentive to preserve your capital as you would yourself. Third, the value of a promise depends on the recourse that one would have if the counter-party failed to make good on that promise. If failure to repay generates a significant cost for the counter-party, the promise has much more value than if the counter-party can walk away freely.

The above highlights the importance of information and agency costs in financial markets. Many of the important characteristics of a financial transaction are unobservable—the true intent of the borrower, the quality of a project to be funded, a project's riskiness and the quality of the management after the investment is made. Consequently, we argue that *pure market-based interactions are not conducive to efficient financial transactions*. In a pure market transaction a large number of equivalent buyers bid to purchase an identical good from a large number of equivalent sellers. If the good is a commodity and all of its characteristics are readily observable, then a pure market transaction will be efficient. But in financial transactions, characteristics of both buyers and sellers (that is, borrowers and lenders) are important to the value of the transaction (see Stiglitz 1985).

In competitive markets we expect that mechanisms will be introduced to reduce the agency cost of financial intermediation. One such important mechanism is the use of collateral. When agents are investing their own equity capital in a project, the adverse incentives that arise because borrowers have limited liability disappear—the investor bears all of the risk and captures all of the gain from the investment. For a number of reasons (which will be discussed in the next section), however, not all investors have sufficient equity capital to finance their projects, and thus most projects will be only partially collateralized with equity capital.

We propose that a central feature of policies designed to overcome agency costs inherent in financial intermediation should be the creation and deployment of reputational capital as a form of collateral. Firms and banks with high reputational capital have a stake in their own long-run existence and are thus more capable of making high-quality promises. A reputation has value only if the owner receives greater utility—and in the corporate context this typically means higher profits—from maintaining that reputation. Thus, *reputation must provide an ongoing flow of super-normal profits*, or what we will call a *franchise value* (see also Caprio and Summers, 1995; Hellmann, Murdock and Stiglitz, 1996b). The capitalized value of this flow of profits—in the reputational capital of the firm—can be substantial. If a firm breaks the promise inherent in a financial contract, its reputational capital will be damaged or destroyed. Reputational capital creates strong incentives to perform well without engaging in opportunistic behaviour.

To illustrate that reputational capital is a powerful instrument for reducing agency costs in financial intermediation, consider the following simple example. A company with no significant assets and no reputational capital borrows $100 at 10 per cent interest. The company has two investment opportunities: project A returns $125 with certainty, and project B returns $150 or nothing with equal probability. Clearly, the socially efficient choice is project A (higher total expected return with no risk), but the borrower will choose project

B, which has a higher private expected return, $20, than project A, $15. This example shows that there are two components to the private returns on an investment: value creation and value extraction. Only value creation has social value. But with a financial contract characterized by imperfect information, borrowers may find it in their private interest to pursue a strategy of value extraction, not value creation.[3]

Consider next the case in which the borrowing firm still has no assets, but has reputational capital (or a franchise value) worth $15. This figure means that the firm expects to be able to make profits in the future that have a net present value of $15. In this case the firm is less likely to engage in opportunistic behaviour. If project B fails, causing the firm to fail, this reputational capital will be destroyed. The investment decision that is privately optimal (project A) now becomes socially optimal as well, because the expected private return to project B has fallen to $12.50.

The functions of financial markets

Before addressing issues of financial policy, it may be useful to briefly review the main functions of financial markets. These can be divided into two categories—allocation and governance. Policy discussions have traditionally focused on the allocation functions. We believe that the governance functions are no less important. The allocation functions are associated with the *quantity* of capital intermediated, while the governance functions are associated with the *quality* of intermediation. In this chapter we will mainly focus on the governance functions because they are less well understood.

Allocation functions

The fundamental problem of allocation is that there are two sets of people (or firms) that do not overlap. The first set is the owners of capital, and the second set is the owners of investment opportunities. The allocative role of financial markets is to bridge these two sets of people (or firms). This job involves five main steps.

First, financial markets must mobilize resources. An economy needs savings to finance investment and growth. Savings can be deployed more efficiently elsewhere in the economy. The financial system mobilizes these resources through the taking of deposits and the primary sale of equity.[4]

Next, financial markets must distribute these financial savings to investment projects. A good distribution allocates funds to projects with the highest social returns. The financial sector has the responsibility for making these choices.

Third, financial markets allocate risk. When individuals and investors are risk-averse, projects with very high returns may not be selected because of their riskiness, that is, they are too risky for any one party to bear. Financial markets allow multiple investors to share the risk, dividing the risk and return according to individual levels of risk-tolerance. This allows for high-risk, high-return projects to be financed.

A fourth role of financial markets is to aggregate capital. The minimum efficient scale of an investment in many industries is much greater than the capital internally available to any individual investor. Financial markets allow for the pooling of capital so that investments can be made at the efficient scale.

Finally, financial markets transform maturities. Providers of capital, such as depositors, often want to make short-term investments, while users of capital, such as corporations, typically want to make long-term investments. Through agglomeration and pooling, financial markets can resolve this divergence of interest between lenders and borrowers.

Governance functions

Because of the severity of agency costs in financial transactions, the providers of financial capital must have some mechanism in place to monitor the users of their capital. Using the framework developed by Aoki, Patrick and Sheard (1994), we distinguish three (abstract) periods during which monitoring takes place. The first is ex-ante monitoring, which takes place before the borrower is given funds for investment. The objective is to overcome problems associated with adverse selection (hidden information). Lenders want to provide funds only to borrowers who are good risks and who have excellent management capabilities. Unfortunately, this information is not directly observable, and, worse, borrowers with negative characteristics may have at least as strong an incentive to seek funds as do attractive borrowers.

The second is interim monitoring. After borrowers receive funds, they may deploy those resources in ways other than what was expected when the loan was made—they may engage in activities that increase risk or they may exert less management time and attention to the project than originally agreed. These are problems of moral hazard (hidden action). Interim monitoring must be designed to limit such moral hazard problems. The third type of monitoring is ex-post monitoring. It is often not clear when a project or a firm has failed and should be shut down. Firms may continue to borrow money long after they start destroying value by their continued activity. Ex-post monitoring is aimed at determining when this point of failure has been reached.

Monitoring is not the only aspect of the governance function. Financial markets must enforce discipline with credible punishments. The most obvious example of this occurs when ex-post monitoring has determined that a firm is no longer viable. Efficiency dictates that the firm be shut down and its assets reallocated to more efficient uses. As we will discuss more extensively later, failure to impose discipline may be the most decisive reason that financial markets in some countries have such poor records—demonstrated by the soft-budgeting problems in many communist and former communist countries.

Government objectives in financial markets

We believe that there is a hierarchy of policy objectives and that the state should first attend to the higher-order objectives before considering lesser issues. We divide the goals into three tiers:

- Tier 1—Establishing an appropriate framework for financial development.
- Tier 2—Creating and enhancing the functioning of the financial system.
- Tier 3—Using the financial infrastructure for industrial policy considerations.

The state's primary objective should be to create the proper framework for financial development, which entails two components. The government bears responsibility for the macroeconomic environment—it should maintain a low and steady inflation rate and exercise fiscal discipline. If the government is extracting significant resources from the private sector, particularly to finance wasteful projects, the returns to investment in the private sector will be adversely affected. This last point deserves additional emphasis when considering the importance of reputational capital for the efficient functioning of financial markets. If the government is extracting resources from the economy, it is very difficult for reputational capital to develop. In addition, the government bears responsibility for developing the legal and accounting infrastructure. Our emphasis on reputational capital and governance underscores this role. A good accounting framework allows for better information gathering, thus facilitating monitoring. A strong legal infrastructure supports the enforcement of property rights and the credibility of governance mechanisms.

The second objective of the state should be to develop and improve the functioning of financial markets. By this we mean that the government should facilitate the creation of institutions that help financial markets better allocate and govern the flow of financial resources. In the third section we will develop a sequence of arguments that shows how various financial policies (interest rate controls, prudential regulation and so on) can be structured to create an environment that is based on the creation and maintenance of reputational capital, among both banks and firms.

The state's third objective falls broadly into the category of industrial policy. With this set of policies the state attempts to shape the deployment of capital. For example, the government may choose to intervene in the allocation of capital to coordinate complementary investment decisions, to help implement new technologies, to promote risk-taking or to facilitate learning. The institutions used to achieve these goals often include long-term credit banks and directed credits. Although there are circumstances in which such interventions are welfare-enhancing, we believe that most governments place far too high an emphasis on these objectives. A government should never pursue these third-tier objectives at the expense of not achieving either of the two higher-tier objectives. Only a government that truly has its house in order will be able to pursue these industrial policy objectives and enhance social welfare.

Four models of financial systems

The debate over financial development has often taken the polar form of comparing a public sector to a private sector financial system. Today, the dominant view holds that financial deregulation, that is, the shift of activity from the public to the private sector, is beneficial. We agree that many state-run financial systems are fundamentally flawed and that private-run financial systems are considerably better. But we resist the conclusion that deregulation and bank privatization are *always* desirable. Our objection is that the

Figure 9.1: Four models of financial systems

	Low governance	High governance
Public sector	**S-banking** soft budgeting *China*	**H-banking** hard budgeting *Republic of Korea*
Private sector	**A-banking** arm's-length markets *The United States or United Kingdom*	**R-banking** relationship-based banks *Japan or Germany*

unidimensional analysis of private versus public ownership misses a second dimension of equal importance: governance.

Financial markets should also be classified according to the extent of governance control exercised in the system (figure 9.1). We describe four financial systems: soft-budgeting banking (S-banking), hard-budgeting banking (H-banking), arm's-length banking (A-banking) and relationship-based banking (R-banking). For each system we can find a representative country. Other countries may fall somewhere among these four stylized categories.

R-banking

Relationship-based banking is characterized by integrated monitoring, performed by banks with a significant stake in the success of the firm. The prominent examples of this model are the Japanese main bank system (Sheard, 1989; Aoki and Patrick, 1994) and the German house bank system (Edwards and Fischer, 1993). A single bank is actively involved in all three monitoring stages: it is involved in the ex-ante selection of clients and their investment projects, it monitors the use of that capital on an ongoing basis and it has a role in straightening out management in the case of poor performance. Because the monitoring agent has a concentrated stake in the success or failure of the firm, his or her incentives to spend resources to efficiently monitor the firm are enhanced. But the costs of concentrated monitoring are that banks cannot pursue optimal portfolio diversification and cannot develop the same amount of specialization in any single monitoring function. In relationship-based finance ex-post discipline may also be somewhat weakened, since the risk-sharing nature of the relationship also implies that a bank would be slower in terminating a borrower.[5]

A-banking

Arm's-length banking is the model usually considered when discussing market-based financial systems. US financial markets are the prominent examples of this model. Under A-banking a large number of liquid financial markets provide most of the financial instruments required by different economic agents. It is also characterized by specialized monitoring. Institutions such as venture capital firms, commercial banks, investment banks and ratings agencies provide different monitoring services for different financial products at different stages in the life cycle of a firm. Financial markets, such as stock and corporate bond markets, are very good at diversifying risk throughout the economy. Because of specialized monitoring and because there is no single agent with both the incentive and the ability to discipline the management of firms, we characterize the A-banking system as having low governance. It is important to recognize that low governance does not necessarily imply bad governance. A specialized monitoring system may be more efficient under certain circumstances because of gains to specialization. There are, however, significant costs. In an A-banking system less emphasis will be placed on reputation and long-term relationships. Also, governance structures may be less stable. This issue is reflected, for example, in the ongoing concerns over the market for corporate control. Despite their differences, there is an important similarity between R-banking and A-banking—in both systems financial intermediaries are privately owned. Thus multiple agents will compete to provide financial resources to firms. As a result no single agent will control whether a given investment project may go forward, increasing the probability that, ultimately, good projects will be selected by the mechanisms of the financial system.

S-banking

The single most important defining characteristic of soft-budgeting banking is its lack of ex-post discipline, that is, the prevalence of soft budgeting. The Chinese financial system is a typical example. Under soft budgeting even firms that are clearly dissipating resources continue to receive financing from the state banking sector. This set up gives managers and workers in the firm little reason to work harder or improve the performance of the firm. Worse, this system destroys any hope of maintaining responsible monetary policy. The loans extended to these inefficient firms cannot generate a positive economic return. The resulting losses are financed by the printing press, creating inflation, and ultimately taxing the private sector and undermining investment and growth. Note that there may be significant "relationships" in this system, but these relationships are based on political influence or corruption, as opposed to performance. We consider this system low governance.

H-banking

Hard-budgeting banking differs from S-banking in its strong ex-post discipline. Unsuccessful firms are cut off from funds and allowed to fail if they cannot improve their performance. The result is that incentives in the private sector are geared towards ensuring the success of the firm. This system is compatible with fiscal discipline—it is not necessary for the government to continually expand the money supply in order to support failing firms. An example of H-banking is the system in the Republlic of Korea.[6] The government owned the financial sector and maintained very close control over the allocation of credit (see also Cho and Hellmann 1993). It emphasized close government-business relationships in this allocation, typically managed by the banks and guided by formal and informal roundtables, such as "Monthly Briefings on Economic Trends", which included senior government officials, bankers and industry representatives. Moreover, the government established merit-based allocation rules, in which credit would be disbursed to firms that could show superior performance. These rules created a contest in which firms would compete fiercely for the allocation of credit.[7]

Transitions and path dependence in developing robust financial markets

Thus far we have described the four financial systems. We will now turn to an evaluation of their relative merits. First, we compare public and private banking. In line with the discussion in the first section, we argue that significant government failures are likely to occur if the government runs the financial sector, and that these failures may well outweigh market failures, especially if markets are properly regulated. The reasons for government failures relate to the difficulty of obtaining information and the difficulty of making decisions solely on the basis of economic criteria.

Comparing S-banking to H-banking, we believe that H-banking is superior. At a minimum, the government must act to credibly enforce ex-post discipline so that failing firms are shut down, assets are redeployed to more efficient uses and private actors in the economy have incentives for performance.

There appears to be a real trade-off between R-banking and A-banking. R-banking allows for strong governance relationship with concentrated monitoring, whereas A-banking allows for specialization of monitoring along functional lines and diversification of risk across agents in the economy. Which system is more desirable depends on a complex comparison of these trade-offs. Allen and Gale (1995) describe this trade-off as one between inter-generational and cross-sectional risk sharing. R-banking promotes relationships that allow for dynamic risk sharing, while arm's length finance allows for better cross-sectional risk sharing.[8]

For either of these systems to function well, private sector agents must possess significant reputational capital. In the case of R-banking the relationship between a bank and a firm is credible only if the bank has positive incentives to maintain a good reputation. A newly formed financial institution cannot immediately initiate an R-banking relationship—it must either develop a reputation over time or make sunk investments that it can recoup only by maintaining a good reputation. In the case of A-banking specialized monitoring will not be credible if the monitoring agents have no reputational capital. Investors trust the ratings of Moody's or Standard & Poors because of their long history and their incentive to maintain their reputation into the distant future. If a rating agency destroys the trust of investors, its service would lose value. But a new competitor cannot simply enter this market. Investors have no reason to value its recommendations. Only after it has proven itself and made investments to develop expertise in monitoring will its ratings have value. Borrowers face a similar challenge in developing reputational capital. A newly formed firm cannot simply sell its stock or bonds to the public. It must first demonstrate performance through years of operation.

Although we recognize that at advanced stages of financial development there is a real trade-off between R-banking and A-banking, we argue that *in the context of financial development R-banking is preferable to A-banking*. The main issue is which system will allow for greater improvement in governance structures and faster accumulation of reputational capital. There are three broad reasons why the R-banking system should be the medium-term goal of financial development.

First, given the complementarities among the different functions of governance, the complex coordination problem can best be solved within the boundaries of a single (universal) bank rather than across multiple specialized monitoring entities. In particular, since the returns to anyone's investment in specialized monitoring capabilities will depend on the level of investment by others performing complementary monitoring functions, there will likely be underinvestment in monitoring capabilities because of coordination failure. In the case of R-banking, with its integrated monitoring, much less coordination is necessary, and all of the coordination needed takes place within a single banking enterprise.

Second, in order for the specialized monitoring mechanisms of the A-banking system to be efficient, the scale of the financial markets must be large. In many developing and transition economies, where the volume of transactions is relatively small, these institutions may not achieve the efficient scale and may thus not function effectively.

Third, we believe that the essential challenge facing the financial system in an economy operating within the international production possibilities frontier is very different from the challenge facing a financial system in an economy operating on the frontier. A developing economy has a clear and reasonably observable target of obtaining internationally efficient production technologies. The financial system must then promote ways to efficiently deploy proven techniques. An economy on the frontier must search for ways to push out the frontier, which is a much more complicated process. Within this context consider the relative strengths of the A-banking and R-banking systems. A-banking promotes contemporaneous diversification, helping an economy to efficiently deploy inputs and technologies that are currently available. R-banking promotes dynamic risk-sharing, facilitating inter-temporal trade-offs. It may therefore be more effective at helping an economy to move towards the frontier, although its relative advantages will be less clear once the economy reaches the frontier.

Our conclusion that R-banking is efficient for a developing economy can be traced back to the arguments of Gerschenkron (1962). Also, more recently, Berglöf (1995) describes how he envisions corporate governance in the context of transition economies. He identifies eight features that are likely to be prominent in the medium-term structure of the financial system (pp. 81–3):

- Internally generated funds will be the most important source of finance by far.
- Most of the external funding will have to come from control-oriented finance.
- Stock and bond markets are not going to play a major role in the provision of funds in the early phases of economic transition.
- Holdings of debt and equity will be concentrated, with little turnover in control blocks.
- Control-oriented intermediaries will use both debt and equity monitoring.
- Both mutual funds and commercial banks will be needed, but banks are likely to be more important in corporate governance.
- The functional specialization associated with some western financial systems may not be feasible in the transition economies.
- The initial choice of a privatization scheme may not be decisive in determining the evolution of the financial system.

Without using these specific words, Berglöf essentially claims that the transition economies will most likely develop R-banking financial systems, regardless of the initial form of liberalization.[9]

One important warning must be given at this point. The medium-term goal of moving towards an R-banking system should not be equated with a recommendation to maintain all existing economic relationships. Many developing and transition economies suffer from a legacy of dysfunctional or corrupt networks that do not allocate resources on the basis of economic merit. The reputation mechanisms in an R-banking system are by their very nature based on economic performance. But how can we guarantee that the old, corrupt networks won't simply lay hold of the R-banks?[10] Because of this, some people argue for an A-banking system. First, we see no reason why an A-banking system would be less vulnerable to this type of subversion (and consider present day Russia a potential example). Second, we believe that there are ways to protect R-banking from these influences. An important issue in the R-banking system is who owns the banks. If, for example, banks are captive organizations of inefficient firms that resist extinction, the banks are vulnerable to being brought down (or even looted) by those firms. To maintain an effective R-banking system, the ownership of banks must remain in the hands of agents that have incentives to preserve the franchise value of these banks.

Our assertion that R-banking should be the medium-term goal of financial development leaves open the questions of the short term and the long term. We begin with the short term (figure 9.2).

Starting from the unfortunate—but for many developing countries, realistic—position of S-banking, there are three possible directions: H-banking, R-banking and A-banking. First, we argue that a direct move from S-banking to A-banking is not possible, or, if attempted, is likely to lead to financial chaos. Imagine attempting to simultaneously create all of the financial institutions currently functioning in US financial markets, without the benefit of a long history of successful financial institutions and firms. Unfortunately, this switch is effectively what some financial liberalization programs attempted, as witnessed, for example, in Chile. Depositors have no secure institutions in which to place their savings, banks have neither experience nor the track records to properly evaluate firms and firms have no history of successful operation in competitive markets. If neither banks nor firms have an existing stock of reputational capital, then both have powerful incentives to gamble or loot the funds placed in their care, with significant adverse effects on the efficiency of investment. In terms of figure 9.2, we claim that there is a cliff between S-banking and A-banking, making the transition between the two very difficult.

What about a transition to an H-banking system? This transition may be effective in the short-run by reducing inflationary pressures and providing stronger incentives for performance in the private sector. The main advantage is that the government may institute good governance structures before turning over the operation of the financial system to the private sector. Whether or not these advan-

Figure 9.2: Transitions between financial systems

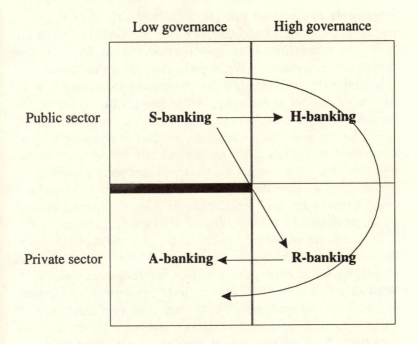

tages will materialize depends on the ability of the government to promote internal change.

Finally, there is the issue of where the financial system should be in the long run. Enthusiasm for R-banking or A-banking seems to track closely the recent economic performance of the United States and Japan: in the late 1980s Japan was being praised for its banking system, while by the mid-1990s it is was being scolded for its banking crisis.[11] Going beyond these short-term mood swings, we argue that the welfare comparison of these two systems is complex, and that the two systems are probably not Pareto rankable. Moreover, whether desirable or not, an economy is likely to move closer to an A-banking system as it develops and as the financial system is faced with greater international competition. We will return to this topic in the third section.

The building of reputational capital

Proponents of financial liberalization implicitly assume that if reputational capital is important for efficient financial transactions, then independent firms in competitive markets will invest on their own to create reputations. We begin by examining this statement.[12] In a competitive market banks will earn zero expected profits in the long run. Consider an economy with no (or very little) reputational capital. How would banks create reputation? A "textbook answer" would be that they sink investments that can be recouped only by continuing to operate with an untarnished reputation. Once a reputation has been created, the bank will earn an ongoing flow of positive profits. Thus the financial returns to the competitive bank entail losses in the early periods that are then exactly compensated by the profits it later accrues because of its good reputation.

There are two important reasons to question the applicability of this textbook answer. First, when banks have little or no reputational capital, we would expect that they face severe finance constraints. After all, who will give banks the equity to finance their investments in reputational capital, particularly when they have none to begin with? Second, banks have incentives to deviate from the textbook behaviour. If a bank can engage in value-extracting activities that allows it to make positive profits in its early years, then it will be privately optimal, but socially costly, for the bank to engage in value extraction. For these reasons we argue that perfectly competitive financial markets may not develop enough, if any, reputational capital. Indeed, a low stage of development is characterized by the lack of endogenously created reputational capital.[13]

If we expect financial liberalization to yield a slow and difficult path to the creation of reputational capital, what does this imply for the scope of government policy? We believe that the government should intervene in financial markets with the explicit goal of exogenously creating or enhancing reputational capital for the financial sector and, in particular, for banks. We discuss this policy—financial restraint—in detail in the fourth section. This intervention, if managed appropriately, will overcome some problems that remain unresolved with a purely free-market-oriented financial liberalization. Governments create opportunities for banks to capture a flow of positive profits over a long horizon. Banks will be able to make investments in reputational capital that would otherwise not be feasible because of binding finance constraints. Furthermore, because financial restraint creates reputational capital for the banking sector, banks have stronger incentives to engage in value-creating activities, rather than in value-extracting activities.

REGULATING THE FINANCIAL SYSTEM

In this section we discuss some of the financial policies that are at the center of current policy debates. We will attempt to present a balanced view of the state of that debate and then provide our interpretation, emphasizing that incentives and governance are critical to understanding and resolving these policy issues.

Interest rate regulation

Financial liberalization is often synonymous with interest rate deregulation and has been the cornerstone of numerous policy reforms. To the neoclassical economist it represents a welcome move towards the ideal of a complete and competitive financial market system. In the first section we showed that this simplistic argument failed to properly account for the trade-off between government and market failures. Moreover, the neoclassical perspective fails to understand why governments choose to rely on interest rate regulations in the first place.

There are three main reasons why governments would want to adopt interest rate regulations. There is a recurrent notion that charging interest is exploitation and that the government should protect borrowers by putting a ceiling on interest rates. This notion has numerous historic roots: both the Christian and Muslim religions repudiate the levying of interest (see also Glaeser, 1995). Marxists interpret interest as capitalist exploitation. Even the Cambridge-Cambridge debate on the aggregation of capital was largely motivated by the question of whether interest could be justified as the price of capital. And modern economists continue to argue that "usury protection" is justifiable if lenders can exert monopoly power over borrowers.

Governments also implement interest rate controls to obtain cheap funds to finance their budget deficits. Put simply, lower interest rates redistribute income from the lender (the private sector) to the borrower (the government). Khan (1995) examines this issue more carefully in an equilibrium asset portfolio model. He shows that in the absence of an effective direct taxation system (a condition commonly observed in developing countries) a government can finance its budget deficit by printing currency, issuing bonds or "taxing" banks by asking them to hold low-interest-rate bonds. If the government wants to avoid creating excessive inflation by printing currency, it will want to use interest rate controls to lower the cost of financing the budget deficit.[14]

A third reason that government may want to impose interest rate controls is to stimulate investment. There has been a lot of confusion about this motivation. The simplest argument holds that investment demand is decreasing in the interest rate. But this argument does not take into account the equilibrium perspective, in which lower interest rates will decrease savings, thus decreasing the availability of funds. If there are, however, positive externalities from investment associated with lower interest rates, the lower savings may be more than compensated by productivity increases in investment. We will examine a more sophisticated form of this argument shortly.

An attempt to understand the origins of interest rate regulations naturally leads to an evaluation of the above reasons. Identifying monopoly positions in financial markets is notoriously difficult. It is true that few financial markets are perfectly competitive because of information asymmetries and agency costs. This local monopoly power, and the associated rents, may perform a useful function in enabling the creation and maintenance of reputational capital. Making a distinction between which rents are necessary for efficiency and which rents constitute exploitation of a monopolistic position is very difficult. We would therefore argue that usury protection is a good argument for interest rate controls in only very select circumstances.

The bid to control interest rates to finance budget deficits is as difficult an issue as the decision to allow addicts to consume addictive substances. If you withhold the substance, the addict will suffer severely in the near term (and may even harm other people). And in the long run the addict may or may not overcome the addiction. If you give the addict the substance, you avoid the short-run cost but undermine the chances of long-run recovery. The same argument holds true for interest rate deregulation. In the short-run we would expect to see increases in the government budget deficit and higher inflation. But over time we hope that the government learns to moderate its fiscal expenses. What becomes evident from the addiction analogy is that instead of fighting symptoms (interest rate controls), we should concentrate on fighting causes (deficits). Policy-makers should focus on reducing the primary government deficit (and/or the development of an efficient direct taxation system) rather than just deregulating interests rates.

So far, we have found only weak endorsements for interest rate regulation. But a variation of the third argument concerning savings and investment has considerable validity. First, we must distinguish between deposit and lending rates, because two separate sets of arguments apply.

Hellmann, Murdock and Stiglitz (1994, 1996b) argue that lower deposit rates are a powerful means of creating franchise value for banks. This franchise value provides strong incentives for banks to invest funds wisely and to monitor the performance of borrowers. The benefit of a sound banking system and the added incentives of banks to mobilize more funds can actually increase the fraction of savings that are channeled through the formal financial system. Certain interest rate restrictions may also increase the incentives of banks to mobilize funds and promote investments in the infrastructure of the banking system—so that aggregate savings may actually increase.

Lending rate restrictions can be used to correct market inefficiencies that arise from imperfect information, lack of reputational capital and weak governance systems. The basic premise of the argument is that the people or firms with the best ideas and projects are not necessarily the people or firms that have the capital to make investments. In the past 20 years the finance literature has featured models of imperfect information that exhibit the resulting investment inefficiencies (see Harris and Raviv, 1992, for a survey). A common problem of those models is that firms with good projects do not necessarily have the collateral and/or reputational capital to prove the quality of their projects, resulting in underinvestment. Lending rate controls, then, may lower the cost of capital, allowing firms to accumulate capital faster. As firms accumulate capital, they are in a better position to use internal resource allocation to signal their confidence to outside investors, resulting in reduced agency costs in lending markets.

The above argument makes an implicit assumption that the firms that generate positive cash flows are in a favourable position to identify superior investment opportunities or to manage those investment opportunities more efficiently. There is, however, some controversy as to why the corporations (or conglomerates) that accumulated capital in the past should have better investment opportunities in the present. We would argue that, especially in economies where managerial talent is scarce, there is likely to be a high correlation between past investment success and present investment opportunities. Firms in growing markets (which will be found in a developing country with good economic policies) are also less likely to make very poor investments. The success of investments is also a function of the flexibility with which retained earnings are invested. In this respect conglomerate structures may out-perform single-unit businesses in a developing country where financial markets have difficulty channeling funds to the most profitable projects. Finally, it is evident that the benefits of faster capital accumulation are a function of governance structures: if firms are properly controlled, they are more likely to identify the most promising investment opportunities and achieve high performance from their investments.

The two arguments above provide a strong rationale for mild interest rate restrictions.[15] We add the qualifier "mild" recognizing that large deviations from market prices will generate two problems. First, the benefits of increased franchise value and faster capital accumulation must be traded off against costs arising from the price distortions on which they are based. It is worth noting that the benefits of interest rate controls can often be achieved with relatively mild distortions. In the fourth section we will provide an example of how an intervention that reduces the deposit rate by just two percentage points from the free market interest rate can dramatically increase the franchise value of the bank. The benefits from this intervention will exhibit diminishing marginal returns, whereas the cost of price distortions will typically exhibit increasing marginal costs, implying that there is some optimal level of intervention. As a second point, it is worth noting that the ease of enforcing interest rate regulations is a function of the size of the price distortion.

In some sense banks will like deposit rate controls—they increase the profitability and franchise value of the financial sector. A bank would want to circumvent a deposit rate control only in order to attract a large number of small deposits or to attract large customers. In order to attract new customers, the knowledge that a bank is offering higher rates must be made public. Thus, it should be relatively straightforward for a supervisory body to identify unlawful behaviour. But the other case—in which a bank wants to offer higher rates to large individual customers in order to obtain or retain business—does not rely on public information. There are typically relatively few customers that fall into this category, however, and regulators should not have too difficult a time monitoring this behaviour. Furthermore, as long as the number of assets that successfully evade deposit rate controls is a relatively small fraction of total assets of the banking sector, the intervention will generate significant franchise value for the financial sector.

There is also a question of legal circumvention of deposit rate controls in terms of non-price competition. Banks may want to offer gifts to new depositors or build fancy buildings to attract customers. The importance of this kind of non-price competition is easily exaggerated. Because the non-price instruments are typically inefficient at attracting marginal depositors, the marginal cost of their use rises rapidly, thus preserving infra-marginal rents and the franchise value of banks. Moreover, depending on its form, non-price competition may be socially beneficial. Hellmann, Murdock and Stiglitz (1996b) showed that non-price competition may take the form of banks spending additional resources to deepen deposit markets (that is, to mobilize funds from areas that have not been reached previously by the formal financial sector). Another potential form of non-price competition may be competition in innovations (for example, checking facilities).

An interesting question to ask is whether there are additional instruments that can be used to create franchise value. Caprio and Summers (1995) argue that limits on competition will increase franchise value (see also Dinc, 1996). The cost of limits is increased pricing distortions due to oligopolistic behaviour. In general, we would want to rely on both types of instruments to induce franchise value. A stronger reliance on limiting entry (such as through higher prices for bank licenses) would create larger banks. Although this may facilitate coordination, it also carries the risk that these large banks are more likely to be "too large to fail".

The formulation and enforcement of lending rate controls are more delicate than those of deposit rates. Lower lending rates create or reinforce credit rationing. This gives loan officers additional discretion in allocating funds—and getting banks' incentives right becomes all the more important. An appropriate lending rate control must also account for risk premia, ideally at the level of the individual firm. This is, however, neither feasible nor desirable, both from a logistical standpoint and because setting firm-specific risk premia would inevitably require the government to micro-manage a large lending portfolio.

In the absence of lending rate controls that are adjusted for firm-specific risk-premia, there may be an anti-risk bias in the allocation of funds: banks will divert funds to firms investing in low-risk, low-return projects. But this argument relies on the assumption that lending rate controls are strictly enforced. Banks may be willing to lend to riskier borrowers if they can levy compensating balances. It is easy to show that if banks are entirely free to levy compensating balances, the effect of lending rate controls can be undone entirely (see Horiuchi, 1984). Not surprisingly, we find that in most countries with lending rate controls, compensating balances are illegal. They are, however, more difficult to monitor. Hellmann, Murdock and Stiglitz (1996b) argue that because compensating balances are illegal, there is no price discovery function. Instead, prices are determined through a bilateral bargaining process. As a result we would expect that compensating balances are likely to undo some, but not all, of the effects of lending rate controls. They may also correct some of the anti-risk bias.

One final point about lending rate controls: if we argue that faster capital accumulation is beneficial, we must justify why we should use financial policies, rather than tax policies, subsidies or income and wage policies. In fact, we would argue that using several or all of these instruments simultaneously can be beneficial. Each instrument has a beneficial effect, as well as a cost in terms of distortions imposed on the economy. An "optimal taxation" approach reveals that spreading the distortions across several markets can be beneficial.[16] Another argument why financial policies may be particularly effective in distributing rents is that the allocation of funds can be linked to an effective governance structure. We will develop this argument more fully later in this section.

It is useful to briefly review the empirical work on the relationship between interest rates and growth. A number of empirical studies have shown a strong positive correlation between growth and a regime of positive real interest rates (Fry, 1988, 1995). These results have been interpreted as evidence supporting a policy of financial liberalization (see McKinnon, 1993). The evidence shows that moving from a regime of financial repression (with very negative real interest rates) to a regime of positive real interest rates is growth-enhancing.[17] Governments should establish interest rate and monetary policies such that the real rate of interest is positive and the rate of inflation is low. The evidence does not show that higher real interest rates are unambiguously better once rates are positive. Rather, some evidence suggests that mild interest rate restrictions may be growth-enhancing (Murdock and Stiglitz, 1993).

Mild interest rate restrictions create significant franchise value for the financial sector, possibly at a cost of a modest distortion in the supply of savings. The reputational capital thus created has positive incentive effects on the investment decisions of banks, which improves the efficient deployment of capital in the economy. Thus the underlying motivation of this intervention is to assist the formation of reputational capital.

Prudential regulation

The challenge of prudential regulation is to provide a framework for a stable and sound financial system.[18] Financial market instability in numerous countries has proven that financial crises can have a huge effect on the health of the real economy. What drives financial market instability? Of course, because the financial system pools a lot of risk, it is always affected by macroeconomic shocks. There are also structural aspects of the financial system that can become a cause of instability. In particular, bank failures may be the result of moral hazard—in which bank managers believe it to be in their interest to choose bank portfolios that are either very risky ("gambling") or are destined to fail ("looting") (see also Bhattacharya, 1982; Kane, 1989; Akerlof and Romer, 1993).[19]

Understanding the behavioural origin of financial instability is key to formulating prudential regulation. Specifically, financial stability cannot be achieved without providing an appropriate incentive structure to bank owners and managers. Prudential oversight is thus directly linked to bank governance.

The literature on the regulation of banks focuses on the restrictions on their capital structure and portfolio allocations. The most prominent regulation is the Basle accord. At the core of this regulation, which has been adopted by most industrial and several developing countries, are two ratios. The Basle accord specifies a maximum leverage (or equity-over-assets ratio) and a risk-weighted capital requirement. The capital requirement consists of a set of rules that classifies different asset categories (on a scale of 0 to 1) according to their riskiness. It then specifies that bank capital should not fall below 8 per cent of the weighted sum of risky assets. Some of the current debate revolves around issues concerning the measurement of risk. In particular, the Basle accord does not recognize interest rate risk and cannot be adjusted to cyclical fluctuations. Moreover, while some economists argue that the 8 per cent capital requirement is much too low to account for the risks faced in many developing countries, others argue that 8 per cent is too high, given the scarcity of capital. A related problem is the inherent difficulty of measuring bank capital, which is amplified in many developing countries by poor accounting practices.

What is the rationale behind a capital requirement? Dewatripont and Tirole (1994) provide an insightful analysis. They begin by asking why the capital structure of banks should matter. They argue that the capital structure can act as an incentive device and as a contingent-governance mechanism for banks that are run by managers who are typically neither large depositors nor significant equity holders. Dewatripont and Tirole make two key distinctions between bank deposit holders and bank equity holders. First, deposit holders are (typically) small, risk-averse savers who cannot be expected to have much information about the banks they choose. Equity holders, on the other hand, are consciously taking risks and can be expected to have a greater ability to collect and interpret information about banks. Second, depositors and equity holders face different incentives in terms of their payoff structure (depositors have a concave payoff structure, whereas equity holders have a convex payoff structure).[20]

This capital structure provides a contingent governance structure. As long as banks are solvent, shareholders remain in control. If the bank becomes insolvent, however, shareholders have a choice of either recapitalizing the bank or relinquishing control to the debtholders. Debtholders then have three choices: they may continue to operate the bank, taking a loss and effectively becoming the new equityholders; they may reorganize the bank, typically selling it to some other entity; or they may liquidate the bank. In the last two scenarios bank managers are likely to loose their jobs and reputation as good bankers. In anticipation of this outcome bank managers try to avoid insolvency. But depositors may not be able to effectively punish poor bank management because of the free rider problem inherent with small depositors and because depositors cannot commit to a punishment. Once a bank is insolvent, depositors may find it easier to simply continue the bank's operations without punishing the incumbent managers.

This is precisely where capital requirements come into play: they are mechanisms for monitoring bank performance and ensuring that the threshold of contingent governance is set at an appropriate level. Regulators ensure that actions are taken whenever bank capital falls below a critical threshold. Regulation is desirable if it improves the contingent governance structure in terms of providing timely and appropriate punishments for poor bank performance. Regulators can be thought of as solving the free rider and commitment problems.

The argument of Dewatripont and Tirole relies mainly on the application of the first ratio in the Basle accord. A second rationale for capital requirements is related to the second ratio which imposes restrictions on the portfolio choices of banks. Consider a simplified bank portfolio allocation problem in which banks decide between private sector lending that carries a risk factor of one (risky) and government bonds that carry a risk factor of zero (safe). The capital requirement essentially sets a limit on the fraction of assets that can be invested in private sector loans. Hellmann, Murdock and Stiglitz (1994) show that such a restriction may induce bank managers to abandon a gambling or looting strategy. There is, however, a cost associated with the restriction. Banks are forced to invest an excess portion of their assets in government bonds, which typically have a lower private (and social) return. To put it more dramatically, the capital requirement poses restrictions on the activities of banks that undermine their function of allocating capital in the private sector.

A natural question to ask is whether there are other tools that regulators can use as a complement (or substitute) to capital require-ments. One answer is direct supervision of bank activities that tries to identify gambling and looting. While some direct supervision is clearly beneficial, it is unrealistic to expect regulators to play "hide-and-seek" with a set of bank managers that have a vast array of complicated gambling and looting strategies at their disposal. Direct supervision should be thought of merely as a tactic that identifies some symptoms of the problem, without reaching its root. Moreover, many developing countries do not have a highly sophisticated regu-latory infrastructure.[21]

We argue that franchise value is a powerful tool for addressing the moral hazard problem. Deposit rate controls and limits on the extent of competition provide strong incentives for banks not to gamble or loot. Hellmann, Murdock and Stiglitz (1994) compare how capital requirements and deposit rate controls affect the behaviour of banks. We show that both tools can prevent gambling, although in different ways and at different costs. Capital requirements impose a cost in generating inefficient portfolio allocation, while deposit rate controls may create a price distortion in the deposit market. If capital requirements are used rather than deposit rate controls, banks will have less incentive to mobilize additional deposits. Finally, these tools differ in their enforceability. We noted earlier that deposit rate controls can be enforced to a reasonable extent. Capital requirements, however, are intrinsically difficult to enforce. While the evasion of deposit rate controls requires that banks publicly offer a higher rate of interest, evading capital requirements simply involves a bank engaging in accounting practices that inflate its equity capital. Because many accounting practices are inherently judgmental in nature, it is very difficult for regulators to observe such intentional evasion.

Deposit insurance

In the aftermath of the S&L crisis deposit insurance has become a hotly debated policy issue in the United States, with some of the discussion spilling over to developing countries. The original argument in favour of deposit insurance was simple: depositors are small, risk-averse, uninformed stakeholders that should be sheltered from the risks of bank insolvency. At the center of the new debate is a claim, made by a significant number of US economists, that deposit insurance forms the root of the moral hazard problem in banking. The argument is based on the observation that, with deposit insurance, bank managers need not concern themselves with the impact of their decisions on depositors. They face a convex return function, which provides them with incentives to gamble. Moreover, insured depositors have no incentives to monitor. Thus bank managers have incentives to gamble and loot, leaving the government with the liability of the failed bank's deposits.

The description of the moral hazard behaviour is accurate. But the conclusion that deposit insurance should be abolished is, in our view, questionable for three main reasons. First, the argument seems to suggest that in the absence of deposit insurance, the preferences of bank managers would not have the convex property that invites gambling.[22] There is, however, no reason to believe that bank managers would have a greater incentive, in the absence of deposit insurance, to consider the impact of their decisions on depositors. This conclusion leads to the second point. Proponents of abolishing deposit insurance argue that bank managers would learn to take depositors' preferences more seriously. Since depositors are at risk, they would spend time and resources monitoring the soundness of banks. Moreover, they would have an effect on bank governance by voting either with proxies or with their feet. We believe that this argument dramatically overstates the ability of depositors to solve the governance problem. It fails to recognize the free rider problem of monitoring—no small investor has an incentive to spend time and resources on monitoring the banks. Moreover, the argument that depositors can simply vote with their feet is not innocuous! This behaviour is precisely what triggers bank runs (see also Diamond and Dybvig, 1983)—one of the problems that financial policy attempts to solve. A third reason to question the abolition of deposit insurance is that it is not a credible policy. A bank that is sufficiently large will be considered "too big to fail", that is, the government cannot credibly commit to not rescue a large bank in case of insolvency. Moreover, if this behaviour is anticipated by banks, it may create a perverse incentive for banks to grow beyond their natural size, in order to become too big to fail.

If we accept the premise that some deposit insurance is necessary, we are faced with the much more difficult question of how to design such a system. One view is that perfect deposit insurance is not necessary. For example, we can insure only small deposits (defined by a size limit). But this policy is ill-conceived, as large depositors can simply split their savings into a series of smaller accounts. A more promising approach is to insure a large constant fraction of all deposits. While depositors will not have any real incentives to invest resources in monitoring, they will at least respond to generally available knowledge about the solvency of banks, thus giving more solvent banks a competitive advantage. However, it is not clear that bank runs can be avoided in this system. It will depend on how aggressively depositors would withdraw deposits that have a small uninsured component.

Another approach is to require that banks hold insured deposits and uninsured debt in certain fractions. The uninsured debt would pay a higher interest rate and would be held by more concentrated investors, who may have an incentive to monitor. Dewatripont and Tirole discuss the difficult question of whether the uninsured debt should be subordinated. They show that subordination would provide stronger incentives to monitor ex-ante, but would provide perverse incentives ex-post (in case of insolvency), in which case uninsured debtholders would essentially become equityholders and have an interest in gambling on the remaining assets. In economies with well-functioning securities markets the uninsured debt component could also be publicly traded. Prices would reveal information to regulators about the market's perception of banks' insolvency risks. It is doubtful, however, that securities markets alone would provide a sufficient signal to identify insolvent banks.

Another intriguing idea is to let private markets provide a fraction of deposit insurance. Again, regulators could use this price information to assess market beliefs of the risk of bank insolvency. This formulation may be the best mechanism for encouraging private sector monitoring of financial institutions. If the private deposit insurance is subordinated to the government's deposit insurance, the insurance company would have strong ex-ante incentives (identified by Dewatripont and Tirole) to monitor the bank. The insurance company, however, would have none of the perverse ex-post incentives that arise from a change in control, because the policies have only a liability and not a control component. Furthermore, the risk borne by the insurance company will probably be greater than that borne by any single subordinated debtholder, so the incentives to monitor will be correspondingly greater.

A difficult issue is determining which deposits qualify for deposit insurance. In the S&L crisis deposits were insured that paid out rates far in excess of the Treasury bill rate. The question arises as to why the government should insure investments that pay a rate higher than the safe rate of return. Our response, of course, is that the deposit rates of banks and S&Ls should be regulated in the first place. But even in the absence of deposit rate controls, the government may want to limit its insurance liability by restricting the benefit of deposit insurance to accounts that pay no more than the safe rate of return.

Another controversial topic is the determination of risk premia that banks pay on their deposit insurance. The issue is whether risk premia should be based on measures of insolvency risk. One set of problems relates to the accounting definitions of risk premia. Here, we are more interested in behavioural issues. On the bright side, lower risk premia reward well-managed banks for their soundness with respect to solvency risk. On the dark side, however, higher risk premia may further erode the capital base of troubled banks and thus increase their temptation to gamble or loot.

It is also important to recognize the inter-dependency of deposit insurance and the governance mechanisms in the financial sector. If relatively little reputational capital has been developed in the private sector and if the governance mechanisms that are in place are relatively ineffective, then the government will have to charge high average premia for deposit insurance. But these high premia reduce the ongoing profitability of the banking sector, making it increasingly difficult to develop reputational capital. Conversely, an intervention such as deposit rate controls will create franchise value for the financial sector, reducing the incentives for banks to gamble or loot. The government will consequently be able to reduce the premia it must charge, further facilitating the development of reputational capital.

The role of securities markets

The last few years have seen the creation of stock markets in a number of developing countries and a dramatic increase in the flow of funds from industrial markets to emerging markets. Policy-makers in developing countries increasingly have to make decisions about the extent to which they want to develop securities markets and, in particular, corporate stock and bond markets.

In order to assess these issues, it is useful to identify the objectives that policy-makers may want to pursue in making these decisions. In light of the argument that strong domestic financial intermediation promotes economic growth (King and Levine 1993a, 1993b), it seems natural to make financial deepening the overarching policy objective. This involves the creation of reputational capital for financial intermediaries and for the firms that require funds. Other objectives include efficiency of resource and risk allocation, and the reduction of transaction costs.

How important is it for a country to develop securities markets?[23] We argue that securities markets are somewhat less important in earlier stages of financial development, when reputational capital is low. To make this argument, we must understand the advantages put forward by the advocates of securities markets. These fall into three broad categories: securities markets provide an attractive source of funds to corporations, securities markets provide investors with better risk diversification opportunities, and securities markets are thought to facilitate inflows of foreign investment.

The first argument is easily overstated. Mayer (1990) shows that even in industrial countries equity markets are an insignificant source of funds for corporations. It is difficult to see how securities would ever become a more important source of funds in developing countries—where they are currently providing an even smaller fraction of corporate funds. Equity markets had a limited role in the United States and virtually no importance in Germany or Japan.[24]

Obviously, if equity markets work well, they can become an attractive source of funds. The advantage of having equity markets as a source of finance is that corporations can reduce their leverage by raising equity rather than debt. Another alternative, however, may be to obtain equity from universal banks.

There are reasons to question whether securities markets are the most desirable source of funds. A potential problem is that they encourage low governance. As the financial claims of corporations are distributed to a wider set of small stockholders, those individual stockholders have fewer incentives to invest time and resources in exercising governance.[25]

This also sheds some doubt on the second acclaimed benefit of securities markets: better risk diversification. While the benefits of better diversification are clearly important, they should be traded off against the less visible loss of governance that accompanies diversification. This trade-off is not easily observable, as bad governance is often not visible until large mistakes have been made. Also, subtle externalities may arise: improved governance of one firm may set an example for another firm or it may affect other firms by intensifying competition. When relatively low-cost firms increase their share of output in their industry, they can have important efficiency effects on the entire economy. This efficiency effect can be much larger than gains in efficiency from more accurate price signals.

The third acclaimed benefit of securities markets is that they attract foreign capital. But it is not clear whether the existence of a stock market or simply an environment favourable to foreign capital attracts most foreign investors (Claessens, 1995b). There is a widespread belief—though not necessarily supported by empirical evidence (Claessens, 1995b)—that at least some foreign portfolio investments are "hot capital flows" that create as many problems as they solve. In particular, it is believed that these capital flows can create exchange rate volatility. Another concern that policy-makers must address is the level and nature of foreign ownership that is politically acceptable.

Securities markets also may undermine some of the franchise value of banks. First, there may be an exodus of households placing their savings into stocks and bonds instead of into deposits. The early introduction of stock markets may thus have some impact on the amount of funds that banks can mobilize. Second, some of the banking sector's most profitable borrowers may choose to raise their funds on securities markets.[26] Dinc (1995) studies the problem of how a bank-dominated economy with R-banking would respond to the advent of competition from a stock market-dominated economy with A-banking. Depending on the parameters, two interesting equilibria may result. In one case reputation in the bank-dominated economy is not strong enough, and the entire economy switches (in a dynamic adjustment process) to a stock market-dominated economy. In another case reputation in the bank-dominated economy is strong enough, and the economy becomes one in which banks and stock markets coexist, although relational banks end up with a smaller market share. Dinc's arguments suggest that even if relational banking is more efficient, it may not be able to withstand the corrosive pressures of stock markets. Thus the development of capital markets, such as stock and corporate bond markets, may indeed threaten the franchise value of banks, especially if they are pushed too early in the process of financial development.

One way to counteract the decline in franchise value of banks is to allow for universal banks. If securities markets induce banks to lose rents on the lending side of the business (that is, the commercial banking side), these banks may recapture some of the lost rents on the investment banking side.[27]

Another interesting hypothesis recently advanced by Demirgüç and Levine (1995) is that securities markets and banks may be complements rather than substitutes. They observe empirically that securities market indicators are correlated with measures of financial deepening. But there are no strong theoretical underpinnings for this view.

A final set of arguments concerns the feasibility and costs of securities markets. The information requirements needed to allow for the public sale of equity are invariably very high, implying that securities markets are a viable source of funds to only the largest companies. Many developing countries also have severe problems maintaining a liquid and transparent market environment. Liquidity is lacking because of the small size of these markets and the relatively few analysts and brokers. And the lack of transparency is related to the overall deficiencies in the legal and accounting infrastructure. The control of insider trading is also notoriously difficult. Finally, the government incurs costs for supervising those markets.

How can we make sense of these different arguments? It is clear that the evaluation of the costs and benefits of securities markets remains an open research question. We would caution against a naïve embrace of the view that the development of securities markets is a policy priority, and we have discussed some of the reasons that are not always recognized in the literature on emerging securities markets. Our own preliminary assessment is that in the early stages of development the costs of pushing for securities markets may outweigh the benefits. As the financial sector develops, the introduction of securities markets, in conjunction with a universal banking system, becomes more desirable. Capital markets provide weak governance incentives for the very reason that they are so valuable in industrial economies: the efficiency with which they diversify risk. Furthermore, the development of these capital markets, by competing with other financial institutions, weakens the development of reputational capital elsewhere in the financial system. Until a sufficiently large stock of reputational capital has been developed in the economy, financial policies should first focus on promoting financial institutions that are more conducive to the creation of effective governance structures.

Directed credits

Directed credits are typically considered to be an important financial policy in developing countries. We argue that they should not be viewed as a financial policy but as an industrial policy. Although they use the financial system as a channel for distribution, they are a way to allocate subsidies to specific firms and industries. If directed credits are used unwisely, they could become a real burden to the financial system: banks are asked to make bad loans to selected firms, even throw good money after bad money, and then bear the costs of non-performing loans. In the process banks see their franchise value eroded, thus losing incentives to perform prudently. If this happens on a sufficiently large scale, the government will have to absorb the losses, typically leading to budget deficits and inflation. From this perspective directed credits seem wholly inefficient. But this inefficiency is the result of misguided industrial policy—the instrument of subsidization is not inefficient, it is used ineffectively or inappropriately.

In examining whether a government should consider using directed credits as an instrument of industrial policy, it may be helpful to return to the hierarchy of government objectives developed in the second section. The government should pursue industrial policy goals (a third tier objective) only if these do not undermine macroeconomic stability (a first tier objective). Developing appropriate incentives to improve the functioning of financial markets (the second tier objective) should be the government's next goal. When directed credits are implemented without deposit rate controls, they simply impose additional costs on the banking system, reducing its franchise value and inhibiting the proper functioning of financial markets. Even with deposit rate controls, if the flow of costs arising from directed credits exceeds the flow of rents captured by the banks from deposit rate controls, then the net effect is negative and the financial sector will have difficulty developing reputational capital.

It is, however, useful to remember that not all directed credit programs have been unsuccessful. Notable exceptions include a number of east Asian economies, such as Japan and the Republic of Korea.[28] In order to understand the reason for directed credits we must answer three questions: Why subsidize? Why use credit to subsidize? And how should we implement directed credits?

The reasons for subsidization are easy to understand in theory, though hard to assess in practice. Subsidies try to remedy the divergence between private and social benefits that arise because of externalities, market imperfections and coordination failures. These include the inefficiencies related to the dynamics of growth, in which private markets may fail to fully account for future benefits of investments in new technologies.

Once the government decides to subsidize the private sector, there are two main reasons why governments would want to use directed credits rather than direct subsidies or tax breaks. First, directed credits are a covert means of subsidization. When a particular firm receives a loan at a low interest rate, outsiders find it hard to determine whether the low interest rate was extended because of a low risk premium or whether it constitutes a subsidy. Moreover, the extent of the subsidy is not visible until a firm fails to perform on the loan. The second, and much more valid, reason for using directed credits is that they may provide a framework for good governance. As lenders, banks want to make sure that firms make good on their promises to back their loans. They therefore have a stronger control motive than a government agency that simply distributes subsidies or tax holidays. And given their greater involvement in control over the firm, banks create a closer linkage between the receipt of subsidies and the accumulation of financial and reputational capital. This argument, however, does not suggest that the government would use direct credit only to implement subsidies. Indeed, a disproportionate use of credit may lead to excessive leverage, which could cause fragility in the corporate sector.

This last point naturally leads to the question of which governance structure should accompany the distribution of directed credits. We argue that banks are in a unique position to distribute these rents—they can be expected to have more information than the government. Banks must then be given incentives to act upon this information, meaning that directed credits should not be distributed unconditionally to specific firms. Rather, directed credits should be targeted broadly. Firms within a targeted industry should then have to compete to capture the credit subsidy, that is, there may be differential subsidization within the industry. In east Asia directed credits (as well as other industrial policy tools, such as export quotas) are allocated in a contest. This contest generates strong performance incentives, stronger possibly than free market competition.

Directed credits remain, however, delicate to implement. Firms will want to change the criteria for their receipt from economic performance to alternate metrics that favour incumbency. Current recipients have incentives to claim that they have a right to subsidies, and government officials are under pressure to continue supporting the firms that they supported in the past. Moreover, with any system that distributes rents, there is likely to be some inefficient rent seeking behaviour.

If a government pursues a program of directed credits, it is very important that the program be designed with the objective of improving the governance mechanisms in place in the economy. Institutions that grant credit subsidies should be designed so that successful firms are rewarded and unsuccessful firms are cut off.

CREATING REPUTATIONAL CAPITAL THROUGH FINANCIAL RESTRAINT

The objective of a policy regime of financial restraint is to exogenously create reputational capital. The government intervenes in the financial intermediation market to create positive profits that are captured by the banking sector. These positive profits can be earned by a bank in every year of operation. Thus the capitalized value of this stream of income can be quite high—creating a franchise value that can be far in excess of a bank's own equity capital. In fact, a bank can have a very high franchise value even when its net worth is negative!

Implementation of financial restraint

There are two primary policy tools that the government must use to implement financial restraint: deposit rate controls and restrictions on competition. By setting the real deposit rate below the free market clearing rate, the government creates large rents that are captured by the banking sector. Controlling the deposit rate alone, however, will not create franchise value for the banks, because subsequent entry may compete away these rents. If the government also prevents or limits entry, these rents may be preserved, thus creating franchise value.

A cursory examination of the mechanism of financial restraint may lead the reader to wonder about the similarities between this policy regime and that of financial repression. These are two very different policies. Under financial repression the government is using the financial sector to extract rents from the private sector to finance its own expenditures. Financial restraint, conversely, is a policy regime whereby the government intervenes to create rents in the private sector.

To understand how we frame the implementation of financial restraint, it may be helpful to return to the discussion of the three tiers of government objectives. We propose financial restraint as a set of second tier policies. By creating franchise value in the banking sector, financial restraint creates reputational capital in the economy and promotes endogenous investment in good governance mechanisms, such as monitoring capabilities. Finally, because of the critical importance of the creation of franchise value, there are explicit limits on the extent to which the government can pursue third tier objectives—that is, industrial policy.

Because of the importance of reputational capital for both banks and firms, there may be some justification for implementing lending rate controls. These lower rates transfer rents to the recipient firms, creating value for firms with good reputations. Lending rate controls, however, are inherently harder to enforce than deposit rate controls, and so they are probably worthwhile only when the economy is in a low state of development, and creating an initial endowment of reputational capital among firms is especially important.

Any government policy risks being corrupted at the level of implementation. The political economy issues of how to create good bureaucracies is beyond the scope of this chapter. We should mention, however, that financial restraint creates relatively few rent-seeking opportunities for bureaucrats, because the government is not involved in the actual flow of funds. It does not collect any revenues, nor does it give out any direct subsidies—it only regulates deposit rates that create rent opportunities within the private sector.

Probably the most difficult aspect of implementation is not the imposition of financial restraint, but the devolution of it. We have stressed repeatedly that financial restraint is a policy that is most valid in the early stages of development. As banks in the economy gain reputational capital, these policies become less important, and possibly obsolete. The difficulty that a government may have in stepping back from its role can be witnessed by the recent experiences in Japan and the slow pace of deregulation in the Republic of Korea.

A practitioner's guide to financial restraint

We have not yet touched upon an important insight as to why financial restraint is so effective at creating reputational capital. Financial restraint creates so much reputational capital because the balance sheets of banks are highly leveraged. Essentially, a small distortion in the deposit market is multiplied by the leverage of the balance sheet to create a very large return on the equity invested in the bank.

To understand this insight better, a numerical example may be helpful. Consider an economy in which there is perfectly elastic demand for capital, earning a 5 per cent return. Let us assume that a bank in this economy is capitalized with 10 per cent equity and 90 per cent deposits. In a free market equilibrium both deposits and equity will earn a 5 per cent return (table 9.1).

Now consider what happens if the government intervenes in the deposit market by placing a 3 per cent ceiling on deposit rates. Depositors suffer a modest loss of income, with their rate of return falling from 5 per cent to 3 per cent. The return on equity, however, increases dramatically, from 5 per cent to 23 per cent! Thus equity

Table 9.1: The franchise value of a bank (dollars)

	Free market			Financial restraint		
	Amount invested	Gross return	Rate of return (per cent)	Amount invested	Gross return	Rate of return (per cent)
Assets	100	105.0	5	100	105.0	5
Deposits	90	94.5	5	90	92.7	3
Equity	10	10.5	5	10	12.3	23
	Franchise value of equity = $0.5/(5%) = $10			Franchise value of equity = $2.3/(5%) = $46		

invested in the banking sector is much more valuable than equity invested elsewhere. We can calculate the franchise value of this bank. Each period, the owners of this bank earn a net return of $2.30. To earn this same return elsewhere in the economy would require investing $46—the franchise value of the bank.

Now consider how this intervention affects the incentives of the owners of the bank. When investing $100 of capital, the owners act as if they have $46 at stake. This franchise value significantly alters the relative return to value-creating and value-extracting activity. Value-extracting activity has a private return for the equity holders only if the loss in a bad state exceeds the value of the equity they invested. Because of the long-term incentives created by this franchise value, we can expect that the bank's activities will be focused on value creation, with little or no activity aimed at value extraction.

Two further points are worth demonstrating. First, the franchise value created by financial restraint is substantial even when bank capitalization is low or negative (table 9.2). Thus financial restraint may be a particularly valuable policy tool to use when the banking industry suffers a severe shock that depletes capital. Second, significant franchise value is created even with very modest interventions in the deposit rate. Consider the value of a bank with a negative 5 per cent capitalization when the government intervenes to set the deposit rate just one percentage point below the free market level (at 4 per cent). The franchise value of this bank is 16 per cent of assets—more than twice the capitalization required by the Basle accord!

Critics of this policy may note that it may induce inefficiency in the supply of savings in the economy by altering the return to

Table 9.2: Franchise value by capitalization for differing deposit rates

Capitalization (equity assets x 100)

Deposit rate (per cent)	10	5	0	-5
5	10	5	0	0
4	28	24	20	16
3	46	43	40	37
2	64	62	60	58
1	82	81	80	79

Note: Assumes a 5 per cent return on assets in the economy.

depositors. While we recognize that this may indeed occur, we present a few points in defense. First, while the expected return on deposits may be higher (5 per cent) in the free market regime than under financial restraint (3 per cent), the former return will have much greater risk associated with it. Given that most depositors are small households with risk-averse preferences, it is not clear which securities are preferable to the household. Second, even if this policy does distort the savings decisions of households, we must ask how important this distortion will be.[29] First, we have shown that the amount of the intervention can be very modest. Furthermore, the benefits derived from this intervention—in terms of improved governance—can be significant. While these benefits are hard to measure directly, the losses incurred in a banking crises give an indication of the possible savings from financial restraint. Caprio and Klingbiel (1995) provide estimates of the cost of a number of bank crises— they range from about 1 per cent to 42 per cent of GDP. Our hypothesis is that the net effect of financial restraint is positive, as long as the magnitude of the intervention is modest.

CONCLUSION

We believe that any consideration of an appropriate policy formulation for financial institutions must begin by first recognizing the fundamental character of financial transactions—that something of real value today is exchanged for a promise of payment in the future. The quality of financial intermediation in an economy will depend critically on the quality of the promises that are made by financial institutions and by their end-users (borrowers). Financial markets function to deliver two outputs—the allocation of capital and the governance of its use. We believe that government policy must place significant emphasis on the development of appropriate governance structures.

One mechanism that can greatly enhance the credibility of financial transactions is the development of reputational capital—the capitalized value of future profitability of the enterprise, attributable to its good reputation. When an enterprise has significant reputational capital, its incentives shift from a focus on rent extraction to a focus on rent creation.

We identify a set of government policies, called financial restraint, by which the government can create reputational capital (franchise value) in the financial sector. The primary mechanisms of financial restraint are deposit rate control and restrictions on competition. By creating significant opportunities to capture rents on an ongoing basis in the future, this set of policies creates powerful incentives for banks to invest their funds responsibly and to intensively monitor the performance of their borrowers. Thus the banking sector can become an important locus for the development of governance mechanisms for the rest of the economy.

In our view complete financial liberalization is not the appropriate policy recommendation for countries just beginning to develop self-sufficient private sector financial institutions. A simplistic view of financial liberalization may push the economy towards a market-based or Anglo-American system before the economy is ready for the required level of sophistication. We have argued instead that developing economies need to invest significant resources in building appropriate reputational capital and governance mechanisms. In our view a banking system resembling the Japanese or German system would provide these institutions and should therefore be the medium-term objective for a developing economy.

Government policy can facilitate the development of institutions and shape incentives so that appropriate governance mechanisms develop. We have suggested a policy framework—financial restraint—which can create these incentives. Much work, however, remains to be done on determining how good governance systems can be developed in financial markets.

NOTES

1. See Stiglitz (1994) for a discussion of this theorem.
2. Moreover, one can argue that the government benefits from lower transaction costs for a number of activities.
3. The example given is an illustration of value extraction through "gambling" . There are other inefficient value extraction strategies, notably looting strategies, where managers seek out covert ways to "take the money and run". Akerlof and Romer (1993) give a fascinating account of some of these tactics.
4. We emphasize the difference between the primary and secondary sale of equities. In the secondary sale there is only an exchange of savings instruments (affecting the distribution of risks), but no new mobilization of funds.
5. The examples of Japan and Germany also suggest that strong bank governance encouraged industrial concentration, which, arguably, may have both benefits and disadvantages. These also depend on the stage of economic development.
6. The Republic of Korea experienced higher inflation than we would consider necessary or desirable, however. Indeed, we would argue that Korea got into trouble when its governance system failed, most notably the refusal to scale down spending on heavy and chemical industries (HCI). It may be helpful to refer to the framework described in the second section to analyze the Korean experience with the promotion of HCI. In pursuing a third tier objective (an industrial policy to promote a particular sector), the government relaxed monetary discipline, thus creating inflation. Since maintaining low and stable inflation is a first tier objective, this policy was mistaken. Worse, during the inflation period banks suffered from undercapitalization, weakening the soundness of the financial system. Thus the second tier objective was harmed as well. Eventually, the Korean government recognized the costs of its policies and took necessary steps to regain control over inflation.
7. One of the most prominent programs were loans for export businesses. Stiglitz (1993b) argues that the emphasis on export markets was important for providing an objective metric of firm performance.
8. See also Baliga and Polak (1995), Dewatripont and Maskin (1995) and Dinc (1995) for further comparisons of these two systems. Mayer (1990) and Mayer and Alexander (1990) provide empirical comparisons.
9. Some recent empirical evidence also supports this hypothesis. Claessens (1995a) finds for the Czech and Slovak Republics that firms with more concentrated owners are valued higher on average.
10. Related to this is the question of "insider control" in transition economies. Again, we would argue that in order to uproot established but dysfunctional or corrupt governance systems, a strong counterbalance, such as an R-banking system, is necessary. At the same time the critical problem is to ensure that the new governance mechanisms (R-banks) respond to economic performance and do not fall prey to the old system.
11. One may be tempted to point out that we base the advantages of the R-system on the example of Japan, which is currently facing a major banking crisis. We see no contradiction. Our claim is that the Japanese banking system was instrumental in the high growth period, up to the first oil crisis (see also Cho and Hellmann, 1993). The development thereafter is a case study in the

difficulties of the system adapting to changing economic circumstances and the difficulties of managing deregulation. Indeed, as we will discuss later in the third section, competition from securities markets undermines the franchise value of banks and may give rise to imprudent bank behaviour.

12. In this section we examine the investment decisions made by banks. A similar logic holds for the choices of firms.

13. The logic of these arguments follows that of Diamond (1989).

14. Hellmann, Murdock and Stiglitz (1996) argued similarly that financial repression, in particular, maintaining a negative real interest rate, is a way for the government to extract rents from the private sector.

15. An intervention placing a ceiling on the deposit rate should be engaged only in an environment of low and stable inflation. Furthermore, the real interest rate should always remain positive.

16. This is true, in particular, if the cost of distortions is convex, such as for Harberger triangles across different markets.

17. The seminal works of McKinnon (1973) and Shaw (1973) discuss the flaws of financial repression.

18. See Vittas (1993) for an excellent overview on this topic.

19. Macroeconomic fluctuations and the moral hazard argument complement each other (see also Caprio and Klingbiel, 1995). In times of recession bank capital may fall below critical thresholds, so that the bank may begin gambling or looting. The franchise value of banks should be sufficiently large to withstand the temptations of moral hazard in recessions.

20. Under perfect deposit insurance, depositors have a constant payoff function.

21. The development of regulatory and accounting infrastructure is, however, very important, as stressed by Caprio (1994).

22. Note that the incentive to loot does not depend on the convexity of returns, but only on the comparison between benefits to looting and the cost of lost franchise value.

23. We will focus here on stocks and corporate bonds. The argument for government bonds is much more persuasive. In Hong Kong, for example, the government created a government bond market with bonds of different maturities in order to establish a yield curve that firms and investors could use for investment decisions.

24. There are theoretical reasons why equity markets may not always work. Greenwald, Stiglitz and Weiss (1984) and Myers and Majluf (1984) show that there may be equity rationing.

25. In the United States this problem has received a lot of attention in the past 15 years. One way that stockholders can exercise control is through the takeover mechanism. This mechanism is surrounded by substantial controversy, the discussion of which would take us beyond the scope of this chapter. The resistance that the takeover mechanism has encountered in the United States and the virtual absence of hostile takeovers outside of the United States, lead us to believe that takeovers are not a viable concept of corporate governance in developing countries. Another theme that has emerged in the United States at the end of the 1980s is the advent of large stockholders, such as pension funds, that exert strong corporate governance through board control and voting rights. This, we would argue, resembles much more closely the corporate governance arrangements needed in developing countries. The irony is that

these stockholders hold larger blocks of equity (and possible bonds) and consider themselves long-term investors. They therefore do not take advantage of two of the characteristics for which stock markets are typically sought: the fact that shares can be sold anytime and that investors can buy smaller stakes to achieve superior diversification.

26. This argument relies on an assumption that banks do not compete perfectly for these firms, or else no additional profits could be made from them.

27. There are, however, costs associated with universal banking that arise from the conflicts of interest between the commercial and investment banking sides (see Rajan, 1992).

28. See Cho (1989) and Kato and others (1994).

29. See Giovannini (1985).

REFERENCES

Akerlof, G. and P. Romer. 1993. "Looting: The Economic Underworld of Bankruptcy for Profit." *Brookings Papers on Economic Activity* 2:1–73

Allen F. and D. Gale. 1995. "A Welfare Comparison of Intermediaries and Financial Markets in Germany and the U.S." *European Economic Review* 39(2):179–209.

Aoki, M. and H. Patrick, eds. 1994. *The Japanese Main Bank System: Its Relevance for Developing and Transforming Economies.* New York: Oxford University Press.

Aoki, M., H. Patrick and P. Sheard. 1994. "The Japanese Main Bank System: An Introductory Overview." In M. Aoki and H. Patrick, eds., *The Japanese Main Bank System: Its Relevance for Developing and Transforming Economies.* New York: Oxford University Press.

Baliga, S. and B. Polak. 1995. "Banks versus Bonds: A Simple Theory of Comparative Financial Institutions." Cowles Foundation Discussion Paper 1100, Yale University, New Haven.

Berglöf, E. 1995. "Corporate Governance in Transition Economies: The Theory and Its Policy Implications." In M. Aoki and H. Kim, eds., *Corporate Governance in Transition Economies: Insider Control and the Role of Banks.* EDI Development Studies 59–95. Washington, D.C.: World Bank.

Bhattacharya, S. 1982. "Aspects of Monetary and Banking Theory and Moral Hazard." *Journal of Finance* 37(2):371–84.

Caprio, G. 1994. "Bank Regulation: The Case of the Missing Model." Policy Research Department, World Bank, Washington, D.C.

_____. 1995. "Dealing with Bank Insolvencies: Cross Country Experience." Policy Research Department, World Bank, Washington, D.C.

Caprio, G. and D. Klingbiel. 1996. "Bank Insolvency: Bad Luck, Bad Policy or Bad Banking?" Paper prepared for the Annual Conference on Development Economics. World Bank, Washington, D.C.

Caprio, G. and L. Summers. 1993. "Finance and Its Reform: Beyond Laissez-Faire." Financial Sector Development Department, World Bank, Washington, D.C.

Cho, Y. 1989. "Finance and Development: The Korean Approach." *Oxford Review of Economic Policy* 5(4).

Cho, Y. and T. Hellmann. 1993. "The Government's Role in Japanese and Korean Credit Markets: A New Institutional Economics Perspective." Policy Research Working Papers, Financial Sector Development WPS 1190, World Bank, Washington D.C.

Claessens, S. 1995a. "Corporate Governance and Equity Prices: Evidence from the Czech and Slovak Republics." Paper prepared for the World Bank conference on Stock Markets, Corporate Finance, and Economic Growth. Washington, D.C. February 16–17.

____. 1995b. "The Emergence of Equity Investment in Developing Countries: Overview." *The World Bank Economic Review* 9(1):1–18.

Demirgüç-Kunt, A. and R. Levine. 1995. "Stock Market Development and Financial Intermediaries: Stylized Facts." Policy Research Department, World Bank, Washington, D.C.

Dewatripont, M. and E. Maskin. 1995. "Credit and Efficiency in Centralized and Decentralized Economies." *Review of Economic Studies* 62(4):541–55.

Dewatripont, M. and J. Tirole. 1994. *The Prudential Regulation of Banks.* Cambridge, Mass.: MIT Press.

Diamond, D. 1989. "Reputation Acquisition in Debt Markets." *Journal of Political Economy* 97(4):828–62.

Diamond, D. and P. Dybvig. 1983. "Bank Runs, Deposit Insurance, and Liquidity." *Journal of Political Economy* 91(3):401–19.

Dinc, S. 1995. "Relationship Banking: Feasibility and Path Dependency." Stanford University, Department of Economics, Stanford.

____. 1996. "A Theory of Competitive Bank Lending." Stanford University, Department of Economics, Stanford.

Edwards, J. and K. Fischer. 1993. *"Banks, Finance and Investment in Germany"* Cambridge, U.K.: Cambridge University Press.

Fry, M. 1988. "Financial Development: Theories and Recent Experience." *Oxford Review of Economic Policy* 6(4):13–28.

____. 1995. *Money, Interest, and Banking in Economic Development.* Second edition. Baltimore: The Johns Hopkins University Press.

Gerschenkron, A. 1962. *Economic Backwardness in Historical Perspective.* Cambridge, Mass.: Belknap Press of Harvard University.

Giovannini, A. 1985. "Saving and the Real Interest Rate." *Journal of Development Economics* 18(2-3):197–217.

Glaeser, E. 1995. "Neither a Borrower nor a Lender Be: An Economic Analysis of Interest Restrictions and Usury Laws." Hoover Institution, Stanford University, Stanford.

Greenwald, B. and J. Stiglitz. 1986. "Externalities in Economies with Imperfect Information and Incomplete Markets." *Quarterly Journal of Economics* 101(2):229–64.

Greenwald, B., J. Stiglitz and A. Weiss. 1984. "Informational Imperfections and Macroeconomic Fluctuations." *American Economic Review* 74(2):194–9.

Harris, M. and A. Raviv. 1992. "Financial Contracting Theory." In J. Laffont, ed., *Advances in Economic Theory.* Sixth World Congress Volume II. Cambridge, U.K.: Cambridge University Press.

Hellmann T., K. Murdock and J. Stiglitz. 1994. "Addressing Moral Hazard in Banking: Deposit Rate Control vs. Capital Requirements." Stanford University, Department of Economics, Stanford.

_____. 1996a. "Deposit Mobilization through Financial Restraint." In N. Hermes and R. Lensink, eds., *Financial Development and Economic Growth: Theory and Experiences from Developing Economies*. London: Routledge.

_____. 1996b. "Financial Restraint: Toward a New Paradigm." In M. Aoki, M. Okuno-Fujiwara and H. Kim, eds., *The Role Of Government in East Asian Economic Development: Comparative Institutional Analysis*. Oxford: Oxford University Press.

Horiuchi, A. 1984. "Economic Growth and Financial Allocation in Postwar Japan." Brookings Discussion Papers in International Economics 18. Washington, D.C.

Kane, E. 1989. *The S&L Insurance Crisis: How Did It Happen?* Washington, D.C.: Urban Institute Press.

Kato, K., T. Shibata, K. Fukui, A. Mogi, Y. Miwa, Y. Niwa, N. Ichikawa and M. Furata. 1994. "Policy-Based Finance: The Experience of Postwar Japan." World Bank Discussion Paper 221. Washington, D.C.

Khan, M. 1995. "Fiscal and Monetary Constraints on Deregulating Commercial Banks; Financial Repression and the Need for Cautious Reform." Stanford University, Department of Economics, Stanford.

King, R.G. and R. Levine. 1993a. "Finance and Growth: Schumpeter Might Be Right." *Quarterly Journal of Economics* 108(3):717–37.

_____. 1993b. "Finance, Entrepreneurship, and Growth: Theory and Evidence." *Journal of Monetary Economics* 32(3):513–42.

Mayer, C. 1990. "Financial Systems, Corporate Finance, and Economic Development." In G. Hubbard, ed., *Asymmetric Information, Corporate Finance, and Investment*. Chicago: National Bureau of Economic Research.

Mayer, C. and I. Alexander. 1990. "Banks and Security Markets: Corporate Financing in Germany and the United Kingdom." *Journal of the Japanese and International Economies* 4(4):450–75.

McKinnon, R. 1973. *Money and Capital in Economic Development*. Washington, D.C.: The Brookings Institution.

_____. 1993. *The Order of Economic Liberalization*. Baltimore: The Johns Hopkins University Press.

Murdock, K. and J. Stiglitz. 1993. "The Effect of Financial Repression in an Economy with Positive Real Interest Rates: Theory and Evidence." Stanford University, Department of Economics, Stanford.

Myers, S. and N. Majluf. 1984. "Corporate Financing and Investment Decisions when Firms Have Information that Investors Do Not Have." *Journal of Financial Economics* 13:187–221.

Rajan, R. 1992. "A Theory of the Costs and Benefits of Universal Banking." Center for Research on Security Prices Working Paper 346. University of Chicago.

Shaw, E. 1973. *Financial Deepening in Economic Development*. New York: Oxford University Press.

Sheard, P. 1989. "The Main Bank System and Corporate Monitoring and Control in Japan." *Journal of Economic Behaviour and Organization* 11:399–422.

Stiglitz, J. 1985. "Credit Markets and the Control of Capital." *Journal of Money, Credit and Banking* 17(2):133–52.

_____. 1988. *Economics of the Public Sector*. Second edition. New York: W.W. Norton & Company.

_____. 1989. "On the Economic Role of the State." In A. Heertje, ed., *The Economic Role of the State*. Oxford: Basil Blackwell.

____. 1993a. "The Role of the State in Financial Markets." In *Proceedings of the Annual World Bank Conference on Development Economics*. Washington, D.C.: World Bank.

____. 1993b. "Some Lessons from the Asian Miracle." Stanford University, Department of Economics, Stanford.

____. 1994. *Whither Socialism?* Cambridge, Mass.: MIT Press.

Vittas, D. ed., 1993. *Financial Regulation: Changing the Rules of the Game*. Washington, D.C.: World Bank.

World Bank. 1993. *The East Asian Miracle: Economic Growth and Public Policy*. New York: Oxford University Press.

10

Public Policy Towards International Capital Flows

JOHN WILLIAMSON

In recent years there has been a strange disjunction between international policy towards international capital mobility, which supports further liberalization, and national attitudes, which have manifest increasing misgivings about the effects of high mobility. Thus the International Monetary Fund (IMF) has become increasingly active in urging convertibility, on capital and current (Article VIII) accounts, and the first stage of European Monetary Union (EMU) required the elimination of controls on intra-European capital movements. In contrast, several European countries have blamed the elimination of capital controls for the crises of the exchange rate mechanism (ERM) in 1992–93, and many emerging market countries are now arguing that Chile's policy of using controls to limit capital inflows has been superior to the unrestricted welcome extended by, for example, Argentina and Mexico. Similarly, the most contentious issue that arose in the Republic of Korea's negotiations for membership in the Organisation for Economic Co-operation and Development (OECD) has been the OECD's insistence that the Republic of Korea liberalize its capital account fully within five years.

This chapter considers the main issues involved in deciding whether and how to depart from complete liberalization of international capital flows. The first section identifies the welfare benefits of capital flows. This section is followed by an examination of the problems that such flows may pose for economic policy. A third section discusses the reasons why market outcomes could be non-optimal. The chapter concludes by examining the menu of policy measures that could be employed to influence capital flows in a benign way.

THE WELFARE BENEFITS OF CAPITAL FLOWS

The literature identifies five welfare benefits of international capital mobility. The classic benefit is that importing capital allows investment to rise above the level permitted by domestic savings in countries where rates of return are especially high. Ideally, it can be pushed to the optimal level determined by the global availability of savings (as reflected in the world rate of interest). Economic history leaves no room to doubt that this benefit has sometimes been very substantial, for example, in what were called "the lands of recent settlement" before 1914, or in the Republic of Korea in the 1960s and 1970s. This source of benefit suggests that capital inflows should be used to increase investment rather than consumption.

A second benefit is that inter-temporal consumption can be smoothed so that a country is no longer dependent on the oscillations of its own output or, often more importantly, on the value that the international market places on that output in a particular year. This benefit can also be important in countries with violent fluctuations in their terms of trade. However, international borrowing is more prone to abuse by myopic governments once the presumption that capital inflows are good only if they increase investment rather than consumption is abandoned.

The other three sources of welfare benefits differ in that they can be realized even with zero *net* capital flows, that is, through gross inflows that are offset by equal outflows. The first of these additional benefits is that the savings of each country can be distributed so as to achieve maximum risk diversification, rather than savers being locked into assets that reflect the particular productive structure of their home country. This helps motivate the international diversification of pension funds. The second benefit is that the domestic financial system will be exposed to the discipline of international competition. And the third is that (as most countries have come to appreciate in recent years) there are advantages in allowing firms to operate across national boundaries, arising from their role in transmitting technology and intellectual property.

In an ideal neoclassical world the presumption is that these benefits will be realized fully only if there are no impediments to international capital mobility. Hence restraints on capital mobility must be justified by demonstrating how the neoclassical assumptions fail, together with a reason for believing that government intervention is likely to make matters better rather than worse.

THE PROBLEMS POSED BY CAPITAL FLOWS

It is convenient to analyze separately the problems that may be caused by inflows and those that may be caused by outflows. The main danger posed by large capital inflows is that they may destabilize macroeconomic management. This can happen if inflows lead to an appreciation of the real exchange rate that causes Dutch disease, if inflows cumulate to a stock of debt that the country finds difficult to continue servicing on the contractually agreed terms or if inflows undermine anti-inflation policy. Another danger is that inflows may cause, or exacerbate, financial fragility.

Consider first the problems that arise from a real appreciation induced by capital inflows. It is traditional to distinguish between the case in which such an appreciation is temporary and that in which it is permanent. A temporary real appreciation *that the public expects to be temporary* is unlikely to have major effects on investment—which one can assume to be governed by long-run expectations. Indeed, the principal effect may be to stimulate an attempt to take advantage of the temporarily low price of foreign capital goods in order to accelerate investment. To the extent that domestically made capital goods (such as buildings) and foreign-made capital goods (such as machinery) are complements, the investment boom will spill over to increase domestic demand as well. Usually, capital inflows will, in any event, tend to be associated with a domestic boom when they result from low foreign interest rates, domestic reforms or a domestic stock market boom. Consumption can be expected to boom as well for similar reasons (as a result of increasing wealth and the complementarity of domestic and imported goods in consumption). And as long as the public has rational expectations, none of these changes should create a policy problem.

Consider, however, the alternative possibility—that the low foreign interest rates or the domestic stock market boom that is responsible for the capital inflows is temporary, but the public does *not* recognize this. Then, the lower profitability of producing tradables will discourage investment in those industries. Either investment will shift towards non-tradable industries, which is perhaps the most likely outcome given that the initiating factor was a decrease in the cost of capital, or the mix of expenditure will shift away from investment and towards consumption. When the capital inflows cease, as they will by virtue of the hypothesis that they were temporary, the economy will find itself in a worse position to service foreign debt than it would have been in the absence of the inflows. In this case a policy of preventing the real appreciation from occurring—of short-circuiting the misleading price signals—would have been beneficial. It will, of course, be practical only if the government is in a better position than the private sector to recognize when capital inflows are temporary.

Consider now the possibility that capital inflows are permanent, for example, because of reforms that make the domestic economy more attractive to foreign investors. Economists have sharp differences of opinion about the desirability of resisting a real appreciation that results from permanent capital inflows. One view is that, just like a resource discovery that induces a real appreciation, such inflows are strokes of good fortune that permit a country to enjoy higher real income—which it can absorb in a combination of increased consumption and increased investment.[1] The other view is that the damage to the tradable goods industries caused by the real appreciation can harm the prospects for development, given that those industries tend to be key to long-term growth. Sachs and Warner (1995) establish fairly conclusive empirical evidence that an abundance of natural resources is actually an impediment to success-ful development. Krugman (1987) has built what is perhaps the best model that shows how dynamic comparative advantage can be created in a world in which industries learn on the basis of cumula-tive experience. In his model an inward transfer that persists for a lengthy period can drive abroad some of the industries with dynamic increasing returns. As a result a country's market share in such industries and its real wage can be permanently reduced—by tem-porary good fortune. Many Latin American economists argue that a key reason for east Asia's superior economic performance is the attention that has been paid to maintaining a stable and competitive real exchange rate (see, for example, Laraín in Group of Thirty, 1994, p. A–78).

In practice, of course, it is often true that neither the public nor the government has a clear view as to whether capital inflows will be temporary or permanent. A rule of prudence recently endorsed by Summers (1995) suggests that inflows should be treated as tempo-rary and outflows as permanent. A second rule of prudence holds that while a government should never adopt a policy that is not viable if expectations *are* rational, it should also avoid policies whose success is *dependent* upon expectations being rational. These rules suggest that a prudent government should treat as a problem capital inflows that could induce a real appreciation big enough to threaten the growth of exports.

Another major macroeconomic problem caused by capital inflows is that they may build up a level of debt that the country suddenly finds difficult to service on the contractually agreed terms, as hap-pened throughout Latin America in 1982 (and again in Mexico by the end of 1994). This potential problem raises two issues: identify-ing how much debt a country can take on and limiting borrowing to a prudent level when the market wants to lend more. The first of these issues is discussed briefly in the appendix, which suggests that a typical country should aim to limit foreign debt to less than 40 per cent of GDP. That figure implies a safe current account deficit in an average year of around 3 per cent of GDP, or as high as 5 per cent in a country with a high growth rate and much of its capital inflows in the form of foreign direct investment (FDI). I discuss various ways in which borrowing may be limited later in the chapter.

Capital inflows have also, on occasion, undermined tight monetary policies intended to reduce inflation—the classic case being Spain in the early 1990s. The market appeared to find Spain's commitment to a fixed exchange rate within the ERM credible, which meant that the high interest rate needed to reduce inflation in Spain attracted inflows whose sterilization was expensive and whose non-sterilization would have jeopardized the degree of tightness believed necessary to continue reducing inflation.

Another major problem caused by capital inflows has come to light recently in several countries that underwent financial liberalization. A large share of capital inflows was funnelled through the domestic banking sector into short-term bank deposits (Calvo, Leiderman and Reinhart, 1994). The central bank credit that banks thus acquired provided the basis for an aggressive expansion of lending, where banks had not yet developed the skills to monitor the creditworthiness of private borrowers. Imprudent and excessive lending poses a hazard to bank solvency, especially if the capital flows out again and loans have to be liquidated rapidly, or if interest rates rise. Such financial fragility can deter a central bank from raising interest rates promptly when the currency comes under pressure or inflation becomes a threat.

There are other possible undesirable consequences of large capital inflows. Inflows may, for example, lead to the development of a speculative bubble in the stock market. One undesirable consequence of such a bubble is a decline in the local saving rate—individuals discover that their asset accumulation objectives are being achieved without the need for anything so tedious as abstaining from consumption. Another undesirable consequence is a financial crisis—and the danger of a recession—when the bubble bursts, especially if inflated asset values have come to underpin the solvency of important financial institutions.

Obviously, capital outflows can also pose major problems for economic policy. If the exchange rate is pegged, capital outflows lead to a reserve loss that requires higher interest rates to maintain the peg. But higher interest rates may threaten a recession or, if reserve inflows were not sterilized and financial fragility developed, a financial crisis. Under a floating exchange rate the currency may depreciate to an extent that significant stagflationary pressures are exerted while offering no compensating benefits in terms of needed improvement in the trade balance. If much of the debt was denominated in foreign exchange, a debt crisis may result. These costs can certainly be large, but they are sufficiently familiar not to warrant extended discussion.

EXPLANATIONS OF INEFFICIENT OUTCOMES

Economists—at least those with a normal quotient of neoclassical instincts—tend to believe that any assertion that a market generates a non-optimal outcome must be accompanied by an explanation of the way in which the neoclassical assumptions fail. Can one point to features of capital markets, of the economy in general or of government policy that explain why free capital mobility may generate the sort of outcomes described above?

In some cases it is possible to point to governments themselves as the creators of distortions that violate neoclassical precepts. The most obvious case is when a government fixes an exchange rate rather than allowing it to be determined by the market. A permanently fixed rate that enjoys full credibility should not create a problem, since the private sector can then disregard national boundaries in formulating plans. But "fixed" rates are typically pegged for the time being, backed by less-than-fully credible promises that the currency will not be devalued. The private sector must assess the probability that the government is going to change its mind about whether to devalue. If a pegged rate appears to be inconsistent with the fundamentals, especially if the exchange rate band is relatively narrow, agents face a one-way option: they stand to lose next to nothing if devaluation (or revaluation) does not occur and to gain a lot if its does, creating classic conditions for a speculative run, which, once under way, virtually compels devaluation (or revaluation).

A second way in which governments may be the source of the problem is by running excessive budget deficits, which are then financed by capital inflows. This observation led Nigel Lawson, then British Chancellor of the Exchequer, to formulate his rule that current account deficits are not a cause for concern if their counterpart is a private sector deficit rather than a public sector deficit. Even if one does not accept the Lawson thesis—on the grounds that the consumption/investment split is at least as important as the public/private split and that even capital inflows that increase private investment can be too big for prudence—there are no grounds for denying the contention that profligate spending by a government can crowd out more productive expenditures.

Government policy may also create the conditions in which it is rational for banks to act imprudently. Deposit insurance, even if only implicit because banks believe they will be bailed out if worst comes to worst, generates moral hazard, which some argue lies behind the observed propensity of newly liberalized banking systems to engage in excessive risk taking.

But one cannot blame everything on misguided government policies. In addition, lenders sometimes over-lend, to the point where the exchange rate becomes so overvalued that it thwarts the growth of exports and generates a foreign exchange crisis; foreign debt builds up to a level that begets a debt crisis; or the stock market develops a speculative bubble. Conversely, lenders sometimes create a financial panic, seeking to get out to a greater extent than justified by the fundamentals, because they believe that their peers are determined to exit, and they want to beat them to it. The question is why capital markets are prone to contagion effects that generate such outcomes.

Both lenders and borrowers find it easy to convince themselves that times have changed and that past rules of prudence no longer apply—until some event triggers a loss of confidence and causes lenders to decide simultaneously that the debtor is no longer creditworthy. The most plausible explanation of this apparently irrational behavior seems to be that lending decisions are made by agents rather than by principals and that the easy test of the agent's performance is whether he or she is doing worse than the market average. A fund manager who misses out on a boom is liable to be sacked, while one whose portfolio loses value in a crash along with everyone else's is unlikely to be fired.[2]

Another reason that private markets may lead to a socially inefficient outcome stems from the fact that private borrowers have no incentive to internalize the diminution of country creditworthiness that their own borrowing brings about. But to the extent that the international capital market ultimately penalizes a country for overborrowing, efficiency requires that borrowers internalize the impact that their actions have on others.

Today, a case for active public policy can no longer be established by simply showing the possibility of private sector failure; it is also necessary to establish that intervention by a public agency is likely to make things better rather than worse. Is there a reason for believing that governments can judge when capital inflows are excessive? If the above hypothesis as to why private markets sometimes get it wrong is correct, then there is a very obvious reason why one could expect governments to be able to do better: they can ask the right question. Instead of asking whether the market is likely to go up further in the short run, they can ask whether it is above the level consistent with the fundamentals in the long run. Even if the question cannot be answered in any precise way, simply posing the question may suffice to limit the errors resulting from contagion effects.

POLICY MEASURES

What can and should be done to control capital flows? I take it for granted that the move towards a world of high capital mobility is irreversible and that the future role of capital controls will be marginal at most. The principal need is to make public policy consistent with the fact of high capital mobility.

Reform exchange rate policy

Because so much of the trouble arises from the attempt to operate an adjustable peg—an exchange rate regime predicated on capital immobility—in an era of high capital mobility, the first step should be to reform exchange rate policy. A fixed exchange rate should be truly and credibly fixed: either by being underwritten by both countries involved, on the model of Germany and the Netherlands in the ERM, or by one party unilaterally pegging its currency to that of another country, but underpinning the promise of a fixed rate by a currency board arrangement governing the issue of domestic money. A rate that floats freely is another viable regime (although it may be politically difficult to maintain this regime when the market drives the exchange rate to a level that is perceived as out of line with the fundamentals and damaging to important interest groups—typically consumers in the case of an under-valuation and exporters in the case of an over-valuation). A further possible regime is a crawling band whose parity is adjusted in line with the fundamentals rather than in accord with speculative pressures. Both a wide band and a crawl that avoids misalignments are helpful in containing speculative pressures, because they avoid one-way options.

Tax international financial transactions

But even countries with exchange rate policies that did not invite disequilibrating capital movements have suffered from excessive flows. The question therefore arises as to what other policy measures may be effective. Perhaps the most popular candidate is the "Tobin tax" (Tobin, 1978). This proposal calls for a small (say, 0.1 per cent) tax on any financial transaction that involves a currency exchange. The argument is that this tax would impose an insignificant burden on traders who needed to buy and sell foreign currencies in the course of exporting or importing, and that it would be similarly insignificant for long-term international investors. In contrast, it would add substantially to the cost of short-term arbitrage and speculative transactions, the bulk of which are reversed within a working day or, indeed, within a few minutes.

Two arguments are advanced in favour of the Tobin tax. The first is that it is a form of international taxation that could raise a lot of money for international good causes. The second is that it would help combat the bad behaviour of foreign exchange markets—that is, decrease volatility and/or misalignments. Both claims depend upon the ability of governments to collect such a tax. It is clear that this would be possible only with wide international agreement, since foreign exchange trading is an activity that can migrate easily in response to financial incentives. But the effectiveness of a Tobin tax would also depend on the elasticity of transactions with respect to the tax. If that elasticity was zero—if the volume of transactions was unaffected by the tax—then a tax rate as low as 0.1 per cent would yield revenue of around $312 billion per year (given that the turnover in the foreign exchange market is now estimated at $1.3 trillion per day, and taking a working year of 240 days). But, in fact, one might expect the volume of transactions to fall off drastically with even a very moderate tax rate, precisely because most transactions are driven by very short-term speculative hopes and portfolio rebalancing following an initial "fundamental" transaction. But even if the volume of transactions fell by as much as 90 per cent following a tax of 0.1 per cent, the tax would yield more than $30 billion per year, a handy sum compared with the needs of most international good causes (other than combating greenhouse gas emissions).

Should we expect a 90 per cent decline in the volume of transactions to help stabilize the market? It is naive to equate speculative or short-term movements with market destabilization. On the contrary, given that trade flows exhibit the *J*-curve phenomenon,[3] the foreign exchange market would be dynamically unstable in the absence of speculation (Britton, 1970). If the Tobin tax was too efficient in killing off speculation, the market could end up becoming more volatile rather than less.

But because for more than a decade it has been conventional to argue that what really matter are misalignments, not volatility, the more important question is whether the Tobin tax would curb misalignments. Perhaps the strongest reason for expecting that outcome is the finding of Frankel and Froot (1990) that during the run-up of the dollar in the first half of the 1980s, most participants in the foreign exchange market recognized that the dollar was above its fundamental value and could therefore be expected to fall in due course. But they nonetheless judged that it was still trending upward and therefore continued to buy. A Tobin tax big enough to make them ask whether the dollar was still likely to be higher in three months might have been helpful in that situation. Frankel (1988) makes the argument in a more general way:

A small tax in proportion to the size of the foreign exchange purchase will not be much of a deterrent to anyone contemplating the purchase of a foreign security for longer-term investing. But it will discourage the spot trader who is now accustomed to buying foreign exchange with the intention of selling it a few hours later. If the destabilizing speculators ... are indeed the short-term traders that the expectations survey data suggest, and the stabilizing speculators are the long-term investors, then the tax may indeed reduce the volatility of the exchange rate. (p. 185)

That argument for the proposal is the most convincing one that I know of. But it remains true that the tax would penalize stabilizing and destabilizing speculators. If the object is to curb misalignments, it seems inefficient to penalize all transactions rather than those that are subverting policy (that is, pushing the exchange rate away from equilibrium). That can be accomplished only through more discriminatory types of capital controls.

In sum, I doubt whether the Tobin tax is a promising way to stabilize the foreign exchange market. Even if it were administratively feasible, it is inferior to more traditional forms of capital controls. And it goes without saying that the minor addition to costs imposed by the tax would be neither here nor there when it comes to defending an exchange rate that the market believes to be out of line with the fundamentals (and therefore to offer a one-way option). It seems equally unlikely that it would do much to restrain capital inflows driven by excessive optimism about a country's prospects.

Improve information and surveillance

Several other policy measures that might be adopted by the international community have been discussed since the Mexican crisis of early 1995. These focus on improving information supplied by debtor countries to international investors and on improving surveillance of borrowing countries by the IMF. There has also been discussion of enlarging the General Arrangements to Borrow,[4] so as to enhance the IMF's ability to help countries that have difficulty maintaining debt service. One danger of that proposal is that it would magnify the problem of moral hazard regarding lenders, who may come to expect further bailouts. A counter to that danger might be found in the creation of a more systematic mechanism for workouts by sovereign debtors, an idea whose study was endorsed by the 1995 G-7 summit. If the problem of unmanageable capital inflows to recently reformed countries does indeed prove to be as general as it is beginning to look, it is difficult to see any other international action that could be remotely adequate for deterring excessive inflows.

Adjust or finance

However, it seems unlikely that any major relief will come from international action in the near future. It is therefore important to examine the options available to a government that confronts large capital inflows. The strategic decision is whether to allow the capital inflows to be translated into a current account deficit so as to finance increased domestic investment and/or consumption. It is rational to allow this when two conditions are satisfied: the rate of return on the additional investment exceeds the rate of interest that will be paid on the debt that is contracted and the additional debt does not imperil creditworthiness (see the appendix).

If the government decides to "make the transfer", it has three polar mechanisms that it can use. The first is the flexible exchange rate mechanism of currency appreciation. The second is the fixed exchange rate ("gold standard") mechanism, whereby an expanding money supply increases demand and thus causes inflation and real appreciation once again. The third is to relax import restrictions, which will also lead to an increased current account deficit, although with the important difference that this will come about through higher imports and will avoid the penalization of exports.

Sterilize

I argued earlier that there are circumstances—if inflows are believed to be temporary, if Dutch disease threatens growth prospects, if the debt is growing so large that it threatens to precipitate a debt crisis, if inflows threaten to expose a fragile banking system to excessive strain or if anti-inflation policy could be undermined—in which it is rational to resist the current account adjustment that would accomplish the transfer. In such cases the natural first resort is to intervene in the exchange market to prevent appreciation and to sterilize the intervention through open market operations. The drawback with sterilization is that it is expensive. Particularly when domestic interest rates are being held up in order to restrict demand, the interest rate that the central bank will have to pay on the bonds that it issues[5] may be much higher than the foreign interest rate that it will earn on the reserves that it acquires. Moreover, in order to persuade the public to hold bonds equal to the whole of the reserve increase, it may be necessary to increase the domestic interest rate. If interest rates are allowed to increase, capital inflows will rise further. Even if they are held constant, there will be no market incentive to reduce inflows.[6]

The central bank can avoid this cost by raising the reserve ratio required of commercial banks. It thus averts the need to issue additional domestic currency bonds while still avoiding an increase in the money supply, despite the increase in the monetary base. This procedure may be particularly helpful if there are worries about bank lending getting out of hand. But beyond some point high reserve ratios impose costs of their own—they diminish the efficiency of the financial system as borrowers are diverted away from those lenders subject to the high reserve requirement and towards others that escape that requirement. Another way of achieving de facto sterilization without issuing additional bonds is to require government-controlled financial institutions (like the postal savings system) to switch their deposits from commercial banks to the central bank. Although this method has proved effective in a number of Asian countries (Fischer and Reisen, 1992), it implies either reducing the return to savers in those institutions or (if the central bank pays the normal domestic interest rate) still imposing a financial cost on the central bank.

Discourage inflows

Another possible policy reaction is to widen the band of permissible exchange rate fluctuations—allowing capital inflows to push the exchange rate to the strong edge of the band, but leaving the private sector with a presumption that the appreciation is temporary. If the private sector believes that, it will have two helpful effects. First, since foreign investors deduct expected future depreciation from the domestic currency return in order to calculate the expected yield in their own currency, this measure will reduce the incentive for capital inflows. This effect will be reinforced to the extent that investors are risk averse, since the wider band will also increase exchange rate risk. Second, the measure will minimize the danger that the appreciation will discourage investment in tradable goods industries, which is influenced mainly by expectations of the long-term real exchange rate.

It is also possible to tighten fiscal policy, either by cutting government expenditure or by raising taxes. A tightening will permit domestic interest rates to be reduced, thus diminishing the incentive for capital inflows without losing control of domestic demand and thus risking inflation. Perhaps the main problem of this strategy is the difficulty of persuading politicians that a surfeit of capital inflows should be countered by fiscal austerity, not provide the wherewithal for a spending binge. Is it conceivable that political resistance would be less to a tax on interest payments, which would permit the cost of domestic borrowing to remain above the international interest rate without attracting more foreign capital? Unfortunately, this option is precluded for many countries by the terms of existing double-taxation treaties, which would have to be revised fundamentally—a change that would also require the agreement of creditor countries.

Rather than tighten fiscal policy, a government could seek institutional measures (as opposed to higher rates of interest) that would increase private savings. The establishment of a postal savings system or of arrangements for the private provision of pensions are examples of measures that might increase savings without requiring higher interest rates. The latter has induced an important increase in savings in Chile, and other Latin American countries are now following Chile's example.

Capital inflows might also be discouraged by withdrawing any measures that inadvertently subsidize inward investment. The two most common examples are probably insurance of bank deposits and grants to direct investors. The grants are presumably intended to attract direct investment because of its job-creating or technology-enhancing features, but there is absolutely no reason, except for accident or inertia, why foreigners should benefit from free or subsidized deposit insurance. Indeed, the problems of moral hazard discussed earlier suggest that even the insurance of domestically owned bank deposits ought to be limited.

We are now in the realm of measures intended to repel rather than finance capital inflows. The classic measures of this type are capital controls. These can take many forms, such as the prohibition of foreign purchase or holding of domestic assets, requirements to obtain administrative permission for a foreign bond issue, minimum maturity periods for foreign bond issues, a dual exchange rate for capital transactions, taxes on purchases of domestic assets by foreigners or on investment income earned by foreigners, negative interest rates on bank deposits held by foreigners or reserve requirements on deposits held by foreigners. If such controls were easy to enforce, there would be no problem of excessive capital inflows. The most important question to ask about proposals for such controls is whether they can be enforced and, if so, at what cost in terms of economic distortions or civil liberties. Belgium offers an example of the limits of such controls in a European country with a well-regarded administrative apparatus. For many years it operated a dual exchange rate system, but problems of evasion began to become significant whenever the two rates diverged by more than 3 per cent.

Some measures applied by middle-income countries in recent years have enjoyed a measure of success, however. Both Chile and Colombia appear to have succeeded at least in lengthening the maturity structure of their debt through the imposition of a reserve requirement applying to foreign loans and foreign-owned deposits of short maturity. This measure has probably also reduced the magnitude of total inflows. Several countries in south-east Asia, including Indonesia, Malaysia and, more recently, Thailand, have also placed limits on the offshore borrowing or the foreign exchange exposure of their banks (IMF, 1995). These limits defend against the aggravation of financial fragility caused by foreign borrowing of banks and restrain the magnitude of total capital inflows.

Control capital outflows

A final possibility is to relax controls on capital outflows. There is, however, some evidence from the experiences of countries like Italy, New Zealand, Spain, Uruguay and Yugoslavia that a blanket relaxation of outflow controls can have the perverse effect of stimulating net *inflows* (Labán and Larraín, 1993; Bartolini and Drazen, 1994). The reason is that investors can become so sure that they will have no difficulty withdrawing their money when they wish to that they actually increase their exposure. It may nonetheless be possible to undertake limited liberalization, for example, by permitting domestic pension funds to invest abroad, while avoiding the danger of provoking a perverse reaction.

Institute a comprehensive program

Chilean experience suggests that the best policy is to employ many instruments, without expecting any one to be a panacea. Sterilized intervention and increased reserve requirements can provide useful short-term relief. The exchange rate band should be widened, imports should be liberalized and fiscal policy should be tightened so that domestic interest rates can be reduced. Capital inflows can be discouraged through controls or taxes, although it is critically important to recognize that all controls leak and will be evaded if the incentive to do so is strong. The most common mistake is to expect too much of capital controls. Certain capital outflows can be liberalized. Together, these measures offer some prospect of enabling a government to maintain macroeconomic control without dousing a potential export boom.

Many of the options facing a government threatened with heavy capital outflows are similar. The government can allow adjustment to occur, either by allowing the currency to depreciate or by allowing interest rates to rise (though it would not be wise to try to adjust by intensifying import restrictions). It can sterilize, reduce reserve requirements or pursue an expansionary fiscal policy in the hope of limiting the impact on the domestic economy—but at the risk of intensifying capital outflows. Or, it can try to restrict capital out-flows, although with scant hope of success, unless it has inherited a functioning system of exchange control.

Most countries faced with heavy capital outflows therefore choose to try and finance at least part of them by borrowing from the IMF or elsewhere. This is not the place to elaborate on that response, except to note the relevance of the alternative possibility mentioned earlier—giving the IMF the responsibility of supervising workout situations for countries that find themselves unable to continue to service their debts on the contractually agreed terms.

Consider heterodox possibilities

In conclusion, it is worth taking a brief tour d'horizon of some more speculative ideas. One such idea is to reduce the scope for tax evasion by those who place funds abroad. This measure would require a network of tax information-sharing agreements or, preferably, a multilateral tax information-sharing agreement. Such an initiative is not likely to be effective if countries like Luxembourg and Switzerland refuse to participate because of their concern about retaining their private banking business. If a multilateral initiative with near-universal participation did succeed, it would be quite important in reducing the incentive for capital flight and in increasing tax equity, but of little relevance to the other dimensions of capital mobility.

A final policy option is to alter the basis for remunerating money managers. If my diagnosis of why financial markets are prone to speculative bubbles is correct, then the solution suggested by the theory of optimal intervention (which says that one should intervene as close to the distortion that causes the problem as possible) is to reward money managers according to the performance of their funds over a long time period, say five years, rather than a short time period, typically three months. This scheme would provide them with a reason to think about whether the market is currently above or below the level justified by the fundamentals—and the ability and incentive to act on their conclusions. But this proposal may be almost as dependent as that of Tobin on the need for universal participation, in which case it is equally unlikely to be implemented. Further, it is not clear that the problem is just managers' short-run motivations. It may be that they actually do make more money, even over a long time horizon, than those with longer-term considerations in mind. This may be possible, despite the famous Friedman (1953) theorem claiming destabilizing speculation to be unprofitable, because of activities of stop-loss traders, who place an order to sell if the price falls below a certain level as a mechanism for limiting their risk exposure in holding assets in a different currency (Krugman and Miller, 1993). Stop-loss traders provide a continual supply of traders who sell when prices fall and buy when they rise, which may enable chartists to prosper by destabilizing the market.

CONCLUDING REMARKS

Governments are currently awed by the power of capital markets. That is a healthier attitude than pretending that these markets can be ignored. Since capital mobility also offers important welfare benefits, it is sensible to start out by asking how governments can adapt their policies to make the best of a world of high capital mobility. But because capital flows are not always driven by the forces that economists assume, it is also sensible to ask whether policy should seek to limit capital mobility. I have outlined several possibilities, ranging from national actions to impose reserve requirements on foreign loans or the limitation of foreign borrowing by banks through the Tobin tax, through to multilateral tax information sharing, to creating a workout facility in the IMF and to modifying the compensation arrangements for mutual fund managers. But I have to say that, at the moment, the advice I would give is to emulate Chile: avoid policy getting swept aside by capital inflows by doing a little bit of each of a series of undramatic but complementary policy actions.

APPENDIX.   SETTING A PRUDENT LIMIT ON
             FOREIGN INDEBTEDNESS

There is not a very satisfying method of estimating the safe level of debt. The best approach still seems to be that based on various ad hoc rules of thumb about the relationship of debt or debt service to variables that influence a country's ability to service debt, such as exports, GDP or the capital stock. The most famous rules of thumb state that the debt-export ratio should not exceed 200 per cent, that the debt service ratio (the ratio of debt service to exports) should not exceed 25 per cent and that the debt-GDP ratio should not exceed 40 per cent. Such rules of thumb should probably be combined in some way,[7] but in the meantime they provide at least a starting point for analysis.

What do these rules of thumb imply about sustainable (desirable) current account deficits? A little algebra will show. Let D = foreign debt and Y = nominal income (expressed in dollars, as debt typically is). A hat over a variable signifies its rate of change, so that $\hat{D}$ is the proportionate rate of change of debt. Consider a developing country that can expect a long-term growth rate of real income of 5 per cent; then, its expected long-term growth of nominal income measured in US dollars (the international currency) will be 8 per cent if one assumes an average 3 per cent dollar inflation. In the steady state the rate of growth of debt must be the same as the growth rate of nominal income. Then, the prudent steady-state current account deficit according to the debt-GDP rule of thumb would be $\hat{D}/Y = (\hat{D}/D)\,(D/Y) = 0.08 \times 0.4 = 0.032$, that is, the steady-state deficit should not exceed 3.2 per cent of GDP. Of course, a country that starts out with a lower debt-GDP ratio than 40 per cent can run a greater deficit for a while. But it is advised to prevent the deficit from getting much larger because of the difficulty of adjusting back as the debt limit approaches. (It is appropriate to focus on the debt-GDP ratio for a country with an export-GDP ratio in excess of 20 per cent and on the debt-export ratio for a country with an export-GDP ratio below 20 per cent to ensure that both constraints are satisfied.)

Of course, a country's vulnerability to capital outflows depends not just on the level of debt but also on the type of liability that is contracted. Foreign direct investment is the least vulnerable to sudden withdrawal. Portfolio equity investment has an important self-equilibrating property: a loss of confidence will lead to a decline in stock prices that will automatically decrease the incentive for further withdrawals. Long-term bonds have the advantage that the principal can be liquidated only as the bonds mature. Bank loans have the advantage that it is relatively feasible to renegotiate the terms of the contract when the need arises. Nevertheless, both bonds (especially those with short maturities) and bank loans expose countries to significant risk of confronting a debt crisis, with consequences that the 1980s showed can be severe.

In view of these differences is it appropriate to count the stock of non-debt foreign claims on the economy—notably, foreign direct investment and foreign holdings of equity claims in domestic companies—on a par with debt itself? They too generate a need for foreign earnings to maintain debt service, so it would seem wrong to ignore such claims entirely. Perhaps the most reasonable procedure is to treat a dollar of a foreign non-debt claim as something less than a dollar's worth of debt—for example, to give it a 50 per cent weight. In any event such figures can provide no more than a very rough guide as to how much borrowing is more than the economy can safely handle—a figure that will also vary with the proportion of capital inflows being translated into investment in general and investment in tradables in particular.

NOTES

The author is indebted to Jeffrey A. Frankel, to participants in the Helsinki meeting, and to two referees for comments on previous drafts.

1. Note, however, that Ground and Bianchi (1988) argue that a resource boom is inherently temporary, because the rents that it generates will ultimately be bid away. This suggests that on some time scale the factors contributing to Dutch disease should always be considered temporary. Nevertheless, if the resource boom or capital inflows are expected to last for 10 or 20 years, it would make sense to adjust the balance of payments to increase absorption rather than to finance inflows, if such an increase in absorption is indeed in the long-run interest of the country (see discussion in text).

2. I recall meeting a banker in about 1983 who told me that he had been promoted twice within five years, the first time for building up a big portfolio of Peruvian paper during the boom years and the second time because he saw the crisis coming a few months sooner than his peers and therefore ran down the portfolio by 10 per cent before his bank got locked in along with all the others.

3. A currency depreciation initially causes a worsening of the trade balance, because exports tend to be denominated in the domestic currency and trade volumes adjust more slowly than prices.

4. The General Arrangements to Borrow consist of lines of credit from 11 major industrial countries, totalling SDR 17 billion, on which the IMF can draw to cope with a major systemic crisis.

5. Or, depending on institutional arrangements, that it sells from its portfolio.

6. Inflows may, however, tend to taper off spontaneously over time to the extent that the stock adjustment model of the capital account is valid.
7. As was done in some of the literature of the 1970s, such as Cline and Frank (1971) and Petersen (1977).

REFERENCES

Bartolini, Leonardo and Allan Drazen. 1995. "Capital Account Liberalization as a Signal." Working paper No. 9, Center for International Economics, University of Maryland at College Park. Forthcoming in *American Economic Review*.

Britton, Andrew J.C. 1970. "The Dynamic Stability of the Foreign Exchange Market." *Economic Journal* 80 (March):91–6.

Calvo, Guillermo A., Leonardo Leiderman and Carmen M. Reinhart. 1994. "The Capital Inflows Problem: Concepts and Issues." *Contemporary Economic Policy* 12(3):54–66.

Fischer, Bernhard and Helmut Reisen. 1992. *Towards Capital Account Convertibility*. OECD Development Centre Policy Brief 4. Paris.

Frank, Charles R. and William R. Cline. 1971. "Measurement of Debt Servicing Capacity: An Application of Discriminant Analysis." *Journal of International Economics* 1(3):327–44.

Frankel, Jeffrey A. 1988. "International Capital Mobility and Exchange Rate Volatility." In N.S. Fieleke, ed., *International Payments Imbalances in the 1980s*. Boston: Federal Reserve Bank of Boston.

Frankel, Jeffrey A. and Kenneth Froot. 1990. "Chartists, Fundamentalists, and the Demand for Dollars." In A. Courakis and M. Taylor, eds., *Private Behavior and Government Policy in Interdependent Economies*. Oxford: Clarendon Press.

Friedman, Milton. 1953. "The Case for Flexible Exchange Rates." In *Essays in Positive Economics*. Chicago: University of Chicago Press.

Ground, Richard L. and Andrés Bianchi. 1988. "The Economic Development of Latin America." In A. Bianchi and T. Nohara, eds., *A Comparative Study on Economic Development Between Asia and Latin America*. Tokyo: Institute of Developing Economies.

Group of Thirty. 1994. *Latin American Capital Flows: Living with Volatility*, A Study Group Report. Washington, D.C.: Group of Thirty.

IMF (International Monetary Fund). 1995. *International Capital Markets: Developments, Prospects, and Policy Issues*. Washington, D.C.

Krugman, Paul. 1987. "The Narrow Moving Band, the Dutch Disease, and the Competitive Consequences of Mrs. Thatcher." *Journal of Development Economics* 27(1–2):41–55.

Krugman, Paul and Marcus Miller. 1993. "Why Have a Target Zone?" *Carnegie-Rochester Conference Series on Public Policy* 38 (June):279–314.

Labán, Raúl and Felipe Larraín. 1993. "Can A Liberalization of Capital Outflows Increase Net Capital Inflows?" PUC-Santiago Documento de Trabajo 155. Santiago.

Petersen, H.J. 1977. "Debt Crisis of Developing Countries: A Pragmatic Approach to an Early Warning System." *Konjunkturpolitik* 23(2):94–110.

Sachs, Jeffrey D. and Andrew M. Warner. 1995. "Natural Resource Abundance and Economic Growth." Harvard Institute for International Development, Development Discussion Paper 517a. Cambridge, Mass.

Summers, Lawrence H. 1995. "Remarks at the IDB Symposium on Capital Flows." US Treasury mimeo. Washington, D. C. October 6.

Tobin, James. 1978. "A Proposal for International Monetary Reform." *Eastern Economic Journal* 4(3–4):153–59; reprinted in Tobin, James. 1982. *Essays in Economics: Theory and Policy*. Cambridge, Mass.: MIT Press.

INDEX

Adelman, I. 219
Africa 16, 149, 152–4, 161, 187 n
  east 154, 157, 186 n
  sub-Saharan 68
agency costs 277–8, 295
agglomeration economies 92, 101, 104,
  135–6, 139 n
aggregate demand spillovers 98–103, 120,
  233
agricultural sector (see rural sector)
Ainsworth, M. 187 n
Albania 52
Allen, F. 286
Angola 255
Aoki, M. 280
Argentina 45, 55, 56, 163, 177, 325
Austrian school 226
Azariadis, C. 140 n

Bank for International Settlements (BIS)
  36
banking sector (see financial sector; central
  bank)
Bardhan, P. 228
Barro, R. 40, 94–5, 117, 158–9, 160, 163,
  175, 187 n
Basle agreements 68, 300, 301, 315
Batista Gomes-Neto, J. 156
Beegle, K. 187 n
Behrman, J. 157
Belarus 51–2
Belgium 340
Berglof, E. 288–9
Berthelot, Y. 6
Bevan, D. 190 n
big push theory 100, 101, 233, 238
Bilginsoy, C. 125
Bils, M. 95
Birdsall, N. 159, 163–4, 172, 188 n
Bolivia 160, 161
Bosnia 255
Boyer, R. 228
Brazil 45, 68, 155, 156, 165–7, 175, 179,
  180–1, 182, 183, 187 n
Breshnahan, T. 113
Bretton Woods institutions 66, 79
Bruno, M. 40

budget constraints
  hard 54
  soft 241, 281, 285
Buiter, W. 4, 5
Bulgaria 51

Caballero, R. 102–3, 108, 125
Cambodia 255
capacity utilization 16, 31, 43
capital
  domestic 94, 96
  flows, international 5, 8, 12, 13, 57–67,
    82 n, 92, 105, 117, 214, 325, 343
    benefits from 326–7
    controls on 8, 13, 61–3, 325, 326–7,
      333–42
    inflows 12, 58–60, 63–6, 327–8,
      332–3, 336–8
    outflows 4, 12, 13, 60, 63, 66, 330,
      340–1
    problems of 327–30
  human 2, 3, 4, 5, 15, 69, 76, 79, 96, 116
    accumulation of 149, 151, 156, 158,
      168, 176–8, 199, 204, 205, 207, 248
    and growth 149, 151, 158–64, 176–8,
      181, 183–5, 240
    demand for 5–6, 151, 162–4, 166,
      176–81, 187 n
    returns to 156, 157, 159, 161–4, 165,
      176, 178, 181, 184
    supply of 5–6, 97, 151, 176, 178
    theory of 152, 158–9
  financing of 5, 74–5, 119, 151, 161,
    172–5, 177, 181, 182–3, 184
  markets 34, 78, 172–4, 178
  physical 2, 12, 15, 31, 32, 33, 42, 57–8,
    69, 70, 77–8, 116, 157, 198, 204 (see
    also infrastructure)
Caprio, G. 297, 316
central bank 54, 55, 65, 256, 263, 264,
  330, 337–8
central Europe 6, 15, 46–52, 68, 73, 226,
  228
central planning (see planning, central)
Chakravarty, S. 233, 234, 238, 239, 241
Chan, V. 125
Chari, V.V. 96

Tanzi, V. 7
tax collection/administration 18–21, 39, 56, 200, 256, 257, 258, 262, 275, 294
technological change 116–17, 198, 205, 206, 207, 213, 218, 240
technology
  adoption of 3, 140 n, 141 n
  capital-intensive 5, 52
  choice of 99–102, 103, 121
  labour-intensive 171–2
Thailand 12, 340
Thatcher, M. 15, 202
Thomas, R. 218
Timmer, C.P. 189 n, 190 n
Tirole, J. 300, 301, 304
Tobin, J. 61, 334
Tobin tax 8, 61, 334–6, 343
Trajtenberg, M. 113
transaction costs 26, 41, 215, 218, 222, 234, 306
transfers 168
transition economies 11, 26, 32, 33–4, 35, 58, 60, 214
  financial sectors in 61, 228, 270, 288–9
  government revenue in 18–21, 46, 56
  reforms in 6, 46–52, 53–6, 68, 73, 83 n, 219, 220, 225–8, 229, 258–9 (see also central Europe, eastern Europe, former Soviet Union)
transportation costs 13, 101, 103, 107–8, 109, 121, 240

Uganda 259
Ukraine 51–2
underdevelopment traps 5, 92, 94, 97, 102, 106
unemployment 16, 31, 33, 39, 43–5, 53, 76–7, 85 n, 86 n, 213, 228

unified banking system 19
United Kingdom 12, 15, 17, 21, 23, 28, 86 n, 107, 135
United States 15, 28, 108, 117, 139 n, 269, 290, 303
urban sector 171
Uruguay 202
Uruguay round (see GATT)

Venezuela 155–6, 182
Vishny, R. 99–102, 103, 233

wage compression 165–7, 184
Warner, A. 96, 328
Weil, D. 96
welfare economics 26
  first fundamental theorem of 15, 82 n, 274–5
  second fundamental theorem of 15, 82 n, 274–5
welfare systems 219–20, 221
West Bank and Gaza Strip 255, 258
western Europe 16, 76–7, 218
Williamson, J. 8
World Bank 36, 68, 203, 231, 247, 248
women
  education of 75, 149, 161–2, 184, 187 n
  employment of 161
World Trade Organization (WTO) 14, 36, 68
World War I 79
World War II 73, 79, 94, 199

x-efficiency 168, 170

Young, A. 98, 114–15
youth deficit 34, 72, 75–7
Yugoslav Republic (former) 20